Impersonating
Animals

Impersonating Animals

RHETORIC, ECOFEMINISM, AND ANIMAL RIGHTS LAW

S. Marek Muller

MICHIGAN STATE UNIVERSITY PRESS | *East Lansing*

♾ The paper used in this publication meets the minimum requirements of
ANSI/NISO Z39.48-1992 (R 1997) (Permanence of Paper).

Michigan State University Press
East Lansing, Michigan 48823-5245

LIBRARY OF CONGRESS CATALOGING-IN-PUBLICATION DATA
Names: Muller, S. Marek, author.
Title: Impersonating animals : rhetoric, ecofeminism, and animal rights law
/ S. Marek Muller.
Description: First. | East Lansing : Michigan State University Press, 2020.
| Includes bibliographical references and index.
Identifiers: LCCN 2019037505 | ISBN 978-1-61186-366-6 (paperback) | ISBN 978-1-60917-641-9
| ISBN 978-1-62895-402-9 | ISBN 978-1-62896-403-5
Subjects: LCSH: Animals—Law and legislation. | Animal welfare—Law and legislation.
| Animal rights. | Ecofeminism. | Animal ecology.
Classification: LCC K3620 .M83 2020 | DDC 344.04/9—dc23
LC record available at https://lccn.loc.gov/2019037505

Book design by Charlie Sharp, Sharp Designs, East Lansing, Michigan
Cover design by Erin Kirk New
Cover art: Flag shaped from origami birds by feoris, from iStock.

Michigan State University Press is a member of the Green Press Initiative and is committed to developing
and encouraging ecologically responsible publishing practices. For more information about the Green
Press Initiative and the use of recycled paper in book publishing, please visit www.greenpressinitiative.org.

Visit Michigan State University Press at *www.msupress.org*

Contents

Acknowledgments

I don't really know how I ended up here. Writing a book was intense and I didn't think that I could do it—I really didn't. Somehow and some way the text is now complete. Completing the challenging process of research, writing, and revising was not accomplished in isolation.

First, I would like to thank my educators—those responsible for turning a naïve, terrified student into a fully developed scholar. Thanks to the members of my dissertation committee for supporting me, pushing me through graduate school, and encouraging the development of my academic self. I could never have written this book without the sharp insights and constant encouragement of Drs. Danielle Endres, Marouf Hasian, Kent Ono, Wanda Pillow, and Natasha Seegert.

Another set of thanks to my family and friends, without whom I would never have been able to get this far, particularly Judy Heller, Mark Muller, Daniel Muller, Anthony Barba, Julie Snyder-Yuly, Kourtney Maison, Taylor Johnson, Joshua Barnett, Jose Angel Maldonado, Ammar Hussein, Michael Foist, Oscar Mejia, Megan Cullinan, and Melissa Parks.

Thanks as well to Dr. Catherine Cocks, my two anonymous reviewers, and the editorial board of the Michigan State University Press for encouraging this project's completion and for making the final product much stronger.

I also owe a debt of gratitude to scholars and activists who I have never met in person, but whose research and activism have been foundational to my own work. Many thanks to Amie Breeze Harper, Christopher Sebastian, Aph Ko, Julia Feliz Brueck, Carol Adams, Greta Gaard, Maneesha Deckha, Sunaura Taylor, and the many other intersectional and/or radical vegans working toward total liberation within and across species lines.

And finally, many thanks to Buttons, Boots, and Francesca—you silly canines are my constant reminders that, despite the difficulty and mental agony of dealing with the dark subject of more-than-human exploitation, this work is necessary and needed.

Rhetoric(s) of Animal Rights and the Law

In response to the irresistible but unacknowledged unleashing and the organized disavowal of this torture, voices are raised—minority, weak, marginal voices, little assured of their discourse, of their right to discourse and the enchantment of their discourse within the law, as a declaration of rights—in order to protect, in order to appeal . . . to what is still presented in such a problematic way as animal rights, in order to awaken us to our responsibilities and our obligations with respect to the living in general, and precisely to this fundamental compassion that, were we to take it seriously, would have to change even the very basis . . . of the philosophical problematic of the animal.

—Jacques Derrida

n 1989, West Hollywood, California, declared itself a "Cruelty Free Zone for Animals." In the following decades, the city would make illegal a number of human-on-animal practices, including but not limited to the use of steel leghold traps on wild animals and the testing of cosmetics on animals. West Hollywood made headlines when it banned the sale of fur products within the city limits, ultimately culminating in a lawsuit with the fashion boutique Mayfair House in which the city emerged victorious (Backus, 2013). The state of California has slowly but surely started following West Hollywood's example. For instance, the city banned selling puppy-mill dogs in pet stores back in 2010. In 2017, California governor Jerry Brown signed AB 485 into law to ensure that every pet store in the entire state would only sell dogs, cats, and rabbits from animal rescue organizations. Elena Bicker, the executive director of Tony La Russa's Animal Rescue Foundation, exclaimed "This is a great law. California is setting the standard and elevating the status of pets in society" (McCarthy, 2017, para. 10).

The American Association for the Advancement of Science composed a "Declaration for the Rights of Cetaceans" in 2011, arguing that species such as dolphins and orcas ought to be afforded "personhood status." Cetaceans, claimed the group, had "the right to life ... the right to freedom ... the right to the protection of their natural environment . . . the right not to be subject to the disruption of their cultures" and are entitled to "an international order in which these rights, freedoms and norms can be fully realized" wherein "no State, corporation, human group, or individual should engage in any activity that undermines these rights" (Helsinki Group, 2010). The AAAS's call for cetacean rights would ultimately come into fruition across the globe in 2013 in India when, in a groundbreaking legal decision, the Ministry of Environment and Forests declared dolphins "nonhuman persons" on the basis that:

> Cetaceans, in general, are highly intelligent and sensitive, and various scientists who have researched dolphin behaviour have suggested that the unusually high intelligence as compared to other animals, means that dolphins should be seen as "nonhuman persons" and as such should have their own specific rights and it is morally unacceptable to keep them captive for entertainment purposes. (qtd. in Hogan, 2015, para. 3)

The ministry advised state governments to reject any and all proposals "by any person / persons, organizations, government agencies, private or public enterprises that involves import, capture of cetacean species to establish for commercial entertainment, private or public exhibition and interaction purposes whatsoever" (qtd. in Hogan, 2015, para. 2). The decision abolished the use of cetaceans in theme parks, leading to the banning of dolphin shows, the withdrawal of dolphin park licenses and the halting of "dolphinarium" constructions around the country (Coelho, 2013).

In 2016, the Oregon state Supreme Court upheld the decision in *State v. Amanda Newcomb,* wherein a woman was convicted of second-degree animal neglect for starving and beating her dog. Newcomb claimed that her rights were violated when investigators took the dog to a Humane Society veterinarian and drew blood from her dog, Juno, to determine if the dog with "no fat on its body" needed medical care. Since dogs are legally considered property in the state of Oregon, Newcomb's counsel appealed, the Humane Society had committed unlawful search and seizure of property. The initial 2011 suit saw circuit judge Eric Bergstrom deny a motion to suppress the blood evidence, agreeing with prosecutor Adam Gibbs that investigators taking the dog to the vet for examination was sufficiently similar to a suspected child abuse victim taken into protective custody. Furthermore, claimed Gibbs, a dog's property status should not render the canine to the status of an empty container that "doesn't contain anything," for within the dog was "more dog," thus doing away with any prerequisite for a search warrant (qtd. in Green, 2016, para. 9). The Supreme Court agreed, noting that "dogs are not 'mere' property and don't require a warrant to search internally" (Green, 2016, para. 2). Oregon's Supreme Court would also rule in favor of the state in *State v. Nix,* an animal abuse case regarding the neglect of twenty horses, specifically the argument that the horses could, for the purposes of sentencing, be considered "victims" (Buff, 2014). These legal victories would lead to Jacob Kamins, Oregon's animal cruelty deputy district attorney, celebrating that "the issue of animal welfare is really coming into its own in the criminal justice world" (qtd. in Green, 2016, para. 13).

The United States District Court of Utah struck down the state of Utah's controversial "ag-gag" law in the summer of 2017, an ordinance that criminalized undercover investigations at factory farms and slaughterhouses. The decision came after Utah-based animal activist Amy Meyer became the first person to be prosecuted under ag-gag legislation after videotaping cow abuse at a local meatpacking company in 2013. The ban was declared unconstitutional on the grounds that it violated animal activists' First Amendment rights to free speech. A similar case took place in August 2015, when the state of Idaho was also forced to dismantle its ag-gag laws due to violating the First *and* Fourteenth Amendments of the U.S. Constitution. These legal victories served as a moral victory for activists against agricultural giants who "sought to keep cruelty to animals a big secret that only the profiteers could see . . . to punish the whistleblowers and eyewitnesses who expose inhumane and illegal conduct" (PETA, 2017, para. 9).

The above cases are mere snapshots of a burgeoning societal interest in the morality of interspecies—specifically, "human" on "animal"—interactions in a so-called "globalizing" world. In the legal realm, more and more litigators are taking the plight of animals seriously—so seriously, in fact, that multiple law schools now offer classes in animal law and have animal law clinics. These students have the chance to graduate and work in many large-scale animal protection organizations such as the Humane Society of the United States, the American Society for the Prevention of Cruelty to Animals, the Animal Welfare Institute, People for the Ethical Treatment of Animals, the Animal Legal Defense Fund, and multiple others. And, while this book will focus on U.S. American contexts, it is important to note that the American animal rights movement does not exist in a cultural vacuum, and is in fact in constant conversation across national borders. The following chapters will evaluate the strengths, weaknesses, and ideological incoherence present in certain U.S. American rhetorics of animal rights and animal rights law with the understanding that transnational conversations about ethics, human or animal, cannot be accomplished without addressing how longstanding, hegemonic, and colonial ideologies can impede social justice advocacy even within the confines of a single "nation-state."

Moreover, this book will interrogate the extent to which traditional welfare and rights-based approaches to animal liberation (to be discussed momentarily) are ultimately insufficient by themselves, particularly when the latter's purported radicalness is left uninterrogated and its colonial roots left unquestioned. As Wolfe (2003) insisted, "one of the central ironies of animal rights philosophy is that its philosophical frameworks remain essentially humanist . . . thus effacing the very difference of the animal other that it sought to respect" (p. 8). What is more, in taking for granted the "rationality" and "objectivity" of the Enlightenment-era tenets still manifest in rights-based rhetorics today, many mainstream animal rights rhetorics engage in renderings of rights and justice that ultimately further inequality rather than quash it. Wynter (2003) importantly explained in her acclaimed genealogy of the Western "invention" of Man how the notion of the "objective human" (or the "overrepresentation of man") must be demolished to unsettle injustice—after all, contemporary renderings of the *Homo sapiens* maintain their historical roots in White colonial rule, specifically the rhetorics used to justify the domination and enslavement of Others due to their supposed "lack" of humanness.

Sitting at the intersection of rhetorical theory, jurisprudential thought, and applied animal ethics, the concept of this book's concluding rhetorical-ontological framework—a critical vegan rhetoric—must be understood as the phenomenological mode of "being" in the world, or more simply, as a "who you are space" (Harper, 2013). I use the term "critical" here as a specific orientation toward scholarship that examines macrolevel systems of power and oppression, discourses of hegemony and exclusion, and how aspects of "identity" (e.g., race, gender, disability, species) are often central to the production and reproductions of inequalities. Critical work might centralize one feature of these systems by looking through the world for a specific subject or object of concern (e.g., critical legal studies looking at the law or critical race studies centralizing race), but draw upon material gleaned from multiple arenas of critical research (for instance, critical legal studies would not exist without insights from critical scholars of race). Thus, while my work dubs itself "vegan" and "ecofeminist," it does so with a critical orientation sensitive to how oppressive systems operate through interweaving discourses and ideologies regarding race, gender, class, sexuality, ability, species, etc. Indeed, as Christopher Sebastian McJetters explained, understanding veganism not as a diet or a lifestyle choice but as a distinct way of being/acting/doing, as "something that defines *who we are* every single time we look at a menu and every time we go to a retail store," allows for a world in which "veganism becomes a verb, not a noun" (McJetters, 2015, para. 14).

I simultaneously argue for ecofeminist legal theory, a theoretical framework emerging from a careful combination of ecofeminism (with an emphasis on vegan ecofeminism), feminist legal studies (with an emphasis on intersectionality and decoloniality), and critical animal studies (with an emphasis on total liberation and intersectional veganism) and defended through ideological rhetorical criticism (an understanding of rhetorical artifacts beyond the "text" with emphasis on a rhetor's situated "contexts"). This stance more seriously interrogates species and interspecies inequalities in a purportedly unbiased, rational, and justice-oriented legal system. It not only seeks to dismantle the Cartesian human/animal binary (humans *are* animals, after all, and even the notion of "animal" is in large part a social construction based on biological politics) but also the unfortunate essentialisms that lump "humans" and "animals" into coherent, unified wholes through liberal humanist discourses inside and outside of the courtroom. "Types" of humans have, through discourse, been deemed more animal than other, just as some animals have, through discourse, been moved toward the realm of the human. I align with critical theorists who argue that this mode of discursive nuance *matters* to such an extent that we must move away from abstract universalisms toward contingent relationalities, a paradigm shift that necessitates a critique (but not necessarily a total abandonment) of hyper-rational animal rights rhetorics as they manifest in varied (and oftentimes "radical") legal arenas.

This book is not an attempt to "reinvent the wheel" of animal rights thought and praxis writ large. On the contrary, despite the liberal humanist, hyper-rationalist, postracial, patriarchal, etc., tendencies of many "mainstream" (or at least mass-mediated) animal rights rhetors in U.S. American contexts, many scholars and layperson animal advocates have been speaking out for years, decades, even centuries in favor of more nuanced and inclusive visions and practices of animal liberation. Contemporarily, intersectional vegan voices of color such as Amie Breeze Harper, Aph Ko, Syl Ko, Julia Feliz Brueck, Nekeisha Alexis, Christopher Sebastian McJetters, and Margaret Robinson have advocated for and engaged in extended critiques of the tacit and, more often, not-so-tacit politics of Whiteness of the United States of America's animal rights movement. Patriarchal leadership, theories, and practices in the United States' animal-oriented organizations and institutions have received resounding critiques from the likes of Carol J. Adams, Corey Wrenn, Lisa Kemmerer, Emily Gaarder, Josephine Donavan, and Richard Twine. Sunaura Taylor, Bob Torres, David Nibert, Steven Best, and multiple others have commented upon, criticized, and offered alternatives to animal rights discourses that overemphasize ableism, capitalism, and other necessarily oppressive phenomena. Maneesha Deckha has been a vocal advocate for the importance of postcolonial and posthumanist theory to American schools of animal law. This book is in conversation with, not a replacement for, such important contributors to animal rights theory and praxis.

What this book *does* attempt to do is introduce principles from the aforementioned authors' resoundingly important work to the field of rhetorical studies. Despite the emergence of environmental rhetoric as a legitimate disciplinary subfield in the latter half of the twentieth century, rhetoric as an overall discipline still grapples not only with the thought that *Homo sapiens* is not the only "rhetorician" that the planet Earth has to offer but also with the fact that the rhetorics used to communicate *about* beings not designated as "human" necessarily affect relationships *across* species boundaries (i.e., how we treat our dog) and *between* them (i.e., how we treat humans frequently compared to dogs). Furthermore, this book seeks to highlight how interdisciplinary scholars interested in animality and animality's relationship to the legal sphere can and should utilize ideological rhetorical criticism as a basis for understanding why a legal argument was created; how it functions within larger, fragmented discursive arenas; and why it succeeds and/or fails to accomplish the rhetor's desired tasks upon dissemination in (multiple and fragmented) public spheres and public screens (Habermas, Lennox, & Lennox,

1974; DeLuca & Peeples, 2002). Finally, this book offers an academic analytic that incorporates tenets from ecofeminism, feminist legal studies, and critical animal studies that will hopefully open opportunities for other rhetoricians (or scholars of other fields interested in rhetoric's force in pursuits of social justice) to engage in discursive studies of animality and its relationship to legal rights in formal and informal judicial settings.

Such studies are more than necessary given contemporary manifestations of animal rights (and "animal rights") practices in a twenty-first-century U.S. American context. At first glance, the United States might appear to be an ever-growing paradise for the human-animal bond. In 2016, U.S. Americans contributed $66.75 billion to the country's booming pet industry, including but not limited to the purchase of food, bedding, medical treatment, and even insurance, clothing, daycare, and spa treatments (APPA, 2017). A 2016 survey by Fortune-Morning Consult revealed that 76 percent of respondents considered their pets to be "beloved members of the family," leading journalist Laura Entis of *Fortune* to run an article provocatively titled "Pets are Basically People." David Grimm, author of the renowned book *Citizen Canine: Our Evolving Relationship with Cats and Dogs,* made the case that, far from being mere "animals," felines and canines in particular might very well become legal U.S. American citizens in the coming years.

Alternative diets and lifestyles based on animal ethics are also growing in the United States. Spurred in part by videotaped undercover investigations at factory farms, explosive animal cruelty and food industry documentaries such as *Cowspiracy, What the Health?,* and *Forks Over Knives,* 2017 saw 6 percent of people identifying as "vegan." Compared to 1 percent in 2014, this statistic represents a 600 percent explosion in plant-based lifestyles in a mere three years (Neff, 2017). One report characterized this trend as representative of increasing "awareness of the impact of meat consumption [and] driving demand for meat-free products substitutes" (qtd. in Neff, 2017, para. 5). Many supermarkets and fast-food restaurants now carry popular meat alternatives such as tofu and seitan as well as "fake meat" brands like Tofurkey and Beyond Meat. Bioengineering companies like New Harvest and Memphis Meats have been experimenting with "lab-grown meat" in an attempt to cut the cruelty out of food consumption altogether.

Yet, at the same time, the United States is a place where concern for animal well-being withers and dies. The dawn of the Trump Administration in January 2017 marked a particular decline in federally mandated legal standards for animal well-being. Two weeks after the forty-fifth president's inauguration, the United

States Department of Agriculture (USDA) removed thousands of documents detailing national animal welfare violations from its website after decades of (at least minor) transparency. The deleted records included annual reports from every commercial animal facility in the United States from zoos to breeders to farms to laboratories. Adam Roberts, the CEO of the animal advocacy agency Born Free USA, told *National Geographic* that "the government's decision to make it harder to access this information further protects animal exploiters in the shroud of secrecy on which their nefarious activities thrive" (Daly, 2017, para. 5).

Quizzical rhetoric praising the act of sport hunting as an act of animal compassion continue to dominate conservationist discourse. A 2017 report by the U.S. Fish and Wildlife Service reported that 40 percent of the population aged sixteen years or older had engaged in "wildlife related activities" such as hunting and fishing in 2016 (Department of the Interior, 2017). Ryan Zinke, the former U.S. secretary of the interior, claimed that "hunting and fishing are a part of the American heritage" before reversing an order banning lead ammunition and tackle on National Wildlife Refuge lands and authorizing the expansion of hunting and fishing options on public lands (qtd. in Department of the Interior, 2017, para. 3). Greg Sheehan, the U.S. Fish and Wildlife principal deputy director, celebrated that "hunters and anglers form the foundation of wildlife conservation in the United States" and added "industry, federal, and state fish and wildlife agency initiatives that focus on hunter and angler recruitment, retention and reactivation are crucial to . . . ensuring the next generation of wildlife enthusiasts have the opportunity, access, and awareness to pursue these time-honored American traditions" (para. 13). The Trump Administration has reversed, re-reversed, and then re-re-reversed a ban on the importation of elephant corpses as "trophies" in international sport hunting (Dwyer, 2018).

And, most significantly of all, animals remain legally confined to the status of *property* in the U.S. American legal system. Absurd as it may sound, under a chattel system, a golden retriever is legally the same thing as a shoe—important only insofar as it has monetary value to a human subject. No species has yet reached the level of the dolphin in India or chimpanzees in Argentina, or even the entire Te Urewara National Park in New Zealand. That is to say, none but the *Homo sapiens* is considered a "person" in a court of law, a distinction with massive implications that the following chapters will explore in-depth.

In this book, I will take particularly seriously the consequences of relegating the "more-than-human world" (Abram, 2012) to the status of "object" rather than "subject," to "property" rather than "person," or to "mere automata" rather than "member of a moral community." The premier task of animal rights practitioners in the legal sphere is, as I and most critical animal theorists argue, the eradication of the classification of animals as property. Such a shift would necessarily mean that the notion of "personhood" would have to expand beyond the confines of the human species. The definitions of moral duties and social contracts would need to expand their reach into the messy realms of interspecies interplays. This approach would have to engage with the posthuman, the notion that humanity-as-moral-center cannot hold, while simultaneously acknowledging that one can never truly understand alterity due to the confines of one's particular phenomenological, fleshy experiencing of the world. To embrace humanity and animality as conditions of subjectivity, where neither is inherently better or worse than the other, is thus a task that requires engaging with not only definitional questions of who is discursively constituted as human but also evaluative questions of why *particular humans* are so constituted as *particularly human* in argumentative opposition to an "inferior" animal form.

In other words, ontological dissolution of animal-as-object must necessarily lead to a reinterrogation of *who* counts, *how* they count, *why* they count, and how that "countedness" ought to be defended in a purportedly (or at the very least, *ideally*) "fair" and "just" judicial system. To do so requires a second glance at not only what is written in the law but also how those laws came to be written in the first place. Reconfigurations of personhood must thus expand beyond questions of "What should be argued in court?" to "Does this argument open doors for future liberation or reify the very oppressive practices that led to this court case in the first place?" And, in this negotiation of animal rights' short-term tactics versus long-term strategies, animal rights lawyers (and anyone interested in "the law" for protective status) must grapple with how even *Homo sapiens* individuals do not have equal access to personhood status, even when such access *appears* to exist. Engaging with animal personhood, then, is not merely a matter of "animals." It is a matter of dissolving the inane binary separating humanity and animality, of critically interrogating a longstanding and de facto legal "sliding scale" of humanity, wherein only certain "bodies" are afforded the full benefits of legal protection. Animal rights law, in its necessary form, is not only a matter of securing rights for non–*Homo sapiens* but also a matter of fighting against every oppressive ism that has enabled an unequal legal system to prosper under the guise of impartiality. Overall, it is a matter of interrogating distinctly *colonial* ontologies that function under the guise of justice, with coloniality in this sense defined not merely as a historical event or time period spurred by the age of exploration and Enlightenment philosophies but as an all-encompassing ontological phenomenon, unending and omnipresent. As feminist philosopher Maria Lugones insisted:

> With expansion of European colonialism, [a] classification [system] was imposed on the population of the planet. Since then, it has permeated every area of social existence, constituting the most effective form of material and intersubjective social domination. Thus, an encompassing phenomenon, since it is one of the axes of the system of power and as such it permeates all control of sexual access, collective authority, labor, subjectivity/intersubjectivity and the production of knowledge from within these intersubjective relations. Or, alternatively, all control over sex, subjectivity, authority, and labor are articulated around it. (Lugones, 2007, p. 191)

This book's task is therefore to use the combined theories of ecofeminism, feminist legal studies, and critical animal studies in tandem with methodologies drawn from rhetorical studies to start this process of ontological reconfiguration. Specifically, it will argue that definitional and conceptual revisions of the "person" and the "rights" afforded to bodies in the rhetorics of animal rights law, and the pragmatic *strategies* and discursive *tactics* that would make such reconfigurations possible, must occur within a broader commitment to intersectionality and decolonization. There are, of course, competing definitions of strategies and tactics ranging from the work of Michel de Certeau (where strategies are used by elites and tactics by the disenfranchised) to critical military studies (where the terms are used in the context of material violence). In this book, I will use these two key activist terms in the style of rhetoricians interested in social movement discourses, particularly by movement "leaders," where, in situations necessitating mobilizing bodies, exerting external influence, and resisting counterinfluence, strategies are most generally understood as *what "we" ultimately want* and tactics as *how "we" will go about getting what we want* (Alinsky, 1989; Simons, 1970; Stewart, 1980). Strategic and tactical commitments must, I argue, be geared toward all species, not some, thus requiring the law to become less anthropocentric and for animal liberation to become more "anthropo-inclusive."

A Microhistory of Animals in the Law

As Cao (2014) has explained, "Human treatment of animals in history has been overwhelmingly a one-sided affair, of total control, dominance and disposal, and of killing and destruction as food and other resources" (p. 170). This book in no way argues that "the West" or "Western law" are somehow the *only* cultural entities with a history of animal exploitation. Indeed,

> one commonality across all cultures and societies is found in our treatment and attitude towards animals. It is a misconception that Eastern cultural and religious notions and practices are kinder and gentler towards animals or that Western culture somehow is particularly cruel towards animals. (Cao, 2014, p.171)

Sanbonmatsu (2011) even posited that the "'need' to annihilate the animal in order to engender 'the human' remains the defining hallmark of contemporary civilization" (p. 39). In this way, the construction and treatment of the more-than-human world as inferior, and thus disposable, to human interests "is as much an existential as a political question" (Sanbonmatsu, 2011, p. 32). Animal exploitation has a global history, and Sanbonmatsu's existential critique of it holds particularly true in Western jurisprudential thought and legal systems (the primary focus of this book due to its boundedness to U.S. American judicial processes), which were created for (some) and are maintained by (some) human beings. Thus, the notion of a totally, completely, and absolutely nonanthropocentric legal system may or may not be possible. However, to argue that animals have no place and have never had a place in Western litigation is anachronistic. Although animal rights, and by extension animal rights law, is considered by some to be a recent phenomenon in a U.S. American linear history of social progress, a search through the annals of "Western" history demonstrates that beings outside of the species *Homo sapiens* have at many moments had their day in court. To quote Mussawir and Otomo (2013), "The significant *disappearance* of the animal from the text of law is a somewhat overlooked phenomenon" (Mussawir & Otomo, 2013, p. 6, emphasis mine).

In other words, Western legal discourses have not always rendered animal bodies to the status of empty vessels devoid of moral relationships to humankind. Grimm (2016) has asserted that the earliest court case involving animal beings was in the year 824, when an ecclesiastical judge excommunicated a group of moles from Italy. A French court sentenced a bull to death in 1314 for goring a man to death and a donkey to burn at the stake in 1575 for bestiality (a bispecies punitive practice carried on in early U.S. American colonies, as detailed by historian William Bradford in the 1642 case of colonist Thomas Granger's active livestock fetish). In 1522, the Black Death had ravaged the European continent. Desperate for somebody, anybody, to blame for their plight, the citizens of Autun in France put the town's rats on trial. The rodents were ordered to appear in court by the town bishop's vicar and were represented by jurist Bartholomew Chassenee. Monsieur Chassenee observed that to punish all rats for the crimes of a few was inherently wrong: "What can be more unjust than these general proscriptions which destroy indiscriminately those whom tender years or infirmity render equally incapable of suffering?" (qtd. in Grimm, 2016, para. 2). The legal proceedings were then adjourned indefinitely, sparing the rodents from formal legal punishment. In one case, explained Grimm, "Due process for animals was so highly valued that when a hangman in Germany took matters into his own hands before the trial of a sow had commenced, he was permanently banished from his village" (para. 3).

Obviously, cases such as these were not and certainly are not the norm. In the contemporary United States legal system, an animal is extraordinarily unlikely to be appointed its own lawyer or granted plaintiff status—although, as any lawyer of dog-bite law can attest, the animal's execution is still a common practice. According to Grimm and rhetorician Greg Goodale, common discourse surrounding the history of U.S. American animal rights law starts its narrative in the realm of Aristotelian ontology, wherein the Greek philosopher proposed a hierarchy of souls; the soul of the human contained some "quality" (typically conceived as rationality) that elevated man's soul over others. This rationale would later combine with a Judeo-Christian understanding of the world in which God created man in His image, leaving humanity to use the fruits of the Earth to his benefit. Aristotelian-Christian ethics bled into Enlightenment philosophy. Social and political philosophers, John Locke and Immanuel Kant included, determined that cruelty to animals should be considered wrong, but only on the grounds that such cruelty would breed interhuman cruelty as well. At most, humans had *indirect* duties toward animals.

Cruelty, then, ought to be addressed in the law through common offenses, such as property damage, from one human party toward another. Enlightenment theorists of law and justice like Jean-Jacques Rousseau at certain points acknowledged that nonhuman beings might have "natural rights" but did not often believe that the possession of those rights necessitated inclusion as subjects in the legal system. Human-centered theories of justice combined with popular binary models of the known universe, such as Rene Descartes's assertion that the more-than-human world was composed of mere automata, so much so that the shriek of a dog was little different than the squeak of a rusty wheel (Goodale, 2015; Grimm, 2016). This notion of cruelty, anthropocentric as its roots may be, would nonetheless form the basis of early animal rights legal theories, particularly Jeremy Bentham, whose ideas regarding the avoidance of animal suffering have rhetorical resonance to this day.

As mentioned above, no history of animal law is complete without a discussion of eighteenth-century act-utilitarian Jeremy Bentham, who inarguably served as a catalyst for Peter Singer's publication of *Animal Liberation*. Bentham rejected Enlightenment notions of natural rights in favor of a system of thought predicated on living beings' push-pull between pleasure and pain. Favoring sentience—the capacity to experience pleasure and pain—as the sole determinate of one's capacity to participate in a moral community, Bentham articulated "the most often quoted footnote in history" (Blosh, 2012, p. 22), in which he drew together the oppression of humans and more-than-humans and advocated for liberation based not only upon social rank but also upon the capacity to feel:

> The day has been, I am sad to say in many places it is not yet past, in which the greater part of the species, under the denomination of slaves, have been treated by the law exactly upon the same footing, as, in England for example, the inferior races of animals are still. The day may come when the rest of the animal creation may acquire those rights which never could have been witholden from them but by the hand of tyranny. The French have already discovered that the blackness of the skin is no reason a human being should be abandoned without redress to the caprice of a tormentor. It may one day come to be recognised that the number of the legs, the villosity of the skin, or the termination of the *os sacrum* are reasons equally insufficient for abandoning a sensitive being to the same fate. What else is it that should trace the insuperable line? Is it the faculty of reason or perhaps the faculty of discourse? But a full-grown horse or dog, is beyond comparison a more rational, as well as a more conversable animal, than an infant of a day or a week or even a month, old. But suppose the case were otherwise, what would it avail? The question is not, Can they reason? nor, Can they talk? but, Can they suffer? (Bentham, 1798/1970, footnote 122)

These European ontological debates ultimately enabled an anti-aristocratic, yet still anthropocentric, Western system of liberal humanist thought that would, over time, carry over state borders through the spread of imperialism (Blosh, 2012). Within this discursive legal framework, dominated by a "rule of kindness," there are "no limitations on how humans can use animals, so there is no need to worry about causing them pain or killing them in order to use them. Rather, humans must only refrain from inflicting gratuitous cruelty on animals" (Blosh, 2012, p. 14).

Of course, rhetorics of animal law are more complex than being merely "law-for-animals," for the more-than-human world is forever classified into smaller and smaller subspecies. This book will demonstrate how notions of animality and humankind's duties toward more-than-human bodies invoke multiple different paradigms. In the case of animal law writ large, we must consider the differentiation between "domestic" animal law and "wild" animal law, for although this binary, even essentialist, conception of animal life is insufficient and vague (see Derrida, 2002), it has nonetheless served as the basis for differential policies and actions in U.S. law. Domestic animal laws have a complex history, particularly since the act of domestication in and of itself is a debated historical "event." For those species used for biomedical research, like cats, dogs, apes, and hamsters, contemporary manifestations of domestic animal protection laws emerged in 1876 with the passage of the United Kingdom's Cruelty to Animals Act. This act, which designated a central governing body to approve animals for research, emerged in response to mass antivivisection campaigns against scientists throughout the nineteenth century, wherein many stray animals (or even "petnapped" owned animals) were brutally killed or tortured in the name of scientific discovery. The United States endured a similar outcry over vivisection throughout the 1960s, resulting in the passage of the Animal Welfare Act of 1966, intended to regulate the sale, handling, etc. of animals used for research purposes. (Notably, those animals most commonly used for experimentations—mice and rats—have historically been excluded from protections.)

Recognizable legal protection of "pets"—most often cats and dogs—dates back to the Victorian era in Europe, when indoor pet-keeping became a more common practice. European societies for the prevention of cruelty to animals (SPCAs) emerged in response to what were increasingly deemed cruel practices, such as the beating of carriage horses or the overworking of dogs as draught animals. When Henry Bergh, an American on assignment in Russia, saw and prevented a carriage horse from being beaten in 1863, he returned to the United States, resigned his post, and decided to dedicate his life to animal protection, leading to the founding of the American Society for the Prevention of Cruelty to Animals (ASPCA) in

1866. As the first domestic animal protection agency in the Western hemisphere, the ASPCA fought for animal welfare legislation and charters ranging from the establishment of municipal animal shelters to the establishment of anticruelty laws against horses, dogs, etc. Currently, the ASPCA (along with other domestic animal protection organizations) runs national and international campaigns ranging from promoting spay-and-neuter campaigns for cats and dogs to the establishment of nationwide "no-kill" animal shelters to the quest to ban the slaughter of horses for meat consumption.

American livestock "protections" emerged primarily in response to Upton Sinclair's groundbreaking book *The Jungle*. Initial response to the book resulted in the Pure Food and Drug Act and the Meat Inspection Act in the early 1900s, but these laws eventually led to the regulation of live animal bodies with the 1958 Humane Methods of Slaughter Act. In 1978, the law was expanded to allow USDA inspectors to stop slaughtering lines if they deemed practices to be inhumane. Current legislative efforts include quests to stop particularly gruesome practices on industrial farms, such as the use of gestation crates for female pigs. (However, most of these laws are consistently under- or unenforced.)

Meanwhile, the basis for a good portion of contemporary wildlife-related laws dates back to medieval and colonial-era understandings of the "wild"—*who* should be allowed to hunt game (usually moneyed White men), *how* (utilizing guns and other "proper," "civilized" hunting methods), and for what purpose (only when "necessary"—although this included, strangely, for sport). These proto-animal rights legislations initially dictated who had the right to hunt wild game in Europe and, especially, in European colonies in tropical climates with new and exciting game. These understandings of game "protections" extended into the United States, much of which can be seen in the writings of both early preservationists like John Muir and conservationists like Gifford Pinchot. Mass extinctions of buffalo—the grand and majestic symbol of the frontier—further ignited the drive to protect wildlife insomuch that, they argued, hunting ought to be allowed only in sustainable circumstances dictated by civilized men. Current wildlife laws and policies, such as mass cullings, the removal of invasive species, and the designation of which species are killable for sport, take clear influence from what was essentially a European animal right-to-kill movement (Muller, 2017).

The above represents an extraordinarily condensed version of how U.S. American animal law came to exist in its current form. Ultimately, a few themes arise: There has emerged a philosophical consensus that animals ought not to be treated cruelly for the sake of cruelty alone. Cruelty can be permitted to the extent that it is necessary—with the term necessary of course defined by instrumentalism. Such instrumentalism is defensible to the extent that animals are not direct subjects of the law, but rather objects of it. Debates about the status of animals in the legal system range across ideological spectrums, from Cartesian conceptions of animals as empty containers devoid of value to medieval vicars' willingness to put animals in front of a jury and assign lawyers on their behalf. However, emergent and long-lasting policies and precedents most typically adhere to the "kindness" principle, which does not so much question if animals *should* be used, but rather addresses the *manner* in which that use should occur.

As I will further explain, most of the aforementioned history has resulted in an incremental animal *welfare* approach to law, one which flies in stark contrast to the radical, revolutionary principles of animal *rights*. In large part, animal law scholarship and practice largely holds "a narrow ideological starting point . . . its idiom has remained largely polemical . . . while its agenda has been decidedly reformist" (Mussawir & Otomo, 2013, p. 1). Not all animal law scholars and practitioners are so decidedly conservative in their approach to justice. However, even the more "radical" conceptualizations of rights too often have difficulty escaping their historical embeddedness in colonial exploitation and liberal humanist universalisms and essentialisms.

Animal Welfare/Animal Rights

Summative discourse regarding U.S. American animal rights law most typically accepts that there are two schools of thought regarding the movement's judicial endgame. The first and most common approach, emerging from the aforementioned anticruelty paradigm, is that of *animal welfare*. The second adopts a considerably more "radical" and "revolutionary" paradigm of *animal rights* (Stewart, Smith & Denton, 2012). Although in public discourse the two are sometimes used interchangeably, they are hardly synonymous legal schools. Central to their differences are opposing communicative strategies and tactics.

The former approach, animal welfare, lives up to its name by concerning itself with the physical and emotional well-being of animal bodies in situ. This approach primarily concerns itself with ending unnecessary suffering in interspecies interactions—the keyword here being *unnecessary,* which in most "welfarist"

(Francione, 1996) discourses is not focused on large-scale institutional critique of *why* animals are mistreated, but rather small-scale legal intervention into *how* they are treated. Animal welfare is thus anthropocentric at its core in that it advocates for compassion for animals on the part of humans, but does not question if it is ultimately natural, normal, right, or wrong to consider animals as chattel with predominantly instrumental value. This lack of questioning, this earsplitting silence, must not be considered a coincidence as much as a rhetorical strategy of absence and invisibility that allows for surface level moral reform while pivoting from difficult questions of systemic, multispecies, and all-too-often state-sponsored violence (Nakayama & Krizek, 1995).

Some of the largest animal-oriented organizations in the United States maintain a distinctly welfarist approach when articulating their visions of animal law. The Humane Society of the United States (HSUS), for instance, prides itself on lobbying and putting moral pressure on agriculture-affiliated institutions to end painful practices in industrial farming. In 2015, HSUS filed a suit against the wholesale supermarket Costco because it had "misrepresented the way its eggs are produced" due to its supplying company, Hillandale Farms, having "deceived consumers concerned about animal welfare and the filthy and unsanitary conditions." The pastoral, peaceful images advertised on the egg crates did not match the reality of the birds "locked in cages so tightly they couldn't even spread their wings, live birds forced to share cages with the mummified remains of their dead cage mates, fly infestations, and deteriorating facilities" (Humane Society of the United States, 2015, paras. 3–4). HSUS decried the unethical treatment of the birds, but ultimately framed their concerns not for the sake of the chickens themselves, but for false advertising and detriments to consumer safety.

One could claim that this discourse was merely a strategic approach to lit-igation, a way to make a human-centered courtroom "care" about the chickens from a rational legal perspective. Indeed, why on Earth would the Food and Drug Administration care about anything other than the safety of consumers? However, a glance through the pages of HSUS's larger history suggests that the organization rarely goes past advocacy that would utterly abolish practices ending in the death of animals for human pleasure. Never has HSUS argued, legally or otherwise, that the act of using chickens for eggs might *in and of itself* be morally questionable. While commending McDonald's for its elimination of gestation crates in 2012 and its proposed shift to cage-free eggs in 2016, the organization did not question how the motto of "billions served" reflects an increasingly unsustainable, on-demand, meat-oriented society. While *some* practices ought to be abolished entirely, such as painful cosmetic experiments on rabbits, or the wholesale slaughter of horses for meat, or the trial of animal abusers as a misdemeanor rather than a felony, a legal paradigm emphasizing animal welfare rarely questions the overarching status of animals-as-objects inherent in a legal system based in human dominance and the protection of human economic interests. Welfarist *tactics,* in other words, are not always connected to overarching *strategies* geared toward an end to species-based discrimination.

This book will not take a welfarist approach to animal law on the grounds that it too often provides surface-level, "bandage" type solutions to larger, systemic problems in human and more-than-human relationships. On the contrary, it will adopt (and simultaneously critique) an animal rights approach to animal liberation. Again, animal welfare stands in stark contrast to animal rights: the latter is considerably more radical in its philosophical undergirding, as it is focused not only on how to *lessen* animal suffering at human hands but also how to incorporate best practices that might *end* systemic, normalized suffering in its entirety. As this book will explain in more detail, a rights approach thus advocates against the use of animal bodies for food, clothing, entertainment, experimentation, and in any other arena in which animals are merely means to human ends. (Certain manifestations are more controversial, however, such as pet-keeping and domestication—as will be explored further in chapter 3.) While an organization and its leader(s) might not file a suit demanding that chicken farming be made illegal immediately (such a case would have nearly zero chance of winning in a court of law at the moment), an animal rights paradigm of law demands that the tactics used by organizations reflect a larger strategy that envisions, over time, the dissolution of exploitative human practices against animal bodies.

An infamous example of a U.S. American animal rights organization (although my case study in chapter 3 disagrees with this label) that emphasizes both activism and litigation is People for the Ethical Treatment of Animals (PETA). The organization claims an "uncompromising stance" on animal rights, wherein "we aren't afraid to make the difficult comparisons, say the unpopular thing, or point out the uncomfortable truth, if it means that animals will benefit" (PETA, n.d.). While the litigation branch of PETA has, admittedly, engaged in lawsuits that might be considered more on the side of animal welfare than rights (for instance, suing Kentucky Fried Chicken for being dishonest about the conditions of its suppliers' chickens), its overarching strategy is to use such lawsuits to bring attention to mass cruelty in order to promote a vegan lifestyle. Similarly, its most prominent and mass-mediated suits are those which unapologetically call for the abolition of seemingly normal, but ultimately unethical, human-animal interactions. Examples include, but are not limited to, suing SeaWorld for keeping captive orcas as literal slaves, thus violating the Thirteenth Amendment (see the conclusion) and suing a photographer for profiting from a photo that a primate actually took with the man's own camera, thus violating copyright law. Although the suits may seem absurd, PETA's many attempts to draw attention to animal subjectivity and inherent value through "image events" (Delicath & DeLuca, 2003) and mass-mediated lawsuits (fauxsuits) ultimately function as an animal rights tactic, whether the litigation is successful or not (and it often is not).

This book contends that the differences in rhetorical strategies and tactics in animal law is not as simple as a welfare/rights binary. Indeed, even conceptualizations of what animals' "rights" are and where those rights come from differ from party to party, ultimately influencing the route individual lawyers and larger organizations take when advocating on behalf of animals. To quote Mussawir and Otomo, "Certain familiar coordinates in jurisprudence" such as "the subject and object of rights, the legal person, the sacred and profane, jurisdiction and territory, normativity, representation" are all "reshaped in the presence of the animal" (p. 3). This reshaping, however, differs across ideological party lines. Within legal and broader cultural communities, the most dominant schools of animal rights theory come from the philosophical schools of utilitarianism and classical rights theory, with the former advocated by Peter Singer and the latter by Tom Regan. The two famed ethicists are hardly bitter rivals—in fact, they are happy to publish together—but their philosophical standpoints have important differences, and thus implications, for animal rights activism and litigation.

Singer, often dubbed the "father" of the contemporary U.S. American animal rights movement, gained fame with his publication of *Animal Liberation* in 1975. What is ironic about this "fatherhood" is that Singer does not really advocate for animal *rights* per se, but rather animal *interests*. All living beings have a shared interest in avoiding suffering. Thus, the only "right" of moral importance is the right of all beings to an *equal consideration of interests*—the act of "weighing" the concerns of interspecies stakeholders in times of moral dilemmas through a nonanthropocentric lens. To advocate for the suffering of another being on the basis of its species is merely a form of discrimination on par with prejudice on the basis of race, sex, gender, etc. Interests can and do come into conflict with one another—such is the basis of day-to-day interaction. Singer's act-utilitarian philosophy requires that, in situations of competing interests between human beings and other species, the interests of the former must not be granted any greater weight than the interests of the latter. Once the two sets of interests are given equal weight, one party's violation of another's interests must be deemed sufficiently necessary in order to gain social or legal credence. Taking this stance, Singer concludes, would force nearly all human-animal conflicts to end in favor of the animal. The desire to eat meat, for instance, is of less utilitarian weight than the interest of the animal in living. The desire to see a lion in a zoo for entertainment is less important than the lion's desire to roam freely in its natural environment. Certainly some rare "lifeboat" instances such as animal experimentation to cure an immediately dangerous disease are more complicated and require greater depth of philosophical thought, but given the realm of alternatives such as artificial human flesh and the documented insufficiencies of analogizing animal bodies to human bodies, almost all animal experimentation would also be unjustifiable.

The key components of Singer's utilitarian framework, then, are the existence of interests, the shared capacity for and interest in avoiding suffering, and the necessity of equal consideration of interests regardless of species status. Of course, as with any hard utilitarian framework, his stance comes with its own set of moral dilemmas. For instance, how, how can one "weigh" species interests equally in a context when nonhumans cannot communicate their interests in ways immediately intelligible to humans? If humans are the interpreters (and thus the assigners) of the interests of nonhumans, are human-led philosophical "weighting games" really all that balanced? And how, exactly, should one assign value to various harms (e.g., monetary harm and job losses from the loss of a fur company versus the loss of mink lives to make fur coats)? Some, but not all, of these questions are rendered moot under the framework of Singer's contemporary, Regan.

Regan gained fame in 1983 by publishing *The Case for Animal Rights.* Unlike Singer, Regan's approach takes seriously the notion of *inherent* rights, as conceived in classical Enlightenment theories of being, as necessary and important to the promotion of species equality. Classical rights theory is, for animal liberation thinkers, a necessary contrast to contractarianism, wherein only those who clearly agree to shared moral principles are entitled to equal rights. Such rhetoric has been unjustly used to defend animal exploitation on the grounds that animals do not agree to human rights and thus humans should not agree to animal rights. Rights are not human constructs, but rather natural and preexisting. These inherent rights thus translate into living beings' inherent value, a key concept in Reganite animal rights, wherein animals, as fully capable subjects-of-a-life, cannot be morally used as means-to-ends for human beings. Instrumentalism is "the basic wrong that attaches to our viewing and treating these animals as our resources," and a vision of animal liberation must therefore favor the total abolition of instrumentalism—for food, for science, for entertainment, for everything—no matter how much a human being might benefit from an animal's exploitation (Regan, 1985, para. 4). The key components here are rights as the protection of beings' primordial, preexisting *inherent value,* the animals themselves as *subjects-of-a-life,* and the pursuit of justice through total *abolition.* Under such a framework, the complicated utilitarian mathematics of Singer's methodology are rendered useless. Animal rights are not a matter of weights and measures, but rather of intrinsic significance. Of course, the question of interpreting animal needs, steeped as they are in alterity, remains an open dilemma—as do questions of how to integrate an antispeciesist, abolitionist framework into broader social justice movements led by humans.

Animal rights versus animal welfare; Peter Singer versus Tom Regan—among the most basic discourses of animal liberation—these would at first glance appear to be the only philosophical, strategic, and tactical controversies of note. However, this simplified narrative is hardly sufficient for either an understanding of the "animal rights movement" writ large or a conceptualization of how the movement might advance in rapidly changing U.S. American sociocultural and legal spheres grappling with the cultural politics of identity.

Moving Beyond the Welfare/Rights Binary

This book seeks to move beyond the prototypical welfare versus rights debate. Furthermore, it expands and explodes the inter-rights controversy over utilitarianism versus classical rights. I do not question the idea that animal rights (that is to say, the abolition of animal exploitation for human gain on the basis of species alone) is a superior ethical stance than animal welfare. I also do not argue that the notions of suffering, interests, inherent value, and subjectivity are of extreme importance in understanding the why and the how of animal rights activism and, by extension, animal rights litigation. What I do take issue with, however, is the distinct *lack of representation* in the "big voices" of animal rights theory and praxis, particularly with regard to how animal issues ought to be handled in the legal sphere, and how that definitive lack has led to an ontological shallowness in theorizing/applying the overarching philosophies, strategies, and tactics necessary for the pursuit of *total liberation,* a concept defined by Steven Best as "a global alliance politics of unprecedented scope and range" wherein "human and animal liberation movements are inseparable, such that none can be free until all are free" (Best, 2007, n.p.). The philosophical dominance of liberal humanist approaches to animal rights—be they a welfarist rule of kindness, an act-utilitarian focus on interests, or a classical rights insistence on inherent value—exclude, by virtue of their European Enlightenment roots, modes of thought and praxis that engage with "difference," well, *differently.* Specifically, my task is an *ontological decolonization* of animal rights legal discourse that aims to better incorporate insights from identity studies of race, gender, class, ability, sexuality, and other so-called modes of "being" human. It is an attempt to make visible, criticize, and revise rhetorics steeped in what Quijano (2000) dubbed the "coloniality of power," referring to the ordering and classification of the world via a process of racialization and the construction of difference via systems of knowledge, hierarchies, and culture. Decolonization must be understood, then, as a mode of "epistemic disobedience," explicated by semiotician Walter Mignolo as:

> The energy that does not allow the operation of the logic of coloniality nor believes the fairy tales of the rhetoric of modernity … decolonial thinking is, then, thinking that de-links and opens … to the possibilities hidden … by the modern rationality that is mounted and enclosed by categories of Greek, Latin, and the six modern imperial European languages. (Mignolo, 2011, p. 46)

Far from being a turn toward anthropocentrism, my orientation toward multispecies justice emerges via a simultaneous engagement with critical animal liberation scholars and ideological rhetorical methods—what I describe as a critical vegan rhetoric.

Firstly, what do I mean by a "lack of representation"? There is little doubt that the stereotype associated with a U.S. American animal rights adherent is a White, middle to upper-class, left-leaning female. And, in terms of demographics, this characterization is statistically somewhat accurate. Numerous studies confirm that those who identify as vegan, vegetarian, or part of an animal rights movement predominantly, although certainly not exclusively, meet these specifications

(Harper, 2012; Mika, 2006; Wrenn, 2017). However, these demographics must not be considered benign or coincidental. Rather, they deserve critical interrogation for two reasons. First, why does "Whiteness" pervade the animal rights movement to such an extent that some social justice activists have dubbed it an "animal Whites movement" (Wise, 2005)? And second, why—despite the clear preeminence of female-identified bodies in the movement—are the most vocal voices in the animal rights movement, particularly in its litigation arm, distinctly *masculine?*

The animal rights movement has, at least within a U.S. American context, tended to embrace a "politics of whiteness" (Giroux, 1997), that discourages racially, ethnically, financially, etc. marginalized persons from joining the movement's ranks. Much of the movement's discourse has tended toward neoliberal frameworks of justice that emphasize the capacity of individualism and consumer choice to achieve animal liberation. An animal rights ethic, from a consumption-oriented framework, necessitates a shift to a vegan lifestyle involving the abolition of all animal products for food, clothing, and cosmetics, as well as a staunch boycott of entertainment events that include animal labor. This boycott/buycott strategy (Pezzullo, 2011) is surely a legitimate means by which to advocate for justice, for divesting in exploitation is necessarily preferable to being financially complicit in it. Nonetheless, a hyper-consumeristic framework of justice risks becoming embedded in the very capitalistic framework that led to the industrial exploitation systems as we know them today.

When individual pocketbooks are understood as the premier mode of animal activism, the animal rights movement must seriously account for the distinct inequalities of race, ethnicity, class, etc. that lead to some having more to spend than others. What often occurs, however, are webpages and blog posts dedicated to living "vegan on a budget" or Facebook disputes over why a vegan diet is inexpensive considering the comparatively low cost of beans and rice. Setting aside the fact that veganism is certainly possible when watching one's money, it is notable how this sort of neoliberal discourse paints the lack of a vegan ethic as an individual moral failing rather than a systemic phenomenon that makes a plant-based lifestyle more realistic for some parties than others. Little is mentioned about food deserts, for instance, or how marginalized communities are often rendered to such states of poverty that successfully buying *anything,* much less a specifically vegan product, must be considered a moral victory. And these parties are, statistically, more likely to be persons of color, single mothers, or other "Others" demonized in larger political individualist discourses.

Furthermore, U.S. animal rights discourse often invokes a postracial approach to discourse that inevitably recenters a strategic rhetoric of Whiteness at the expense of communities of color (Nakayama & Krizek, 1995). Prototypical examples of postracial activist tactics include People for the Ethical Treatment of Animals' 2011 exhibit entitled "Animal Slavery," which contrasted violent images of the transatlantic slave trade with contemporary images of industrial agriculture; large-scale animal rights campaigns against "low-hanging fruit" events sponsored by Indigenous populations, such as the Makah Whale Hunt; and, of course, the adoption of liberal humanist "rights" frameworks, such as act-utilitarianism and classical rights that have, since their roots in the Enlightenment, been strategically deployed to eliminate non-White persons from the realm of moral consideration.

To be clear, there are distinct material similarities between the horrific history of American slavery and the contemporary conditions of animal agriculture. And, of course, any animal killed for the sake of "tradition" is a tragic event that should require serious and self-reflexive interrogation. But, when articulated within a movement already renowned for its mostly Caucasian demographic, when set beside a movement seemingly disinterested in the contemporary slaughters of Black bodies outside of chattel slavery, and when apparently unquestioning of the settler-colonialist environment that has sought to destroy indigenous knowledges and practices for centuries, rhetorics of animal rights ultimately fall short of a vision of liberation attractive to anyone but those who already feel free. This state of affairs, as people of color, gender and sexual minorities, disabled persons, and other systemically disenfranchised members of the animal rights movement have consistently critiqued (and I will consistently reiterate), is representative of a movement currently lacking and in massive need of a critical vegan rhetoric.

To the second question—why is a women-dominated movement subordinated, particularly in questions of litigation, by the voices of (White) men?—I offer two possible answers. (I do note, of course, that using "women" and "men" are incoherent terms at best, and that my use of these categories is meant to reflect demographic survey/interview data collected by past scholars, not to assert the singular existence of two genders or sexes.) The first reason has to do with the preeminence of White-centered, patriarchal epistemologies in the legal profession itself. A 2017 report by the American Bar Association demonstrated the homogeneity of the United States' professionalized legal sphere. Using data recorded from forty-six states, it was determined that licensed legal professionals were majority male (65 percent). Furthermore, data from twenty-six states suggested the institution's

White-centeredness, with 85 percent of respondents identifying as Caucasian. It is worth noting that since 2007 the number of women in law has increased by 4.9 percent and people of color by 5.5 percent. However, these modest gains do not negate the fact that the United States' legal institution is, demographically, not representative of an ever diversifying U.S. American "public" writ large. This demographic imbalance does not necessarily have to be a problem if we ignore the staunchly different "realities" that we inhabit by virtue of our unique subject positions.

Much like the animal rights movement, the "great speakers" of the U.S. American legal sphere—lawyers, judges, and other lawmakers—speak from a majority White, paternal subjectivity within an institution developed from that same set of ontological Enlightenment principles. There is little push or pull toward judicial overhaul in large part because those in charge of the institution were, demographically, raised within the very identity categories the United States' laws were designed to benefit from the country's start.

However, the innate maleness of the U.S. American legal sphere still does not fully account for the lack of women's voices in animal rights law. The problem (and it is a problem) is more insidious and in fact goes to the very roots of the animal rights movement. Indeed, the U.S. American animal rights movement is steeped in discourses and practices of patriarchy that require serious interrogation—a stunning revelation given the historical preeminence of women in the movement (Gaarder, 2011). At the time of writing, the animal rights movement is in a furor over the resignation of Wayne Pacelle, the CEO of the Humane Society of the United States, after multiple allegations of sexual harassment. People for the Ethical Treatment of Animals continues to come under fire for the use of "sex" to "sell" animal rights through the controversial use of pornography-as-activism. Acclaimed vegan feminist Carol J. Adams and others have even joined the viral feminist #MeToo hashtag movement, coining #ARMeToo in an attempt to deal with the casual culture of sexual inequality, harassment, bullying, and assault within the rank-and-file of animal rights organizations.

Such discourses are particularly notable given that the history of animal rights activism in Western contexts has been led in tandem with feminist causes and/ or female leadership—for instance, the social movement bridging between the women's suffrage movement and the antivivisection movement in the nineteenth century, the founding of the "Vegan Society" in 1944, and the defunct Feminists for Animal Rights organization of the 1980s and 1990s. Gaarder (2011) has proposed that structural sexism might account for contemporary manifestations of male dominance within the animal rights movement, particularly as activism moves from localized grassroots activism to large-scale, often multinational, nonprofit organizations wherein gendered divisions of labor are often more pronounced:

> It is common for women to create and lead grassroots movements, only to see the leadership turn over to men as the movement or organization becomes national or institutionalized.... Other patterns include a tendency for women to be the "organizers" while men occupy the public stage as the "leaders." ... Within revolutionary movements that utilize extreme tactics and guerilla warfare, men generally occupy the front lines while women remain in the background in positions of support. . . . These divisions frequently involve a devaluing of the work women do, and a valorization of the methods and imagery of "masculine" work. (Gaarder, 2011, p. 94)

Gaarder explained that, for some activists, they "believed the presence of male activists might be encouraging to men outside the movement, that they brought an air of 'legitimacy' to the cause, or that men conveyed an image of strength and power" so much so that "they were hoping that men with a more masculine image would join the movement" (Gaarder, 2011, p. 104). To do so, these activists claim, would do away with gendered understandings of animal rights as overly sentimental or emotional: "Making rational or intellectual arguments was deemed more respectable.... Language that emphasized respect, rights, or justice was preferable to being emotional about the suffering of animals" (p. 106). And, although the devaluation of sentimentality is hardly unique to animal activism, the result for this moment has led to the preeminence of male speakers at events, to the promotion of male figures to public roles in massive organizations, to the point that, according to one woman surveyed, "so it's like one man in charge of a lot of women" (p. 114). Ingrained gender roles and internalized sexism function on theoretical and practical levels in which emotions must be expunged in pursuit of rationality, and that rationality must be expressed via male bodies in order to have mass influence because direct action and confrontation are assumed to be masculine activities, thus necessitating the use of maleness for peak rhetorical effect.

This book takes seriously the claim that, far from being an incidental demographic occurrence, these differences in both movement membership and movement leadership *matter.* A distinct lack of diversity within animal rights is important on a practical level—a level best revealed through a serious engagement with ecofeminist thought. As critical sociologist Corey Wrenn has explained:

> Failure to diversify could have the effect of limiting participant numbers, skills and innovation, and access to other resource pools. Further, it runs the risk of hypocrisy in advocating for species-inclusive diversity, while simultaneously being unable to achieve human diversity in its own ranks. If only a particular demographic appears to support rights for other animals, a lack of diversity may also drain the movement's cultural capital. (Wrenn, 2016, p. 47)

A politics of Whiteness and patriarchy also risks an ontological homogeneity within animal rights theorizing that insufficiently accounts for the potential and necessary nonhumanist theorizations required for composing a coherent liberationist philosophy. Maneesha Deckha articulated how a genuinely multicultural (and, by extension, anti-anthropocentric) approach to animal rights necessitates a paradigmatic shift that must

> necessarily involve an awareness of colonial legacies paired with a self-reflective inquiry and consistency in critique. It will develop through good faith consultation and collaboration with marginalized cultural communities and will often result in partial claims, rather than universal ones. It does not, however, require a hands-off approach to cultural practices simply because they involve culture. Nor does it adopt a human-centered approach. The model strives for contextualized analysis of a particular problem from a space that recognizes the domesticating effects of universalist propositions and western discursive interventions in adjudicating and controlling Other cultures, while also seeking to rehabilitate the animal Other from subaltern status. (Deckha, 2007, p. 228)

And, as this book will demonstrate, this ontological expansion is of extreme importance for animals in judicial arenas. The necessity of such a paradigmatic shift, when placed in tandem with insights gleaned through ideological rhetorical critiques of animal rights legal leaders, guides my ultimate formulation of a critical vegan rhetoric.

A Defense of the Law

Given the rather pitiful representation of the U.S. American citizenry in the legal sphere, given the discourses of anthropocentrism that dominate even in discussions of animal welfare, and given the historical use of the "rule of law" to elevate the privileged to higher social status while institutionalizing the inferiority of the marginalized, some will undoubtedly argue that for this book to advocate from within the law at all is a wasted effort. For instance, some rhetors consistently argue that legal reform is insufficient, and that only revolutionary overhauls such as total police abolition, jail abolition, and the utilization of communal social-policing are sufficient to achieve justice writ large; still others maintain that criminality would not exist if not for the creation of a police state and that the dissolution of the law as we know it would necessarily lead to peace vis-à-vis the dominance of natural law (Ferrell, 1987; Newman, 2005; Osterfeld, 1989; Pepinsky, 1978; Stringham, 2011). And, in terms of legal "rights," some assert that the concept is so steeped in Whiteness, patriarchy, and other forms of oppression that it is ultimately useless as an organizational framework. To purport to work within an anticolonial framework vis-à-vis the utilization of legal institutions is naïve at best, pernicious at worst (Menon, 2004; Spade, 2015).

However, I argue that, for all its historical and contemporary deficiencies, the U.S. American legal sphere not only *might* be refurbished but *must* be. It is, of course, a historical anachronism to suppose that the law is a construct of the Western world. For instance, to accuse Hammurabi and his famous code of institutionalizing White European colonial values is quite a reach. To argue that laws are merely human constructs that legitimize the exploitation of others does little to account for the safeguards, retributions, and restitutions the legal system provides for those (exceedingly limited) subjects who have benefitted from its protections—albeit unfairly and disproportionately. Indeed, while the human-made legal systems have been far from historically equitable through time, space, or place, it is silly to ignore how codified principles of morality have ensured—albeit imperfectly—the protection of some from the physical and/or epistemological violence of others. For all the racism still in existence in the United States, persons cannot be legally held as chattel. For all the ableism, apartment complexes cannot legally deny tenants their service animals. For all the heterosexism, violence against others for reason of sexuality is legally classified as an especially heinous class of "hate" crime. To put it simply, the law has historically been used to codify oppressive ideologies.

However, legal reforms seek to replace these ideologies with properly liberatory ones—admittedly, with varying levels of success.

One could easily argue that social discipline as enacted through the law is a colonial endeavor when used by majority parties to oppress subalterns, that perhaps a return to traditional, localized tribal justice as evidenced by indigenous praxis is better suited to social justice. I argue that this distinction between "big" law and "local" law need not be an either-or but rather a both-and. The maintenance of a large-scale judicial system need not displace the value of localized, more culturally coherent organizations. I further suggest that an *entirely* stateless approach—prototypically understood as a distinctly libertarian anarchist approach to justice—where "live and let live" is the goal and any intervention from the state unto the self is undesirable, does little to promote a genuinely empathetic public. Social discipline is not merely naturalized and normalized through legal codes, but quite literally natural and normal as evidenced through ethological studies of how the more-than-human world exists morally (and differentially) "outside" of "society." The self does not exist outside of the social, and in a social comprised of upward of seven billion people and hundreds of billions of more-than-humans, every self must learn to exist in a manner that caters to, not works against, those with whom it shares the planet—a manner that this book will describe as a critical vegan rhetoric.

I recognize that at stake in these questions is a dispute between over whether humanity is inherently good or inherently brutal, whether the law is a natural defense against humanity's drive to injure or an unnatural precursor to domination and violence, whether Thomas Hobbes or Jean-Jacques Rousseau had it right all along. However, outside of the realm of philosophy, outside of scholarly navel-gazing and lengthy Facebook arguments, people and animals really *do* die at the hands of others. They really *do* experience violence based upon ideologies of superiority and inferiority. And this violence, whether it exists innately or by virtue of some external corrupting factor, is agreed to be undesirable by those who claim to be in favor of social justice. What exists in the here and now, not in the idyllic and imaginary, is a legal system that has done both desirable and undesirable things, that has both helped and hurt, that has behind it a history replete with revolutions and reformations. Barring some sudden, massive uprising, some idyllic fulfillment of Karl Marx's socialist revolution or Errico Malatesta's anarchist upheaval against a well-defended, nuclear-armed American security state, the law as we know it is not going anywhere. Therefore, no matter how "bad" or "good" humanity is, the composition and codification of laws will, almost certainly, remain a strategic necessity in the pursuit of social justice. Can the law be perfected, made good, made equitable? To be frank, maybe, maybe not. Must we try? Yes, because doing nothing is not an option.

Legal "reform," however, can become a legal revolution. But this revolution must happen from within and without, from the top down and from the bottom up. Courts, from Supreme to local, must enact decisions that set legal precedents conducive to long-term change. This process must involve greater representation among legal professionals and a clearer vision of what the law must be to promote long-term justice instead of an ethically incoherent status quo. There is a difference between trying animal abuse as a misdemeanor versus a felony; there is a difference between compensating owners of a murdered pet for the value of dog-as-property versus the inherent value of dog-as-morally-important-legal-subject; and there is a difference between setting in place species-arbitrary, unenforced rules of animal testing for cosmetics or poorly thought-out grad-school experiments and banning animal testing altogether. There is a difference between banning trans fats versus ensuring that even impoverished schoolchildren have access to healthy lunches; there is a difference between accepting an outdated law banning debtors' prisons versus eliminating a corrupt bail bondage system relegating the impoverished to long-term imprisonment or forced plea deals; and there is a difference between outlawing murder versus genuinely holding law enforcement accountable for using excessive force against persons of color.

But at the same time, the powerful cannot (and likely will not) enact substantial legal reform without sufficient calls to do so from below. Vernacular rhetorics and grassroots activism are in and of themselves forms of legal praxis, putting moral pressure on others to resolve incoherent, unethical behaviors (Merry, Levitt, Rosen, & Yoo, 2010). Animal welfare will not become animal rights until the public has sufficiently accepted the moral warrant that species discrimination is undesirable. This warrant will likely not emerge unless and until other codified isms are exposed, interrogated, and castigated in the court of public opinion.

Ultimately, legal reform-as-revolution must emerge from a reciprocal feedback loop of institutional, professional, local, and interpersonal strategies and tactics working within and among each other in the pursuit of total liberation. This stance does not advocate for the dissolution of structural interdependences tout court, but rather the creation of more positive bonds and relationships among individuals and the systems in which they function. Within an animal rights paradigm of total liberation, "it is not enough to democratize power if political change does not also eradicate the pathologies of speciesism and domineering humanism, for this only *redistributes the authority and capacities to exploit and kill*" (Best, 2007, n.p.). Speciesism (Singer, 1975) is not separate from, but rather foundational to, legal and social justice. After all, "humans are animals, but we have made ourselves non-animals in order to feel superior and distinguish ourselves from other animals" (Cao, 2014, p. 170). There are severe ontological consequences of such a seemingly normative stance. If indeed speciesism is "the central organizing principle of human life," then it comprises a "total stance toward life, a total project forming the ontological ground of human identity and purpose" centered around "the idea of murder itself, the affirmation of mass killing" (Sanbondmatsu, 2011, pp. 31, 41). Thus, this book stands by the following tenet of social justice:

> Not only that people change their views of one another, but also that they make a *qualitative leap* beyond humanism to rethink their relations to animals and the natural world. It argues that species boundaries are as arbitrary as those of race and sex and seeks to move the moral bar and boundaries of community from reason and language to sentience and subjectivity. By extending rights to sentient (not merely "rational") beings to protect them from human exploitation, by advancing deeper and more encompassing notions of moral equality, by developing a broader notion of community and citizenship, by forging a more profound and holistic mode of critical thinking, and by promoting changes in the human diet that have enormous positive consequences for human health, social justice, hunger, peace, and ecology, the animal liberation movement is a key catalyst of social change and moral progress and a necessary part of any revolution worth its name. (Best, 2007, n. p.)

And, in the spirit of these values, the rest of this book will utilize an ecofeminist approach to law and an ideological approach to rhetoric in order to demonstrate the axiological and teleological value of a critical vegan rhetoric.

Contributions to Rhetorical Studies

Rhetoric is perhaps the oldest form of communication studies scholarship. This book contributes in particular to the work of those rhetoricians interested in taking a rhetorical, specifically a *critical* rhetorical (McKerrow, 1989), approach to studies of environmental discourse in U.S. American contexts. To suggest that species other than the esteemed *Homo sapiens* might be capable of agentic, persuasive communication (or to be deserving of rights in relation to these communicative capabilities) might have, in decades past, seemed an erroneous thesis. After all, the root of the academic's rhetorical tradition is most often credited to the ancient Greeks, not the ancient ape from whom humankind is said to have evolved. The purported "father" of Western rhetorical theory is Aristotle, whose *Rhetoric* distinguished humans as the only speaking animals. According to Aristotelian theory, ethos, pathos, and logos are the three essential persuasive elements in any given rhetorical transaction. Logos, the use of "logic" in argumentation, has been accepted in argumentation scholarship as the premier trait of effective persuasion—a phenomenon that has led to a distinct "logocentrism" in rhetorical scholarship that claims humans are the only rational, and thus logical, animals (Goodale, 2015). This "tyranny of logic" sustained itself via the purported "Age of Science" during the Enlightenment era (Goodale, 2015, p. 13). And, even though neo-Aristotelianism has lost its preeminence as the model of rhetorical scholarship, other "big names" in rhetorical theory continually elevate "humanity" above animals by virtue of their capacity for rhetoricity. For example, Kenneth Burke's perspective on the human/nonhuman binary is subsequently reflected in his theory of "symbolic action," which is premised upon the superiority of human beings as the only "active agents" (Goodale & Black, 2010).

Nonetheless, as rhetorical scholarship has grown, scholars have broadened their minds and opened up their discipline to new possibilities, among them the idea that humans are not unique in their particular communicative abilities or, subsequently, their particular moral merits and entitlement to rights. As many contemporary environmental rhetoricians have argued, not only do animals engage in intentional communication with one another, their linguistic and extralinguistic capabilities have distinctly rhetorical qualities (see Milstein, 2008; Plec, 2012). Goodale and Black (2010) rightly claimed that the humanistic arguments so prevalent in traditional rhetorical scholarship "are rarely premised on fact, but rather on long held assumptions and the effectiveness of many tropes that have not yet been studied in depth" (p. 3). Fortunately, for rhetoricians willing to look beyond a narrow, logocentric understanding of persuasive discourse, much evidence exists outside of traditional rhetorical theory to account for the subjectivity of animal beings. Spurred by George Kennedy's seminal manuscript "A Hoot in the Dark: The Evolution of General Rhetoric"—"untimely" though it was (Hawhee, 2011)—his assertion that "rhetoric is manifest in all animal life and existed long before the evolution of human beings" provided a useful origin point for the understanding of more-than-human and interspecies communication (Kennedy, 1992, p. 4). Rhetoricians since then have taken Kennedy at his word by studying extradiscursive communicative acts performed by the more-than-human world that have had persuasive effects on human beings (see Milstein, 2008; Schutten, 2008; Seegert, 2014; among others).

More-than-human rhetoric has now been examined from many angles and given many names. Plec (2013) called this rhetorical phenomenon "internatural communication," which she defines as "the exchange of intentional energy between humans and other animals as well as communication among animals and other forms of life . . . about the construction of meaning and the constitution of our world through interaction" (p. 6). Other names include "animate rhetoric" (Seegert, 2016) and "bestial rhetoric" (Gordon, Lind & Kutnicki, 2017; Hawhee, 2011). Whatever its name, realizations of more-than-humans' capacity for rhetorical agency have and should continue to encourage rhetoricians to take seriously the role of what was once deemed a static environment in rhetorical transactions, wherein human "culture" constructs through discourse the boundaries of the more-than-human world, and yet that world simultaneously molds and changes humankind through its distinctive communicative abilities. Rhetoric manifests itself across species lines "in the survival instincts of animals who face ravaged ecosystems and the existential threat of mass extinction" (Gordon, Lind, & Kutnicki, 2017, p. 222).

By integrating critical animal studies into environmental rhetorical studies, rhetoricians can be encouraged to take on a critical, ethical stance on imminent issues regarding environmental degradation, mass extinctions, and the role of anthropocentric rhetoric in the construction of species and interspecies inequalities. This book builds upon those possibilities not by proving, once again, that animals can communicate rhetorically, but rather by pinpointing the rhetorical mechanisms by which animal rights oriented rhetors can simultaneously speak *for* or *on behalf of* animals in manners that are unintentionally detrimental to their well-being.

Despite many rhetoricians' anthropocentric biases, scholarship has grown increasingly interested in the rhetoric of activism geared toward the more-than-human world—particularly since the "social movement turn" in rhetorical studies (see Griffin, 1952). Among these movements is American environmentalism and, as an implicit subsection, the U.S. American animal rights movement. Critical and historical analyses of the birth and flourishing of these two movements have not only cast the more-than-human world as a subject of interest for communication scholars but also revealed the pernicious nature/culture binary that has been rhetorically constructed to ideologically separate humankind from the more-than-human world (see DeLuca & Demo, 2000; DeLuca & Slawter-Volkening, 2009; Oravec, 1981). This book builds upon such work, particularly in that it goes beyond constructions of the "environment" as some far-off, untouched wilderness and interrogates those moments of liminality wherein food, pet-keeping, and other human/more-than-human interactions muddle the murky waters of pristine wilderness. Distinctions between "nature" and "culture" are erroneous, often reliant upon constructions of a "wild" and "untouched" natural world that is merely a rhetorical fabrication based upon the intentional erasure of indigenous and more-than-human histories (Cronon, 1996).

Significantly, this book aligns itself with Robert Cox's assertion that environmental rhetoricians have an "ethical duty" to pursue prescriptive, justice-oriented scholarly projects given the environmental crises of our time (Cox, 2007). As a morally conscious, justice-seeking environmental rhetorician, I fuse critical cultural communication scholarship with analyses of environmental discourses, heeding Raymie McKerrow's 1989 call for rhetorical prescriptive, rather than descriptive, scholarship. Like Plec (2007), I call upon environmental rhetoricians to examine how issues of exigency, representation, and sustainability are implicated in broader critical cultural environmental politics. Like Danielle Endres and Phaedra C. Pezzullo, I call for an explication of the interconnections between human oppression and environmental degradation, putting environmental rhetoricians in conversation with what is called the U.S. American "environmental justice" movement (see Endres, 2009a, 2009b, 2009c; 2013 and Pezzullo, 2003a, 2003b, 2009a, 2009b).

The animal rights movement in particular does not, sadly, garner as much attention as environmental justice in communication studies. While environmental justice is a necessary addition to engaged environmental communication scholarship, it is not always considered alongside the U.S. American animal rights movement as either a part of or a partner to human justice in relation to the more-than-human world. This omission is hardly surprising given the communication field's general lack of engagement with the animal rights movement at all, much less as a crucial component of environmental communication's supposed ethical imperative. Of the generally few writings available on rhetoric and animal rights, authors do not generally examine the rhetoric of animal rights for its moral merits or ethical imperatives, but rather as opportune case studies to elucidate new rhetorical concepts (see Atkins-Sayre, 2010; Black, 2003; Stewart, 1999). Some scholarship confuses and conflates animal rights and environmentalism, struggling to find where the movements intersect and depart (see Corbett, 2006). In many cases, it is difficult to determine the extent to which these authors have been influenced by or interpret animal rights through a welfarist paradigm, a rights paradigm, or a vexing conflation of the two.

Most available essays on animal rights *for* animal rights' sake are confined to Greg Goodale and Jason Edward Black's anthology *Arguments about Animal Ethics*. There are, however, some other standout writings that not only offer contributions to rhetorical studies and/or environmental communication but also make an attempt to probe the undergirding ideologies of the U.S. American animal rights movement to gauge how their discourses function in larger paradigms of civic engagement, social justice, and total liberation across species lines (see Broad, 2013; Doyle, 2016; Freeman, 2010; Olson & Goodnight, 1994). Some have emerged with an interest in the intersection of animal ethics and ethically imperative social justice endeavors, seemingly aware of the important connection between environmentalism, environmental justice, and animal liberation (see Broad, 2016; Freeman, Bekoff & Bexell, 2011; Milstein & Dickenson, 2012; Rogers, 2008; Singer, 2016). Consistent among these critiques is a staunch understanding among scholars that "solidarity" between humans and those deemed "animals" is essential in the pursuit of larger liberationist goals:

> We [should premise] our concept of membership of a human/animal solidaristic community on a division between a pre-political relation of solidarity through internatural communication, corresponding to care, and a more generalizable institutionalization of those insights. (von Essen & Allen, 2017, p. 11)

In line with the aforementioned authors' orientations toward animal rights scholarship, this book attempts to offer an in-depth exploration, analysis, and critique of what is ultimately an understudied social movement with massive implications for the pursuit of social justice in the twenty-first century.

This book further argues that, even if environmental rhetoricians do not identify themselves with "animal rights" per se, their scholarship will suffer without a firm understanding of anthropocentric ideologies and the impact of those ideologies not only on animal beings but also on human beings. We might consider, for instance, how racial minorities have been consistently cast as "too animal" to be treated as equals in colonial projects, a pattern that continues even in a purportedly (and erroneously) "post" colonial era. A parallel consideration to be addressed is how the all-too-common critique that oppressed persons are treated "like animals" implies that animal bodies may be treated instrumentally and inhumanely while human beings should be immune to such treatment. While some might deem this turn in scholarship to be "too political," it is equally valid to argue that decidedly "apolitical" scholarship constitutes complicity in oppressive structures. Environmental rhetoricians, whatever their stance on the politicization of the academy, have nonetheless grown in number and gained ideological support from this prescriptive scholarly orientation. This book supports that scholarly orientation by critically engaging with the U.S. American animal rights movement via a critical vegan rhetoric, thus offering environmental scholars unfamiliar with ecofeminism, feminist legal studies, and/ or critical animal studies a means by which to conceive of animal liberation legal rhetorics as part of a larger social justice endeavor in need of consistent ideological interrogation via rhetorical criticism.

I ultimately hope that this book will contribute to animal liberation as both a theory and a praxis. As time goes on and the Earth's capacity to sustain life plummets at ever-faster rates, reconceptualizing the role (and even the definition) of the human in a definitively more-than-human world is perhaps the most important issue facing us all. As the reach of capitalist exploitation spreads through the many tentacles in the many pots of "post" colonial globalization, interspecies conflict is at an all-time high—industrialized cruelty, after all, has no moral limits. Nonetheless, without an approach to animal rights that incorporates the perspectives of the traditionally invisible both to the "movement" and to the colonized world at-large—women, people of color, etc.—animal liberation and, by extension, total liberation will forever be usurped by patriarchal, Whiteness-bound, hyper-humanist, and ultimately shallow conceptualizations of justice. Animal rights and human rights ought not to be conceived of as separate branches of legal theory or social praxis, for neither can flourish without the other's direct involvement. The courtroom is only one arena of many that requires a deeper engagement with the interconnectedness and institutionalization of oppressions between and among species. This book will hopefully be the first of many projects to examine the rhetorical constructions of inclusion and exclusion permeating the many paradigms and projects of animal rights law in order to better advocate for ethically coherent top-down and bottom-up approaches to total liberation.

CHAPTER 1

Critical Refurbishments

Ecofeminist Legal Theory and Rhetorical Methodologies

The master's house is taking up all the land. If we are going to build a new house it has to be on this same plot, and most of our building materials will be recycled from his house. We cannot ignore his tools, or we will constantly trip over them; but we can dismantle and rework them.

—Sarah Koopman

U.S. American animal law has traditionally fallen into two theoretical camps: animal welfare litigation and animal rights litigation. I have made clear that my ethical stake is in the latter camp, as the former does little more than put a cheap bandage on eons of ever-increasing more-than-human degradation and suffering. However, this chapter suggests that, on a basic theoretical level, classical animal rights theory and its subsequent partnership with liberal humanist, legal positivist understandings of the American legal system are ultimately insufficient for producing lasting social change and justice. While I do not wish to understate the substantial influence that theorists like Peter Singer and Tom Regan have had on the production of an ever-burgeoning animal rights movement, this chapter argues that, from both an ecofeminist and a rhetorical perspective, their tenets ultimately match all-too-well with the classical legal theories that have long permitted the exploitation of the human and more-than-human world under the guise of objectivist justice. Thus, to engage with animal rights law from a strictly classical perspective of "rights"—and of the function of the law more broadly— misses valuable insights from hitherto silenced voices that have experienced and continue to endure the imitations of the rule of law. This distinct lack, in turn, risks *re*-relegating animals, and those human bodies historically deemed to be closer-to-animal, to the status of object.

Singer's act-utilitarianism and Regan's rights orientation are connected to each other and to prototypical legal theories by virtue of their adherence to liberal humanist ideals. Applying rhetorics of "interests" and "rights" as commonly conceived through liberalism is a common approach to seeking justice for marginalized groups. It is, in fact, quite rare to read substantial critiques of liberal orientations in animal law scholarship other than its central focus on human issues (Deckha, 2011). However, as Maneesha Deckha has explained, while respecting interests and securing rights can and often do offer surface-level protections for the more-than-human world, they will not ultimately "disrupt the subhuman/human boundary zones that enable violence in the first place," for, "as feminists very well know, a mere extension of rights with nothing more does not interrogate the logic of exclusion contained within traditional moral/ethical categories" (Deckha, 2010, p. 28). The theoretical adherence to liberalism omnipresent in Singer's and Regan's notions of animal rights, and subsequently in their lawyer followers' legal strategies, is not an inherently evil partnership. It is in fact admirable that animal rights law has come so far in an arena that so degrades the more-than-human world. Indeed, advocating for new rights and the protection of existing rights is, has been, and should be a fundamental part of an American legal system purportedly committed to equality.

Law—or at least the liberal conception of law—is, nevertheless, an anthropocentric arena (Burdon, 2010; Deckha, 2011; Francione, 2010). It must be, for liberal lawyering is "to participate in and reproduce a professional consciousness that avoids actively engaging in the full range of possible alternative social relationships" (Hasian, Condit, & Lucaites, 1996, p. 325). It worships sets of "scientific" (which is to say, purportedly objective and universal) principles that purposefully exclude those bodies understood as "subhuman"—principles such as rationality and autonomy, principles that in their initial conceptualizations were thought to be possessed by Man (specifically White, heterosexual, able-bodied, Judeo-Christian men) alone. As Marouf Hasian, Celeste Condit, and John Lucaites have explained, classical legal theory—the main theory utilized in the professionalization and education of U.S.

American lawyers—works under the "assumption that the law is an independent discursive field occupied by trained specialists who participate in, apart from, and above the body politic" (Hasian, Condit, & Lucaites, 1996, p. 324). Free from the taint of politics and its special interests, those trained to "think like a lawyer" attempt to reflect the "image of an apolitical legal forum . . . capable of withstanding the public pressures" (p. 324).

Therefore, "liberalism as a theoretical home for animal-centric, or even animal-friendly theories lays out a superficial welcome; perhaps animals can be guests from time to time, but . . . they can never comfortably reside there for the long-term" (Deckha, 2011, p. 234). The U.S. American liberal legal system is based on the social production of difference—not out of respect for difference, but rather as an adversarial means of deciding who "counts" and who does not: "Animal law is thus a hybrid variation of oppression-based critiques in law, adopting a difference-based framework *without problematizing liberalism's conception of difference*" (p. 235, emphasis mine). I thus adhere to Marya Torrez's call for animal-centric legal minds to not only litigate for animals in the courtroom but also critically question and identify "the ways in which we are contributing to maintaining the systems that we are trying to dismantle" (Torrez, 2013, p. 302). Researching the law without overvilifying or underinterrogating the notion of legal rights or de jure personhood is essential to envisioning possibilities for meaningful social change. As Marouf Hasian has long insisted:

> Perhaps the "cultural thinker" needs to find an art that both disassembles and reconstructs new formations, knowing that she will have to maintain a stance that preserves self-criticism. Laws, like other social constructs, are neither completely indeterminate nor immutable in form. They are simply "influential" in their ability to inhibit or invite political change within a range of policy alternatives. (Hasian, 1994, p. 349)

As one such "cultural thinker," I agree with the need to break away from Singer especially and Regan to a smaller extent in order to better interrogate the possibilities and perils of animal rights law. Luckily, much like the U.S. American animal rights movement as a whole, conceptualizations of animal law do not emerge from an ideological monolith. Just as critical legal scholars have sought to question the innate rationality and impartiality of the rule of law, critically minded animal rights thinkers have critiqued traditional, Enlightenment-style theories of justice, ethics, and morality as both productive and counterproductive to an agenda of total liberation. Of interest to this book is the ecofeminist perspective. While mass-mediated depictions of animal rights litigation suggest that Singer's act-utilitarian and Regan's classical rights approaches are the sole paradigms in play, canonical and emerging ecofeminist literatures provide extensive criticism of the innate hypocrisies of liberal legal orientations to animal rights (Gaard, 2002). As Josephine Donovan has observed:

> Regan's and Singer's rejection of emotion and their concern about being branded sentimentalist are not accidental; rather, they expose the inherent bias of contemporary animal rights theory toward rationalism, which, paradoxically, in the form of Cartesian objectivism, established a major theoretical justification for animal abuse. (Donovan, 1990, p. 351)

Liberalist conceptualizations of animal rights and, subsequently, animal rights law thus have notable limitations. Their hyper-rational tenets impose a "machine-like grid" upon reality that allows some subjects into the realm of moral consideration and excludes others almost entirely. Thus, exploring animal rights law in this fashion invokes familiar patriarchal hierarchies that place man over nature, demanding that justice for animals be attained via paternalistic and colonial modes of human intervention. Put simply, despite being more inclusive and compassionate than a welfarist approach, a classical rights–based paradigm of animal law and its corresponding rhetorical tactics highlight Enlightenment values at the expense of those deemed too "irrational," like care, empathy, and kinship. Doing so may ease entry into prototypical formalist legal discourses but ultimately and ironically utilizes the same "objective" and "scientific" discourses Singer, Regan, and their adherents so denounced in the first place. An ecofeminist addition to these legal frameworks would hope to replace cold Cartesian hierarchies in favor of an interconnected sense of ecology among all beings. It would engage in a "complex reevaluation of corporeality and emotionality as signposts" for feminist, and subsequently legal, politics (Twine, 2010, p. 400). Additionally, it would refuse the classical insistence on universalized morality and abstract, idealized rules in favor of a relational, contextual, and ultimately much more complex vision of animal rights litigation.

The law is, as Lucaites (1990) insisted, "only one such locale in a grand system of social relations" (p. 442). It is a "primary site at which social and political understanding and normative commitments interact to empower and legitimize one set of interests and concerns over another by constituting the range of acceptable public meanings for social experience" (p. 442). Thus, in response to the introduction's critique of the lack of marginalized *Homo sapiens* voices in the "spotlight" of animal rights law, this chapter invokes an approach to legal thought that refuses to leave unexamined "the broader oppression based on species and oppression based on other presumed biological markers . . . as well as other categories of difference" (Deckha, 2011, p. 224). I argue that without such an approach, without "attentive investigations of difference *beyond* species difference" (p. 224, emphasis mine), animal rights law is ultimately limited in its capacity to reproduce *lasting* social change. Relying solely upon a system of thought that has at once advocated for justice while intentionally denying it to others, a system composed and maintained by colonial ideals, would seem to ignore the multiple rhetorics of the marginalized, the systemically silenced, the "subaltern" (Spivak, 2003) that show how "getting" equality via the liberal legal process is not the same as "receiving" equality after the gavel has been put aside.

The rest of this chapter completes two tasks: First, it outlines the necessity of a distinctly intersectional, decolonial, and ultimately *ecofeminist* legal theory to supplement, and ideally decenter, classical theories of the law that have so dominated traditional animal rights rhetorics to this point. To develop a nuanced understanding of an ecofeminist legal theory, I draw upon scholarship from ecofeminism, feminist legal studies, and critical animal studies. Second, this chapter outlines the benefits and process of my *rhetorical* approach to legal critique, specifically in the form of ideological rhetorical criticism.

Conceptualizing Ecofeminist Legal Theory

Conceiving a multifaceted, more-than-human, less-than-liberal legal paradigm capable of engaging with theories and practices of animal rights is an interdisciplinary endeavor. I argue that the most potent disciplines with which to engage these legal discourses are a combination of ecofeminism, feminist legal studies, and critical animal studies. When put in tandem with one another, these schools of thought compose what I call an ecofeminist legal theory: a critical, intersectional, and decolonial understanding of law as a manifestation of national ideologies— ideologies that, if left uninterrogated, would inevitably perpetuate the racist, sexist, heterosexist, ableist, classist, and ultimately *speciesist* thought systems that justify oppression and impede the pursuit of justice. Furthermore, this understanding of the law specifies that the liberation of the more-than-human world is essential to legal praxis—but that, paradoxically, to engage with animal litigation as a subfield separate from law proper dangerously and disingenuously disengages animal rights from the multitude of human oppressions in which they are entangled. In the text that follows, I introduce the teleological value of ecofeminism, feminist legal studies, and critical animal studies for the development of an alternative school of animal rights law capable of engaging with the many shortcomings of classical, liberal theories of "rights," "law," "equality," and "justice."

Ecofeminism: Dualisms, Domination, and the Oppression of Not-Man

To discuss ecofeminism as a singular concept is something of a misnomer. Like most disciplines, and like most "feminisms," it is composed of many branches of thought, each with its own scholarly gang seeking converts. Nonetheless, there are a few guiding principles linking ecofeminists, the first and most obvious being the stance that there is an undeniable connection between environmental degradation and women's oppression. These connections reveal themselves in the material world—as in the disenfranchisement of female farmers in the Global South with the introduction of industrialized farming (Shiva, 1988), or the pattern of advertising fast-food burgers as exceptionally masculine in contrast to plant-based foods (Rogers, 2008). These material manifestations, however, are ultimately a result of long-held masculinist ideologies privileging dualist thought, specifically Cartesian notions of man/woman, nature/culture, and human/animal. Normal or natural as these divisions may seem:

> The moral distinction between humans and nonhumans is no more a scientific fact than any other distinction used to justify oppression and exploitation of a certain group. Rather, it is socially constructed and has its genesis in the same philosophies and schools of thought that have served to oppress women and other marginalized groups for much of human history. (Torrez, 2013, p. 267)

Carolyn Merchant has argued that these dualisms emerged during Europe's Scientific Revolution and era of colonization and contributed to mindsets advocating for and justifying the use of the more-than-human world for instrumentalist ends (Merchant, 1980). Others directly connect such mindsets to Christianity's maintenance of hierarchy on the supposed orders of God (Gaard, 1997), still others to the ancient Greek conceptualization of some as natural slaves (Smith, 1983), and some even to the advent of agriculture (Eisler, 1987). Regardless of "when" the justification of patriarchal domination of humans and more-than-humans emerged, most ecofeminists agree that notions of women being "closer to" the more-than-human world have directly contributed to their oppression. And, conversely, the idea that the "environment" (construed as an arena occupied by Not-Man) ought not to be considered a moral subject, but rather a collection of automata to be used for human advancement, has led to environmental degradation. These "logics of domination" (Plumwood, 2002) ought not to be accepted. As dominion has so consistently been associated with the pernicious distinction between Man and Not-Man, any feminist truly interested in social justice must acknowledge the centrality of environmentalism in fights for liberation.

Some critiques of ecofeminist thought are that ecofeminism essentializes "women" into a singular category, placing it into the same troubling school of thought as second-wave feminist "sisterhood" that displaces relevant difference in the pursuit of some homogenous transvaginal alliance, and that ecofeminism relies too heavily on a grand, spiritual notion of one's inner Earth goddess, relegating it to the realm of a self-help philosophy more so than a theory of social justice (Jackson, 1993; Thompson, 2006). However, as Greta Gaard has explained, these critiques demonstrate a lack of engagement with contemporary ecofeminist writings—particularly those of vegan ecofeminists—that have long since moved past these admittedly troubling issues that were less than prevalent, but still admittedly present, in early scholarship. Indeed,

> there is no lack of eco-justice issues to interrogate, theorize, organize around, and transform using the analyses of an ecological feminism: Global gender justice; climate justice; sustainable agriculture; healthy and affordable housing; universal and reliable health care, particularly maternal and infant health care; safe, reliable, and free or low-cost reproductive technologies; food security; sexual self-determination; energy justice; interspecies justice; ecological, diverse, and inclusive educational curricula; religious freedom from fundamentalisms; indigenous rights; the production and disposal of hazardous wastes; and more. (Gaard, 2002, p. 44)

Of most interest to this chapter, and subsequently this book, is engaging and advancing the vegan ecofeminist trend of rejecting essentialism and resituating *species* as the premier category of feminist deconstruction. This theoretical pivot point, often referred to as "animal ecofeminism," "vegetarian ecofeminism," or as I will refer to it "vegan ecofeminism," acts as a "logical outgrowth of both feminism and ecofeminism" that is surely "feminism's third generation" (Gaard, 2002). Keeping in mind the insights of early ecofeminists that pinpointed the necessity of defining women as Not-Man in order to oppress them, vegetarian ecofeminists posit that this Man/Not-Man binary engages with differences of race, class, gender, sexuality, ability, and most definitively species. The inclusion of species in the various axes of power under feminist consideration is important because "as long as society accepts certain forms of violence as tolerable, other forms of violence will continue. As long as oppression of those individuals classified as 'nonhuman' is tolerated . . . there will always be humans placed on the other side of the human/nonhuman divide" (Torrez, 2013, p. 267). Indeed, an examination of species-as-construct demonstrates how such processes as "dehumanization" and "animalization" function to not only oppress other humans but also maintain the unfortunate assumption that to be Not-Man is to be innately inferior and unworthy of moral consideration. This distinction merely reifies the "western construction of human identity as 'outside' nature" (Plumwood, 2002, p. 2). After all, to be dehumanized or animalized "refers to that indistinct zone of the inhuman where life is rendered brute" (Seshadri, 2012, p. 21).

Vegan ecofeminism, with its intensive focus on the rhetorical construction of species as a key construction justifying the oppression of living entities, allows for a broader focus on how race, sexuality, ability, and other such "markers" become implicated in the discursive manufacturing of a Man/Not-Man dichotomy. After all, the "rhetorical field of the brute" manifests in "the process of rendering a living creature into something indistinct . . . a brute . . . founded on power's ability to manipulate the indeterminacy that haunts all identity" (Seshadri, 2012, p. 25). With such a "sliding scale" of moral significance, those consistently allowed the opportunities to oppress and exploit inevitably fall under the preferred categorization of "Man" while the oppressed and exploited slide, with varying degrees, toward Not-Man, with the communicative construction of "animal" placed securely at the end of the scale. (Notably, the placement of and differentiation between "insects," "plants," and "natural objects" as Animal, Not-Animal, or something in-between has been employed inconsistently over time by multiple parties—but that is a subject for chapter 4). As Val Plumwood explained, it is no wonder that "the forces directing the destruction of nature and wealth produced from it are controlled overwhelmingly by an unaccountable, mainly white, and mainly male elite" (Plumwood, 2002, pp. 11–12). Those deemed closer to "nature"—by virtue of gender, race, species, etc.—are justified as inferior and thus oppressible, casting Not-Man as "a field of multiple exclusion and control . . . casting sexual, racial, and ethnic differences as closer to the animal and the body construed as a sphere of inferiority" (p. 4).

Of course, to merely explain how the discursive designation of animality works to oppress various human beings is not the sole task of vegan ecofeminists. Such a task would be unconscionably anthropocentric. Vegan ecofeminism is both a theory and a praxis that asks its adherents to apply the battle cry of "The personal is political!" to the seemingly "everyday" interactions that cast species outside the realm of *Homo sapiens* as inherently oppressible. After all, "there is no greater privilege than human privilege" (Torrez, 2013, p. 298) as "human relations to nature are not only ethical, but political" (Plumwood, 2002, p. 13). Most advocate for the relinquishment of human privilege by boycotting the consumption of animal products and stopping the use of animals for experimentation and human entertainment. While a vegan world is, by this standard, an ideal one, vegan ecofeminists emphasize the complexities and contingencies of the "real" world. They pivot from such straw-man arguments that "veganism is ___-ist" by advocating for what Deane Curtin called a "moral contextual vegetarianism," wherein:

> It is one thing to inflict pain on animals when geography offers no other choice. But in the case of killing animals for human consumption where there is a choice, this practice inflicts pain that is completely unnecessary and avoidable. The injunction to care, considered as an issue of moral and political development, should be understood to include the injunction to eliminate needless suffering wherever possible, and particularly the suffering of those whose suffering is conceptually connected to one's own . . . one's body is oneself, and that by inflicting violence needlessly, one's bodily self becomes a context for violence. (Curtin, 1991, p. 70)

And, as the rest of this book will demonstrate, this "injunction to care" is essential to the construction of a critical vegan rhetoric.

The feminist, and subsequently vegan ecofeminist, ideal is centered upon notions of an "ethic of care" (Donovan & Adams, 2007), specifically in the form of "caring for" as opposed to "caring about." The latter invites one to show sympathy for the oppressed but does not always find how one relates to the marginalized subject in day-to-day life. It is by no means an ignorant approach to social justice. For example, those of us in pristine U.S. American academic offices do not often have the chance to interact with, say, a subsistence farmer across the globe. However, given the prevalence of species degradation in nearly everyone's day-to-day life, it is a caring-for approach—the act of appreciating how everyone's own context and history necessarily implicate them in a series of oppressions—that allows for the defamiliarization of those "everyday" practices that reify anthropocentric hierarchies. It is in many ways a pivot from a classical rights–based approach (prevalent in law, animal rights, and in the feminist movement itself) and instead emphasizes the messiness of particular contexts and conjoined histories (Curtin, 1991). This is a far cry from a mere "prevention of cruelty" in that feminist empathy asks more than just "How can we be nicer?" Rather, an ethic of "caring for" extends its concern to broader systems of domination that necessarily influence interpersonal interactions, and thus moves to more fruitful interrogations of justice, asking "How did we become so cruel?" and "What broader, systemic, cultural, and moral changes must emerge to prevent similar cruelties from emerging in the future?"

Ultimately, an ecofeminist approach to social and more-than-human justice avoids the liberal pitfalls of hyper-humanism, moral universalism, and hyper-rationalism by adding the more-than-human world to the realm of moral consideration; by noting how the "eco" and the "feminine" are not the only qualities implicated in the logics of domination used to discount others as Not-Man, thus opening ecofeminist thought to issues of race, class, sexuality, ability, and species; and by embracing those affective values hitherto deemed too "effeminate" for proper philosophical discourse. These include care, empathy, and relationality. Better still, a vegan ecofeminist lens explicates "human" and "animal" as "relationally performed, re- and co-produced" (Twine, 2010, p. 401). A theory maintaining an increased focus on the plight of those designated as "animal" is thus a theory necessitating a clear and cogent praxis: interpersonally, it calls for a culturally contingent, brutally honest reassessment of one's complicity in the perpetuation of the Man/Not-Man binary via the direct or indirect exploitation of animals for food, experimentation, fashion, or entertainment; systemically, it calls upon broader institutions—the legal system included—to reintegrate the more-than-human world into the realm of moral consideration, not by virtue of what animals might do for us, but what we owe to them.

Feminist Legal Studies: Engaging with Intersectionality and Decoloniality

But how, then, might an ethic geared toward empathy, relationality, and moral contextualism apply to the American legal system? Indeed, to take such an approach is counterintuitive to prototypical judicial rhetoric, which, as described previously, prefers to think of the rule of law as an objective science. This approach, dubbed "legal positivism," is an "article of faith" that dominates American judicial proceedings (Hasian, Condit & Lucaites, 1996, p. 323). It defines the law as "a science" that is "ruled authoritatively" by "abstract categories or doctrines" and is impervious to the many "external factors such as the natural world" (Burdon, 2010, p. 63). As the story goes, "over time, a community of legal specialists supposedly 'discover' the correct legal decisions in complex cases because they are guided by non-political rules and logics that operate outside of the contexts of individual interests and human discretion" (Hasian, Condit & Lucaites, 1996, p. 325). This "professionalist privileging" of the law thus frees the legal system from "profane 'politics'" and becomes "increasingly accurate and precise as time and experience allow us to uncover its latent structures and implicit wisdom" (p. 323, 325). In other words, law is *logos,* and to treat it as anything other than that is to sully the legal system in its entirety. Feminism, and particularly vegan ecofeminism, seemingly have no place in legal theory, discourse, and practice (Bartlett, 1990; Scales, 1989).

However, as dominant as legal positivism is in law schools and, subsequently, in the courtroom, it is far from the only theoretical lens with which to view, critique, and alter the rhetorics of the rule of law. The emergence of critical legal studies, critical race theory, queer law, feminist legal theory, and other "critical" orientations to judicial institutions have done much to "demystify the professionalization of 'the law' as a unique and unified discipline of knowledge" (Lucaites, 1990, p. 442). These schools of thought emphasize the concept of ideology in the formation and maintenance of the law and the pursuit of justice. Law is thus "a significant description of the way a society perceives itself and projects its image to the world" (Burdon, 2010, p. 62): it creates a *nomos,* "a socially constructed normative universe" (Matambanadzo, 2012, p. 81); it is a "dominant ideology" representing "a narrow, exclusive range of sociopolitical and economic interests" (Hasian, Condit & Lucaites, 1996, p. 323); and, perhaps most importantly, it "has the power to not only to *regulate culture* but to *limit possibilities* by imposing a narrow understanding of the intelligibility of persons, i.e., *who counts* and *how we take account of them*" (Matambanadzo, 2012, p. 81, emphasis mine). A critical approach to the law thus critiques hegemonic discourses and practices in the judicial system, specifically when those discourses and practices pivot away from and render invisible alternative possibilities for judicial decisions that might empower the historically marginalized. It is an effort to democratize an inherently *un*democratic legal system via the deconstruction of legal texts, showing those moments where the "logic" of the law is steeped in contradictions and incoherencies that are just as steeped in politics and power relationships as anything else (Hasian, Condit & Lucaites, 1996).

Of most interest to this chapter and to U.S. American animal rights law in general is feminist legal theory, particularly as it has been influenced by women of color and global feminisms. Feminist legal theory is, unsurprisingly, a critical orientation to the law from the standpoint of gender studies. A feminist jurisprudence thus rejects the patriarchy inherent in the rule of law and devises systems with which to escape its clutches. As Katharine Bartlett explained:

> Traditional legal methods place a high premium on the predictability, certainty, and fixity of rules. In contrast, feminist legal methods, which have emerged from the critique that existing rules overrepresent existing power structures, value rule-flexibility and the ability to identify missing points of view. . . . Positionality rejects both the objectivism of whole, fixed, impartial truth and the relativism of different-but-equal truths. It posits instead that being "correct" in law is a function of being situated in particular, partial perspectives upon which the individual is obligated to attempt to improve. (Bartlett, 1990, p. 832)

I argue that the successful integration of ecofeminist praxis into the hyper-rational American legal system requires a situated, empathetic, and thoroughly *messy* understanding of how oppression operates. It must therefore take seriously two concepts drawn from women-of-color feminist theories: "intersectionality" and "decoloniality."

The origin of the concept of intersectionality is in the work of legal scholar Kimberlé Crenshaw. Crenshaw offered intersectionality as an approach attempting to outline the interdependencies between socially constructed identity markers and the differential power relations that go along with them. Her initial exploration of how oppressions can be simultaneous and mutual constitutive came in an exploration of Black womanhood in the American courtroom, specifically how legal rhetorics called upon defendants/plaintiffs to be either Black or female, but not both, in articulating a case. Intersectionality has since been extended to multiple "matrices of domination" including, but not limited to, race, gender, class, sexuality, and ability. An intersectional paradigm is

> widely applicable to various relations of marginality and privilege . . . it foregrounds a richer ontology than approaches that attempt to reduce people to one category at a time, it treats social positions as relational, and it makes visible the multiple positioning that constitutes everyday life and the power relations that are central to it. (Dhamoon, 2011, p. 230)

Put simply, one can be oppressed from multiple angles, privileged from multiple angles, and in most cases simultaneously privileged *and* oppressed. For instance:

> To look at white, middle-class women as subordinated as women is accurate as far as it goes, but their experience of oppression is not interchangeable with the oppression of non-white, non-middle-class women. The whiteness and middle-class status supply privilege even as the femaleness conveys oppression. (Grillo, 1995, p. 19)

Strands of identity are inseparable. Neither are they additive. Rather, they are mutually constitutive and forever indebted to the White supremacist, patriarchal, heterosexist, etc. ideologies that "allowed" these identity categories into existence, and therefore into judgment, in the first place. And, as this book will demonstrate, it is important to understand "species" as yet another identity category in need of interrogation and complication.

From a legal perspective, then, intersectionality stands in defiance to rhetorical essentialisms constituting clients as generic characters in a legal drama: "This fragmenting of identity by legal analysis . . . is the subject of the intersectionality critique" (Grillo, 1995, p. 17). Instead, it encourages a legal praxis that examines legal subjects for who they are in situ, how their particular contexts and situated histories have produced the subject under consideration at that moment. After all, "law derives legitimacy from belief in its capacity to govern the messy complexities of everyday existence. This presupposes that law accurately captures and reflects those complexities; that they are, in some sense, within the sphere of law's operation" (Conaghan, 2008, p. 28). Intersectional analysis of the law emphasizes the "messy" part of the construction of legal subjects and their identities, fighting against rhetorical shortcuts that essentialize those subjects for the purposes of a simple legal strategy. Law should therefore carry with it a *telos,* and that *telos* requires a thorough understanding of how we are all necessarily entangled in interlocking systems of oppression. Intersectionality is, at its barest minimum, an exhortation to do better.

Despite the value of intersectionality as an analytical tool, it is not without its flaws—particularly given its increased cultural capital in social justice discourse. Despite the concept's theoretical inclusivity, in practice it creates its own areas of inclusion and exclusion by specifying what differences matter (Deckha, 2008). Sandy Grande has explained how sometimes the anti-essentialist, antidualistic paradigm of intersectionality becomes reabsorbed into rhetorics of oppression and exclusion, often under the guise of social justice. In the case of Whiteness-bound, liberal feminist projects, she argues that intersectionality's broadness is appropriated as "a convenient rhetorical device that not only relativizes difference but that also allows white women to deny their shared complicity in the colonialist project" (Grande, 2003, p. 330). In other words, if *everyone* is in some way oppressed, then reflecting upon one's own collusion in oppressive systems is of lesser importance. To do so would be akin to taking on an "Oppression Olympics" paradigm of social justice wherein the goal is to find who has suffered "the most"—a most unproductive means of persuasion! Admittedly unhelpful as an oppression-as-additive contest may be, the "whitestreaming" (Grande, 2003) of intersectionality risks "whitewashing" a concept developed specifically from Black feminist thought. Indeed, "it is this idea of marginalized peoples being structurally implicated in hegemonies of power that often gets obscured by feminist theorizing of intersectionality" (Dhamoon, 2015, p. 31).

However, as Rita Dhamoon has explained, intersectionality recuperates itself when placed into conversation with notions of transnationalism and settler colonialism, culminating in a *decolonial* paradigm of total liberation (Dhamoon, 2015). Decoloniality is, at its essence, a demand for the dissolution of colonial modernity. It is, as rhetorician Darrel Wanzer claimed, a call to dismantle the "constitutive feature of Western modernity that structures exclusionary modes of power, knowledge, and being—it is the dark underside of modernity, which influences both first and third world people" (Wanzer, 2012, p. 652). It is both a literal call for the return of Indigenous lands and a theoretical paradigm that calls for the disintegration of what Vandana Shiva called "monocultures of the mind"—a troubling assumption that Western, paternalistic ways of "knowing" and "doing" are the *only* ways (or, *prima facie,* the best ways). While intersectionality engages with oppressions in situ, a decolonial perspective forever remembers how the situation "came to be" at all.

Remembrances of imperialism and colonization thus hold everyone accountable to their ancestors' histories, noting that while one relatively privileged subject may not have been "there" when the "bad things" happened, they nonetheless still profit from it years later in the form of institutionalized oppressions codified in political, economic, social, and legal systems. A transnational vision of intersecting oppressions therefore "prompts urgent issues about how to navigate gendered, capitalist, colonial global forces of neoliberalism and racism, settler formations of the nation-state, and non-state forms of nationalism simultaneously" (Dhamoon, 2015, p. 33).

An emphasis on the discourses and ontologies of settler colonialism prompts reengagement with Indigeneity, subsequently reimagining the "nation-state" and its role in the (dis)possession of land, labor, and bodies. Further, it moves against the "erasure or conflation between racisms and colonialisms even in some antiracist circles, which ultimately overlooks, for example, the variations of racisms and colonialisms" (Dhamoon, 2015, p. 23). To "decolonize" metaphorically and literally is thus to engage with intersectional attributes of oppression from a historical perspective, one which evaluates how the increasingly globalized world "came to be" in the context of imperialism, forced migration, diaspora, neoliberalism, and White supremacist projects cloaked by rhetorics of humanitarianism and in some cases environmentalism. Pragmatically, decoloniality is not an effort to "return to the past," to promote a praxis anachronistically idealizing some unspoiled precolonial era. Rather, it is a call to envision alternative possibilities that fall outside of the master tropes within "progress" narratives of history, a motion to conceive of societal betterment in ways often counterintuitive to the naturalized, normalized values of neoliberalism. And, within the context of this book, it is a demand to deconstruct binary notions of human/animal that name the former as subject and the latter as object, notions that, when traced back to their ideological roots, are rife with colonial configurations. If indeed the "native as object is a key element of the postcolonial dichotomy" (Alley-Young, 2008, p. 317), then the discursive linkages between native and animal in the construction of some morally superior "human" must be interrogated further if social justice is to be achieved across species lines.

Engaging at once with intersectionality and decoloniality is essential to the projects of animal liberation and, subsequently, total liberation through the law. Both take seriously the conception of the Other through which "the Western self makes sense of its own identity, defining the Other in contrast to how it wishes to see itself" (Deckha, 2008, p. 217). In examining the matrices of domination that mutually constitute one another, an ecofeminist vision allows the integration of "species" as an observable "identity" category that serves as a mirror to Otherhood. Looking via a colonial gaze across the courtroom at an Other tacitly purports that differences are not only innate and natural but also markers of moral variance. These essential differences serve as "a vital element of colonial and legal logic that socially constructed groups as inferior and uncivilized" (Deckha, 2008, p. 218), differences that ultimately rest upon how "human" the Other is in comparison to the standards set by Enlightenment thought (Wynter, 2003). As Richard Twine has explained, "In line with the feminist argument that intersectionality is not an additive but a mutually constitutive phenomenon . . . categories of 'nature' and animality have contributed a power of disgust to intrahuman constructions of hierarchy and separation" (Twine, 2010, pp. 398–399). Just as decolonial thought acts as a helpful, historically cognizant metaconcept that helps guide intersectional praxis in situ, species is a massive "category" that ultimately encapsulates all that has been dubbed "wrong" with those unable to meet the standards of a White, male, heterosexual, able-bodied Judeo-Christian subject. Ultimately, difference-as-wrongness is bound to a notion of sameness-as-rightness, a sameness based in a notion of a distinctly *human* subject set against everyone else. As bell hooks insisted:

> violence is inextricably linked to all acts of violence in this society that occur between the powerful and the powerless, the dominant and the dominated . . . it is the Western philosophical notion of hierarchical rule and coercive authority that is the root cause of violence. . . . It is this belief system that is the foundation on which sexist ideology and other ideologies of group oppression are based; they can be eliminated only when this foundation is eliminated. (hooks, 1984, p. 118)

The "foundation" of which hooks speaks relies entirely upon troubled notions of species, anthropocentrism, and ultimately, speciesism. And, as Aph and Syl Ko asserted in their extension of Sylvia Wynter's work on the racialized colonial constructions of Man, "racism (and other 'isms') are merely functions of a grander territory . . . discussing the human-animal divide helps us gain entry to that space . . . needless to say, the less 'individuality' we perceive, the less is their moral worth" (Ko & Ko, 2017, pp. 164–165). Speciesism, in other words, is foundational to understandings of power, inequality, violence, and justice.

But perhaps the most cogent explanation for why animal liberation's alliance with intersectionality and decoloniality is so important comes from Billy-Ray

Belcourt's work on animal rights and settler colonialism. Per Belcourt (2014), "an animal ethic is important to decolonial thought by re-framing animality as a politics of space and introducing anthropocentrism to [theorizations] of the logics of white supremacy" (p. 3). What is more, inscriptions of animal status are both "a speciesist rendering of animality as injuring," and representations of how an anthropocentric logic is "militarized through racial hierarchies that further distance the white settler from blackness and indigeneity" (p. 5). Put simply, the task of fusing feminist legal studies with animal rights law is one of renegotiation, one that partners an ethic of total liberation with a politic of decolonization. To advance in theory and praxis requires seriously questioning a "civilized" Western rights paradigm as the premier model of human/animal relations and instead recentering both "indigeneity" and "animality" as sites of decolonial possibility and decolonial praxis.

In short, ecofeminist legal theory has little to offer animal rights thought and praxis without a strong commitment to intersectionality and decoloniality. After all,

> we have to wrap our heads around *the modes of thinking* that were designed precisely to ensure certain humans, animals, and other nonhuman life remain outside our moral and social communities. This is not a precious, academic, intellectual activity. This is absolutely necessary for real change . . . as at least one way to truly *radicalize* [the animal rights] movement. (Ko & Ko, 2017, p. xx)

If indeed "the category *animal* was also a colonial invention that has been imposed on humans and animals" (p. xviii) with the intent to injure and oppress, then species can and must be integrated into social justice projects dedicated to the abolition of matrices of oppression across and between species boundaries.

Critical Animal Studies: Toward a Radical Vegan Praxis

Intersectionality and decoloniality are valuable theoretical tools with which to interpret, reinterpret, and subsequently critique animal rights law and the various discourses of "species" surrounding it. However, as Twine (2010) warned, "It is one thing to include the nonhuman in one's understanding of intersectionality, another also to accept the nonhuman into the political and *act accordingly*" (p. 400, emphasis mine). Indeed, one cannot claim to transcend the Power Paradigm while benefiting from the Patriarchy. It is not enough to give up materialism: if we do not deal with personal power and dominance relationships, we are part of the problem, regardless of our degree of empathy, political awareness, and transcendental purity. (Birkeland, 1993, p. 51)

To break out of the realm of theory and into the world of praxis, this chapter offers a third "theoretical" paradigm that not only identifies the intersectional complications of colonial thought and species-based oppression but also advocates on-the-ground solutions on the personal, interpersonal, and institutional level. This field is critical animal studies.

Critical animal studies is a theory-to-action approach to human-animal scholarship that emphasizes praxis and direct action over abstract theorizations alone. It is distinct from similar fields such as "animal studies" and "anthrozoology" in that, while all emphasize notions such as a "human-animal bond," only critical animal studies examines such notions from a critical, activist-oriented perspective. As animal activist and critical animal scholar Steven Best so emphatically (and cuttingly) asserted:

The recipe for the "success" of animal studies—immersion in abstraction, indulgent use of existing and new modes of jargon, pursuit of theory-for-theory's sake, avoidance of social controversy (however intellectually controversial it may often be), eschewing political involvement, and keeping a very safe distance from "extremists" and "radicals" agitating for animal rights—is also the formula for its failure, upon being co-opted, tamed, and neutralized by academia. Consequently, the profound ethical, social, political, and environmental issues of animal exploitation are buried in dense theoretical webs; the lucidity and power of clear communication is oiled over with jargon and inscrutable language accessible only to experts; politically charged issues are depoliticized; and theory is divorced from practice, resistance, and struggle. (Best, 2009, p. 12)

Critical animal studies assumes total liberation as its ultimate goal, pursuing animal liberation strategies and tactics that maintain a keen eye towards larger intersectional social justice objectives. The Institute for Critical Animal Studies, the semi-official "home base" for critical animal scholars, asserts that the permanent goal for animal liberationists ought to be a complete disintegration of racist, sexist, homophobic, ableist, classist, colonialist, and speciesist practices in the name of creating a fair and just world. While this is certainly a large and intimidating endgame, framing critical animal studies around total liberation has allowed the field to embrace intersectional politics over single-issue analyses, thus expanding the relevance of "animal rights" into other liberation-oriented areas of study—the law included. Such is the task of this book, massive as it may be.

Central to all critical animal studies scholarship is the concept of speciesism. Peter Singer famously defined this infamous ism as "prejudice or attitude of bias in favor of one's own species and against those of members of other species" (Singer, 1975, p. 7). In other words, it is a system of oppression on par with racism, sexism, etc. that privileges the *Homo sapiens* over all other living species for no legitimate reason. The dissolution of speciesism is the central task of critical animal studies scholarship. Speciesism manifests itself in a variety of ways. The renaming of dead animals as objects—such as the shift from "dead body" to "meat," "cow" to "beef," or "murder" to "slaughter"—creates an absent referent that disallows the inclusion of animals-as-subjects when thinking about the social construction of food (Adams, 1990). Speciesism is also inherent in basic interhuman communication, such as using animal-based insults to insult others ("she is such a pig!") as if to suggest that to "become animal" is to become "less than." The ways in which journalists write about animals can be speciesist when it denies their subjectivity (Freeman, 2009), as is the notion that "wilderness" ought to be managed by man vis-à-vis the sport hunting of autonomous animal subjects (Munro, 2004).

The abolition of speciesism is central to a critical animal studies paradigm. However, this abolition is not an easy task, and mere theorizing is likely not enough to destroy this ideology. Thus, the field serves as an academic bridge between the "ivory tower" and the "real world," articulating best practices for the betterment of humankind (where humankind includes every being traditionally excluded from the confines of Man and relegated to Not-Man instead). According Best (2009),

[Critical animal studies] seeks to illuminate problems and pose solutions through vivid, concrete, and accessible language. It openly avows its explicit ethical and practical commitment to the freedom of well-being of all animals and to a flourishing planet. It opposes all forms of discrimination, hierarchy, and oppression as a complex of problems to be extirpated from the root, not sliced off at the branch. It supports civil disobedience, direct action, and economic sabotage. And it promotes bridge-building and alliance politics as the means to promote the large-scale social transformations that alone can free the continuum of animal life and the dynamic natural world from the elite's colonization and conquest and the building furies of global climate change. (pp. 12–13)

Central to this book, however, are three aspects of critical animal studies as they apply to the rhetorical formulations of the law. First and foremost, a critical animal studies perspective presupposes that the welfarist discourses of animal law described in the previous chapter would be considered a speciesist manifestation of the law. This is because legal fights for animal welfare are ultimately toothless, allowing for *less* suffering, but not the abolition of animal exploitation, on the shaky grounds that animals can be used as means-to-ends in manners that humans cannot merely on the basis of their innate animality (Wrenn, 2015). To argue, for instance, for larger battery cages for hens on industrial farms does little more than tacitly agree to the imprisonment of the hens themselves, conveniently ignoring their shortened lifespans, the denial of their innate desire to walk around, the acts of "debeaking" to prevent hen-on-hen violence as a result of their psychological distress, or the inevitable slaughter of any male chick unable to become a battery hen in the first place.

Second, critical animal studies advocate for legal change from a strictly *vegan* perspective—or, more specifically, an *ethical vegan* perspective, which is not merely a "diet" or "lifestyle choice" but rather an overarching tenet that rejects the normative ethic of speciesism. Ethical veganism, defined according to the Vegan Society, is "a way of living which seeks to exclude, *as far as is possible and practicable,* all forms of exploitation of, and cruelty to, animals for food, clothing, or any other purpose" ("Definition of Veganism," n.d., para. 1, emphasis mine). This definition does not mean that any human-on-animal interaction is inherently objectionable, rather that normalized modes of interspecies interaction within a U.S. American and increasingly global capitalist paradigm must be critically evaluated for perverse power relationships in which only one party—Man—genuinely benefits from that interaction. Further, it does not mean that a totally, completely, and absolutely vegan lifestyle is possible for every individual—for instance, a sick person taking medicine previously tested on animals would still be vegan due to this "lifeboat" situation. Notions of "possible" and "practicable" thus fuse a critical honesty toward one's situated contexts and capabilities in an imperfect world to a staunch liberationist ethic with idealistic visions, forgoing moral absolutism but denying moral relativism. Viewing legal battles from an ethical vegan lens thus provides a clearer vision of what is welfarist versus what is actually liberatory for animal subjects. Within the context of the law, then, legally mandating an increase to the size of battery cases would be welfarist and in opposition to a vegan ethic. Making battery cages altogether illegal in agricultural settings, however, is consistent with this approach.

And finally, critical animal studies understands that, despite the vegan ideal, interhuman equalities based in race, gender, class, ability, etc. do not place every person on an "equal playing field" from which to embrace and adopt a vegan lifestyle. Using intersectionality and decoloniality as guiding lenses, critical animal studies asserts that the fight against speciesism cannot go on without simultaneously fighting against all other isms. Legal fights against animal exploitation, then, need not necessarily have animals directly involved in the case. Police brutality lawsuits challenging state violence against people of color are just as important as the prosecution of animal torturers, as both are based in the same ideology that sanctions violence against those deemed, tacitly or overtly, "less-than-human."

Outside of academia, this school of thought is usually dubbed "intersectional veganism." To quote Corey Wrenn, this mode of thought understands that

> oppression is intersectional, but all oppressions are not identical in design or impact. Suggesting that human inequality is on par with nonhuman inequality could diminish the tremendous suffering that is unique to the nonhuman experience. Likewise, pulling on human frameworks to construct a grand narrative of suffering is likely to alienate disenfranchised human groups, especially as they have historically been likened to Nonhuman Animals in an attempt to naturalize their disenfranchisement. "Species-blind" ideologies that reduce difference ("we're all animals") can distort and distract. The goal of diversity in claimsmaking and institution-building is not to erase difference in a "melting pot," but rather to respectfully acknowledge differences in access, interests, and needs. (Wrenn, 2017, p. 32)

A legal perspective that takes into account the advice for theory and praxis offered by critical animal studies, especially the work done by intersectional vegans, thus stresses "the interconnections, not simply the parallels, between human and animal issues. It is thereby better positioned to convince those who discount animal issues or prioritize human issues that animal issues should matter more" and is therefore "a hopeful tool for subverting the marginal position of animal issues in the justice sphere" (Deckha, 2011, pp. 235–236). Using the "intersectional idea of coalition" (p. 223), animal rights law need not exist merely as law school elective courses or fringe legal clinics. It can be part of everyday personal and interpersonal practices that, once adopted by a sufficient number of likeminded justice advocates, will necessarily influence which lawsuits make it to a judge, which legal strategies are most likely to succeed within a broad ethic of total liberation, and which judges are likely to respond in favor of the oppressed. For, as Albright (2002) has predicted, "Once policymakers have recognized the importance of our moral obligations and emotional relationships with nonhumans, legal rights for animals will necessarily follow" (p. 937).

Rhetorical Methodologies: Discursive Fragments as Ideological Critique

With the above theoretical paradigms in mind, my book will utilize rhetorical methods based in the study of "discourse," "persuasion," and "power" to advance its central arguments. Specifically, it will invoke ideological rhetorical criticism, which analyzes texts chosen through purposive sampling in order to gauge which explicit and/or implicit ideologies guided the composition of and reaction to those texts once disseminated.

As opposed to a more traditional textual analysis of great speakers saying great things, which in rhetoric is referred to as a "public address" methodology, ideological criticism moves "outside the barriers of intent" when examining the meaning, message, and implications of a rhetorical artifact (Wander, 1984, p. 214). That is to say, ideological critique takes seriously both authorial intentions and the ways through which artifacts can be interpreted despite initial whims of authors, who are not only implicated in worldviews of which they may not even be conscious but also have little control over what audiences "do" with texts after their dissemination. It invokes a "rhetorical consciousness" (Hasian, 1993) that allows for the investigation of how larger public cultures become involved in the creation of supposedly closed systems such as the rule of law. Rhetorical formations, be they from a "great speaker" or a subaltern group, act as discursive "fragments" that "allow critics to trace discursive reconfigurations that are adapted to changing social conditions" (Hasian, 1993, p. 349). This orientation carries a major critical component that allows scholars to uncover "primary and secondary meanings" of artifacts (p. 350). It is done in the name of pursuing "critiques of domination" and "critiques of freedom" (McKerrow,

1989), where the former refers to the identification of oppressive power structures and the latter to how purportedly "liberatory" discourses are not always benign. And, as this book will no doubt demonstrate, critiques of freedom are extremely important to analyses of animal rights law, even when the lawyers involved truly wish to see the liberation of all beings.

Within the context of rhetorical history, "ideological criticism" is a troubled technique. After all, this method is often associated with traditional Marxist interpretations of ideology, wherein (to put matters simply) there exists a "dominant ideology" ruthlessly disseminated by those in power in order to create a "false consciousness" in the masses (Artz, Macek, & Cloud, 2006). Rhetoricians have largely (although not completely) moved beyond this dichotomous conception of ideology, instead embracing Ernesto Laclau and Chantal Mouffe's concept of "subject-positions" wherein many ideologies can exist among and against one another, often collaborating in one rhetorical situation and dispersing in another in the pursuit of hegemony. When certain ideologies gain preeminence over others in larger cultural arenas, often to the sociocultural detriment of those who oppose that ideology, this can be called a "hegemonic ideology." The most ideal way to analyze competing ideologies in discursive arenas is during moments of cultural rupture, or antagonism (Laclau & Mouffe, 2001). In rhetorical scholarship, this interpretation of ideology-as-discourse is often termed "articulation" (DeLuca, 1999).

A rhetorical approach to ideological critique functions mainly as an interpretation of an interpretation, drawing conclusions from the many ways that an "event" in the world has been mediated through various cultural ideologies and how those ideologies intersect and interact with one another (McGee, 1990). A rhetorical critic's version of ideological criticism, as embraced by scholars like Philip Wander and Michael Calvin McGee, emphasizes the complex systems of power relations within particular historical contexts, especially in spaces of public deliberation with the intent to create change or preserve hegemony (McGee, 1980; Wander, 1984). Ideology exists not as a dark cloud hovering over the nation-state, but rather as a series of discursive fragments representative of a heterogeneous, ever-changing culture that can, with careful study, be pieced together and interpreted (McGee, 1990). In short, this method utilizes purposive sampling of chosen texts to provide insight into how societies mediate and make sense of their lived experiences and to, at times, offer prescriptive insight into how to better communicate those experiences in an increasingly interconnected, mediated, and globalized world. Ultimately, rhetorical criticism "produces a sense of what is not being addressed and how those issues might be brought into a sphere where discourse and debate become possible again" (Goodale & Black, 2010, p. 7).

One arena in which rhetorical ideological criticism is of utmost importance is in analyses of the U.S. legal system. I invoke the "rhetorical turn" in legal studies as utilized by scholars like Hasian, Condit, and Lucaites. Specifically, it integrates critical legal scholarship with rhetorical theory in order to propose a methodology less focused on a singular dominant ideology and more upon the identification and critique of ideological antagonisms within and outside of the courtroom via textual analysis. This rhetorical turn argues that the law is not simply a dominant ideology, but rather a historically situated, hegemonically crafted rhetorical culture wherein interested parties make compromises that function as the boundaries within which the law takes on public meaning. The law is neither a "closed system" based on clear, objective rules and principles nor a simplistic dominant ideology that dupes foolish masses. Ideological critique of legal discourses from a rhetorical perspective is therefore well suited not only to critiquing particular cases at particular moments in time but also to deconstructing the rule of law as it is created by powerful, politically loaded "ideographs" (McGee, 1980) such as "person," "rights," "bodily liberty," and "equality."

Understanding law in such a manner better enables critics to investigate and possibly implement procedures "that would democratize the legal system, giving better access to the voices of those whose interests are disproportionately underrepresented in both the public rhetoric and the translation of that rhetoric into law" (Hasian, Condit & Lucaites, 1996, p. 338). This book enacts the call to "look to see how legal provisions are enacted in particular social dramas" via "the discursive tracing of how selected legal mythic tales have evolved, paying close attention to the ways in which constitutions and other texts set up conflicting ideals within a community" (p. 350). Such a methodology should, if successful, improve understandings of the ways in which judicial relationships emerge, how they are accepted and rejected by communities, and how they might change in order to benefit the disempowered.

Rhetorical methodologies are also of premier importance to the study, deconstruction, and critique of speciesism. Rhetoricians Greg Goodale and Jason Edward Black have explained that methods such as ideological criticism provide "a particularly valuable perspective for understanding arguments surrounding the human/ nonhuman animal relationship. Those arguments are rarely premised on fact, but rather on long-held assumptions and the effectiveness of many tropes that have not yet been studied in depth" (Goodale & Black, 2010, p. 3). Ideological criticism, with its focus on discursive fragments and those fragments' inevitable relationship to their historical contexts, notes the "outdated but historically influential Cartesian dichotomy separating humans from all other animals based on its arbitrary notion of humans as conscious souls and animals as mere automata" (Freeman, 2010, p. 7). Rhetorician Carrie Packwood Freeman argued that close textual analyses with an eye toward the discursive construction of a human/animal dualism reveals how

> like racism or sexism, speciesism operates on the basis of discrimination where a group elevates its status by lowering the status of "other" groups, and there are strong parallels in how women and people of color have been discriminated against by being compared to so-called lowly and irrational animals. . . . Biases enable hierarchies, which often lead to mistreatment, where the "superior" group feels justified sacrificing the major interests of the "inferior" group to satisfy their own minor interests. (Freeman, 2010, p. 8)

Where speciesism is manifested through legal discourse, therefore, "questions may be raised about the configurations of rights and duties that seem to 'preclude marginalized groups from developing an emancipatory, political consciousness" (Hasian, 1993, p. 349). Advocates concerned with the law-as-ideology and ideology-as-discourse must subsequently "refuse to accept automatically the existing social, political, and economic relationships established in part through judicial edicts" because they "understand that when a culture's sacred myths are attacked, ideology emerges to justify the world views that have been adopted with a particular community" (p. 349).

Such a stance would deepen communication scholarship's rather limited understanding of "animal rights" as both a social movement and a rhetorical trope to this point. As I alluded to earlier, scholarship across communication literatures thus far has primarily, although not exclusively, used animal rights practices as effective but one-off case studies that concretize abstract theories and methods but do little to examine the ideologies necessary to promoting total liberation. In other words, scholarship engaged with animal rights more often than not has used the movement to articulate a rhetorical methodology rather than an ideological rhetorical methodology to articulate the movement. There are, as in any field, important exceptions to the rule, such as animal-oriented rhetoricians Garrett Broad, Carrie Packwood Freeman, and Greg Goodale. Nonetheless, past literature on the animal rights movement in communication studies is representative of a larger trend, both inside and outside of the academy, to imagine the animal rights movement as a single-minded group of people with a set of common strategies and tactics. Precious few scholars have sought to scrutinize animal rights as anything other than an ideological monolith, and even fewer seek to interrogate conceptualizations of speciesism as it functions in broader institutions such as the law. Thus, although the aforementioned communication scholarship seems like an extensive, far-reaching analysis of animal rights theories and praxis, it barely scratches the surface of what is a complex, multivocal, and fiercely divided social movement.

Only by analyzing the full depth of the movement's ideologies and discourses can scholars of communication, or of any discipline, hope to engage in a legitimate critique and subsequent revision of animal rights' theories, strategies, and tactics. And, given the world's current state of environmental degradation and agricultural industrialization, now more than ever, it is important to interrogate, critique, rethink, and apply the ideas of environmentally oriented movements, particularly those discourses most typically cast aside as too radical for contemporary society.

What is more, ideological criticism can, with proper care, act as a decolonial methodology. And, as mentioned previously, the task of this book is to decolonize the rhetorics of animal rights law. Multiple rhetoricians have engaged with theories of decoloniality in their efforts to compose prescriptive scholarly works capable of promoting transnational social justice. Wanzer (2012) in particular noted how rhetoricians must practice "epistemic disobedience" in the pursuit of praxis that "de-links" the study of rhetoric from colonial ontologies. Ideological criticism invokes a "decolonial turn" when it "highlights the epistemic relevance of the enslaved and colonized search for humanity. It seeks to open up the sources for thinking and to break up the apartheid of theoretical domains through renewed forms of critique and epistemic creolization" (Maldondo-Torres, 2008, p. 7). Among these domains are those that perceive themselves as liberatory and justice-bound. A decolonial "critique of freedom" (McKerrow, 1989) will thus "shift attention to the ways in which theories themselves (including some that underwrite postcolonialism) reinscribe coloniality in our present era" (Wanzer, 2012, note 32).

Rhetoricians have worked to expand the vocabularies of scholars interested in colonial discourses past, present, and future. Specifically, they have devoted much attention to the differences, overlaps, and interconnections between colonialism, postcolonialism, and neocolonialism. According to Shome (1996), the invocation, deconstruction, and critiques of these terms and their discursive/material manifestations are not only relevant to rhetorical scholarship but also necessary to the field's development:

> By working from a postcolonial perspective, I suggest that as we engage in rhetorical understandings of texts, or produce rhetorical theories, it is important to place the texts that we critique or the theories that we produce against a larger backdrop of neocolonialism and racism, and interrogate to what extent these discourses and our own perspectives on them reflect the contemporary global politics of (neo) imperialism. . . . Whereas in the past, imperialism was about controlling the "native" by colonizing her or him territorially, now imperialism is more about subjugating the "native" by colonizing her or him discursively. (Shome, 1996, pp. 41–42)

McClintock (1992) famously warned scholars about the pitfalls of applying the prefix "post-" to any field of study, particularly those having to do with lived histories and legacies of unequal power relations. Indeed, the post- in postcolonialism risked erroneously implying through its name alone that the era of colonization is in the past, done away with for good via the release of some settled states from European control during the 1900s. In an effort to combat such an anachronistic progress narrative of history, communication scholars have sought to highlight postcolonial criticism's potential to interrogate contemporary colonial manifestations in an increasingly globalized, mediated world. One such means to analyze contemporary coloniality is through the study of neocolonialism, defined by intercultural rhetorician Kent Ono as a "ghost-like presence" in a media-dependent world that acts as a "re-tooled, and therefore more relevant and effective, colonial discourse adapted to meet present-day conditions" (Ono, 2009, pp. 2–4). Indeed, as Kelly (2012) explained:

> To investigate representations of race, gender, capitalism, and empire is to peer into our repressed colonial histories . . . [and] placing media texts in neocolonial contexts yields latent connections between media culture and the persistence of Western hegemony. When these connections are exposed, it becomes possible to disrupt seamless narratives of liberal progress in which colonialism is portrayed as a relic of a distant past. (Kelly, 2012, p. 345)

Particular discursive and/or mediated contexts—be they movies, blogs, journalisms, memes, etc.—can under the right conditions convince their audiences to "unlearn the infamous history of mass slaughter" (Buescher & Ono, 1996, p. 127) and relearn how those histories impact marginalized groups to this day or are cloaked/rendered invisible by majority parties.

Rhetorical ideological criticism is particularly suited to decolonial studies and neocolonial artifacts due to this method's roots in McGee's theories of fragmentation, wherein notions of the "public" or the "people" are "more of a *process* than *phenomenon*" (McGee, 1975, p. 242). Fragmented publics and their reliance upon ideographs are intimately connected to "social imaginaries," which Charles Taylor defined as "the way ordinary people 'imagine' their social surroundings . . . carried in images, stories, and legends" (p. 91). According to Enck-Wanzer (2012), "connecting ideographs with social imaginaries and their attendant concern with stranger relationality can rehabilitate and extend the usefulness of [both concepts] . . . link[ing] modern social imaginaries to coloniality and demonstrat[ing] how ideographic shifts can function to decolonize the imaginary" (p. 3).

Utilizing these concepts in partnership with McGee's fragmentation thesis, ideological rhetorical critics can engage critically with notions of "circulation," wherein the means by which an artifact is disseminated is ultimately just as important as what is presented in the artifact itself (Stuckey, 2012). One benefit in assessing the circulation of rhetorical artifacts in a high-speed, mass-mediated U.S. American context is that scholars can gain better understandings of the text's "authenticity"—which is to say, the extent to which interpretations of a rhetorical artifact have been manipulated and/or coopted by others to create different meanings—often in stark contrast to the intent of the original rhetor (Black, 2009; 2012). Such appropriative processes might be in service of domination (i.e., the cooptation of "intersectionality" by animal rights activists not particularly interested in fighting antiracist, antisexist thought and praxis despite the concept's initial orientation toward liberating Black womanhood under the law) or in the service of freedom (i.e., taking a concept used to oppress and changing its meaning in the service of empowerment, such as the extension of intersectionality rhetoric to include "species" as an identity category in need of deconstruction *in tandem with* and *in relation to* racism, sexism, and other such isms). Studies of rhetorical circulation in colonial and neocolonial contexts enable scholars to navigate "a 'both/and' structure wherein the appropriation of dominant languages is imbricated with subaltern reinterpretations that decolonize the colonial context" (Black, 2009, p. 81).

Ideological rhetoric criticism is thus an ideal means by which to assert the mutually constitutive effects of texts and contexts in the social construction of realities—realities that, in systems of unequal power relations and conflicting notions of what it means to be "fully human," are in terrible need of de- and reconstruction. As Wanzer (2012) explained, "On a practical level, this means that rhetoricians . . . must begin *hearing* those voices excluded from our theorizing and the discourse communities we study, *internalizing* their thought, and *seeking* ways to delink from modern[ity]/coloniality" (p. 654). It can both gauge the intended "meaning" of a text and serve as a way of acknowledging the inevitable polysemy of that meaning within individualized, situated contexts of unequal power relations and disparate material realities. Examining coloniality's "postmodern condition" is essential and insightful to interrogations of global justice:

> While it is clear that law occupies a prominent place in the global society because most of the global exchange of persons, capital, and culture is managed through legal forms, it is not clear where the place of justice is in this new world order. Although justice seems to serve as a standard to which law is held accountable, it is an elusive and slippery gauge against which law and power are measured and tested. In this contingent, ever moving, and asymptotic relationship, justice can both challenge and underwrite legal power. (Silby, 1996, p. 209)

The rhetorical decolonization of artifacts must therefore be more than descriptive, particularly if scholars and their adherents take seriously the need for a revisioning of law and justice in the twenty-first century. Like Cox's insistence that environmental communication scholars have an ethical duty to perform lifesaving, justice-oriented, environmentalist scholarship, so too decolonial rhetoricians need to compose prescriptive work engaged with the quest for social justice. For a "story of justice" (Silby, 1996, p. 209) to emerge from the haunting legacies of colonial thought and praxis, engaged and prescriptive scholarly inquiry "is the minimal prerequisite for engaged action on behalf of justice" (p. 233). To do such work, insisted Ono and Sloop (1999):

> Necessitates social change and the crossing of social boundaries. Indeed, it necessitates cultivating an interest in experiences of cultures other than one's own. It also necessitates appreciation and respect for logics that, because of one's own experiential limitations, may appear quite absurd at the outset. (Ono & Sloop, 1999, pp. 534–535)

Hasian (2001) concurred, for "readers may cringe at this blurring of the line between scholarship and political action, but one could argue that the very absence of such engagement is itself the tacit acceptance of existing social, cultural, and economic conditions" (p. 27).

This book thus advocates for a particular subset of "voiceless" subalterns (those animals excluded from the boundaries of human language despite their own linguistic capabilities) and notes the conceptual insufficiencies of traditional legal strategies and mainstream vegan rhetorics due to the silencing of a multiplicity of colonized human voices. A rhetorical decolonization of animal rights law is a necessary component of and for a critical rhetorical understanding/ethical application of animal liberation discourse.

To conclude, in this book, I look at key rhetorical "texts" written/spoken/performed by animal rights lawyers, philosophers, and activists; mediated depictions of these lawyers and cases in various outlets such as television news, documentaries, etc.; and the tangible, material effects that these discourses have, have had, or might have on the world around them. I acknowledge not only what is present in the texts but also what is absent. I critique stated and unstated ideologies present in animal rights law, not stopping at critiques of speciesism, but critiquing the critiques made by antispeciesists for their inherently colonial values. By invoking rhetorical ideological criticism, I am able to pinpoint ideological structures linguistically and extralinguistically at play in controversies over animal rights law. And, in doing so, I critique not for the sake of critique alone, but to advocate for a specific set of strategies and tactics better in line with an intersectional, decolonial *telos* of animal rights.

In this chapter, I articulated and defended my theoretical and methodological approaches toward the study and critique of animal rights law. In contrast to the classical theories of animal rights—and, subsequently, the prototypical liberal conceptualizations of the rule of law—I offered a teleological lens focused less on abstract, universal principles of objectivism and rationality and more on contextual, contingent relationships based in context, contingency, and empathy. Ecofeminist legal theory consists of a theoretical commitment to ecofeminism, feminist legal studies, and critical animal studies. Methodologically, I invoked ideological rhetorical criticism. This rhetorical stance reveals that legal strategy is a series of discursive fragments, and these fragments are understood as partial representations of broader ideologies situated in particular historical moments.

To quote Audre Lorde, "The master's tools will never dismantle the master's house. They may allow us to temporarily beat him at his own game, but they will never enable us to bring about genuine change" (Lorde, 2003, p. 26). Nonetheless, standing outside the house and glaring will not stop the master's atrocities in a timely fashion. As Sarah Koopman observed, "We cannot ignore his tools, or we will constantly trip over them; but we can dismantle and rework them" (Koopman, 2008, p. 299). A shrewd animal liberationist should therefore strive to break inside, steal the deed, swipe the tools, and totally remodel before the master is any the wiser.

CHAPTER 2

All Animals Are Equal (but Some Are More Equal than Others)

Speciesist Personhoods in the Nonhuman Rights Project

If, as W. E. B. DuBois noted, the problem of the twentieth century was the color line, one could argue that the problem of the twenty-first century will become the lines we draw in law between persons and nonpersons.

—Saru Matambanadzo, "Embodying Vulnerability:
Toward a Feminist Theory of the Person"

On March 16, 2017, acclaimed lawyer and animal rights activist Steven M. Wise argued in front of the New York Court of Appeals that two chimpanzees, Tommy and Kiko, should be considered legal persons under the law. Subsequently, he claimed, under New York's habeas corpus statute, they should be released from captivity and sent to a Florida animal sanctuary to live out the rest of their lives (Fermino, 2017). Of fundamental concern in this particular appeal was a prior ruling by the Third Judicial Department that these chimps were not entitled to legal rights due to their inability to bear duties and responsibilities—an "erroneous assumption" (Wise qtd. in Fermino, 2017, para. 5) that, if applied to all living beings, would deny multiple human beings, such as infants and the intellectually disabled, their right to go to court as well. According to Wise, "It was unfair, and it's not backed up by science" (para. 7). He argued his case and responded to questions from the judges for over fifteen minutes, including queries as to why, after so much time, effort, failures, and court appeals, he continued to insist that his animal clients deserved legal personhood under the law. As the hearing drew to a close, Wise commented:

> All our arguments are grounded on fundamental ideas of justice. And I think when the judges sit down and look at them, they'll see the truth in what we're saying. The reasons that humans have rights are the same as to why nonhumans should have rights. I am eternally optimistic. (para. 11)

The 2017 appeal was the latest in a long series of suits filed by Wise and his nonprofit group, the Nonhuman Rights Project (NhRP). Tommy and Kiko represent two of the group's clients, consisting of four chimpanzees and two elephants, all of whom, Wise argued, have a "fundamental right to bodily liberty" and, as "autonomous beings, they have the right to be released from captivity and sent to an appropriate sanctuary" (Wise, 2017, para. 2). Both chimps have been represented by Wise for years, and both have yet to see much success in the courtroom. Tommy was the group's first client. The NhRP described first meeting Tommy while he was living alone in a cage in a shed (with walls painted to look like a jungle) on a trailer lot along Route 30 in Gloversville, New York. Tommy had only a television as company, since as his owner Patrick Lavery claimed, "He likes being by himself" ("Client: Tommy," n.d., para. 1–2). Kiko was found caged in a cement storefront in Niagara Falls, New York. A former animal "actor," the chimp was rendered partially deaf as a result of beatings suffered during the filming of *Tarzan in Manhattan*. Photos of Kiko show him with a steel chain and padlock around his neck ("Client: Kiko, n.d.). Litigation for both clients began separately in December 2013 and has continued through today. On June 7, 2017, the First Judicial Department ultimately ruled against Tommy, Kiko, Wise, and the NhRP. The judges unanimously agreed that the chimps were not entitled to rights, and that despite the "laudable" goal of Wise and the NhRP, Tommy and Kiko "lack sufficient responsibility to have any legal standing" (qtd. in Brown, 2017, para. 4). Wise stated that he would appeal the decision to New York's highest court.

As of today, Tommy and Kiko still live in captivity, but the NhRP has vowed to keep fighting until they can be sent to Save the Chimps Sanctuary in Fort Pierce, Florida. Despite setback after setback, Wise made clear his intent to appeal until victory is achieved. Tommy's and Kiko's stories continue to capture American headlines just as they have for years. Journalists have been intrigued not only by Wise's tenacity (appealing the cases over and over again in response to denied petitions of habeas corpus) but also by his end goal to achieve legal personhood (and subsequently legal rights) for Tommy, Kiko, and other chimpanzees. Back in 2013, *Wired* reported of Tommy's initial hearing, "What Wise and the members of his Nonhuman Rights Project assert is both simple and radical: that personhood . . . should no more be based on species classification than it is on skin color" (Keim, 2013, para. 4). When Tommy's suit was rejected, the journalist followed up on his previous article by quoting multiple scientists and legal scholars disappointed with the decision, noting how "the decision touched on a deeper discomfort with extending a traditionally human concept to a non-human" (Keim, 2014, para. 22). A *Gizmodo* reporter agreed, "It would appear that the judges ruled against Tommy simply because of his biological status as a chimpanzee. Subsequently, it's a decision that will very likely not stand the test of time" (Dvorsky, 2014, para. 11). The author followed up on the case after the June 2017 ruling, scolding how "the justices, unwilling to establish a bombshell precedent at the state justice level, simply hand-waved the Nonhuman Rights Project's arguments aside, and ignored the mountain of scientific evidence presented at the case" (Dvorsky, 2017a, para. 9). Other outlets reporting on Tommy, Kiko, and the other clients of the NhRP have included the *Huffington Post, Washington Post, New York Times, New York Law Journal, New York Daily News, Pacific Standard, Al Jazeera America, Associated Press, Wall Street Journal, Washington Examiner, NBC News, NPR, Live Science,* and even the acclaimed academic outlet *Science,* sponsored by the American Association for the Advancement of Science, which has to date published seven different articles on cases sponsored by the NhRP.

Some judges have been sympathetic to the NhRP's goals, even while denying their petitions. When the New York Supreme Court rejected the NhRP's plea to make Hercules and Leo, the group's two other chimpanzee clients in 2015, legal persons under the law, Judge Barbara Jaffe wrote in her decision that "not very long ago, only Caucasian, male, property-owning citizens were entitled to the full panoply of legal rights under the United States Constitution" (qtd. in Grimm, 2015, para. 5). She concluded with a callback to Supreme Court Justice Anthony Kennedy, "Times can blind us to certain truths and later generations can see that laws once thought necessary and proper in fact serve only to oppress" (para. 5). The NhRP has been similarly encouraged by the fact that, while chimpanzees do not possess rights or personhood in the United States, an Argentinian judge ruled that the animals were "beings" with "nonhuman legal rights" in November 2016 (Lovelace, 2017). As the twenty-first century proceeds, giving certain animals additional legal privileges is, quite possibly, seemingly inevitable in America's judicial future.

As I mentioned in the introduction, animal rights litigators and the overall movement's adherents must ensure that their philosophies, strategies, and tactics are not only coherent but also in line with visions of total liberation—which is to say, liberation for *all* and not just for *some*. Given the intense visibility of the NhRP and the ever-increasing media prominence—from newspaper interviews to Sundance documentaries—of Wise, and given the increase in national/international interest in cases of chimps, dogs, dolphins, and elephants deemed too "human" to ignore, this chapter uses Wise as a case study to delve into the issues stemming from taking a legal formalist approach to animal rights. Specifically, it uses a rhetorical approach to ideological criticism to seriously question the purported "radicalness" and liberatory potential of Wise's discourse, specifically as employed in his public attempts to secure "legal personhood" for particular animal species on the basis of those species' similarity to *Homo sapiens.*

This chapter argues that, despite Wise's genuinely goodhearted and legally sound intentions, his and the NhRP's project is hardly as "critical," "radical," or even "liberatory" as they and their adherents seem to believe. Indeed, while Wise's emphasis on "legal personhood" has strong historical and legal precedent for giving disenfranchised groups legal rights, his theories of justice, reliant as they are on Enlightenment-style, humanist notions on positive/negative rights and characteristics of formal personhood, often obscure larger barriers prohibiting liberationist, particularly *animal* liberationist, politics. While this chapter *does not* make the claim that invoking the terms "personhood" or "rights" are condemnable animal liberation tactics, it *does* question the *specific* rhetorical tactics used by Wise and the NhRP in the name of procuring animal liberation, and by extension total liberation, through litigation prioritizing human-animal cognitive similarities.

Specifically, the following chapter utilizes the principles established in chapter 1's explanation of ecofeminist legal theory to perform a rhetorical ideological criticism of public texts composed regarding and/or distributed by Wise and the NhRP. It critiques the vexing, and too often contradictory, philosophies, strategies, and tactics at play when hyper-rational animal liberation rhetoric meets U.S. American legal positivist practices. This criticism identifies ideologically incoherent strands of thought running through Wise's theory of legal personhood for animals that, when pushed to their limit, ultimately risk replacing one form of human domination over the nonhuman world with another, only *marginally* different, model. By consistently identifying certain "higher" animals as those most deserving of legal personhood, Wise and the NhRP attempt to gain rights for the animals sufficiently similar to human beings. This tactic is intensely contradictory to broader animal liberation, and certainly to total liberation, by once again privileging the colonial conceptualization of the "human" as the most desirable and most moral body, and thus recentering the Cartesian, humanist logics that consistently justify oppressing animal (and human) others.

At stake in this critique of Wise and the NhRP is a not so carefully disguised hyper-humanist ideology ripe with speciesism. According to Carrie Packwood Freeman (2010), "American society is rhetorically constructed on humanist principles that celebrate humanity's specialness and define it in opposition to animality" (p. 12). Wise's approach to animal liberation is no exception. In this chapter, I note the rhetorical formulations through which, as legal scholar Saru Matambanadzo (2012) noted, "Legal disputes in a variety of areas can be understood as determinations about who counts and how we should take account of them" (p. 45). Such critique should not be considered divisive, but necessary to the furtherance of animal liberation vis-à-vis the U.S. American legal system. Scholars and activists have a duty to determine the "best" tactic (which I will tentatively define as the most "morally consistent" tactic at a given moment in time) through which to secure animal rights. After all, as Goodale and Black (2010) rightly argued:

> The rhetoric of those activists who champion "animal" rights, or welfare, or liberation, or abolition, and of those who argue that humans should be permitted to use "animals" must be examined for failures, assumptions, and exploitations if we are ever to have an honest debate about the relationship between humans and other animals. (p. 7)

By analyzing and critiquing Wise and the NhRP for their ideological insufficiencies and ethical contradictions, this chapter applies ideological rhetorical criticism's power to produce "a sense of what is not being addressed and how those issues might be brought into a sphere where discourse and debate become possible again" (Goodale & Black, 2010, p. 7). And, in this instance, what is not being addressed is the necessity of finding "a way to respect the diversity represented in the animal world (in groups and individuals) so as to avoid creating new hierarchies or revised notions of 'the animal other' ... to call for human ethical behavior without eliciting elitist notions of 'humanity' in opposition to an implied brute animality" (Freeman, 2010, pp. 12, 19). In other words, while this chapter does not seek to "trash" (Kelman, 1984) legal rhetorics of rights and personhood, it aims to interrogate the extent to which certain orientations toward those concepts might ultimately work against the goals of lawyers purportedly in favor of animal liberation, and certainly those working toward total liberation.

Steven Wise, the Nonhuman Rights Project, and Legal Personhood

Nearly two decades ago, acclaimed food activist Michael Pollan (2002) suggested that "animal liberation is the logical next step in the forward march of moral progress" (para. 4). The efforts of Wise and the NhRP would seem to echo Pollan's claim as they attempt to use the legal precedents set through centuries of American judicial proceedings to argue that a proper understanding of justice must avoid speciesist logic with as much fervor as the logics of racism, classism, sexism, etc. Wise famously, tenaciously, and unapologetically has argued that civilizations cannot possibly establish proper protections for animals while they are considered mere property. Thus, the most important goal for animal rights activists ought to be to establish legal personhood for nonhuman beings.

Wise has practiced animal protection law throughout America for over thirty years. According to him, back when he started practicing in 1980, "the whole idea of animal rights was completely bizarre. People would literally talk about animal lovers as little old ladies with tennis shoes who would fill their house with cats" (qtd. in Kaufman, 2016, para. 6). He became interested in animal rights after reading Peter Singer's acclaimed *Animal Liberation,* which encouraged him not only to become a vegetarian but also to shift his legal focus from criminal defense/personal injury to animal protection litigation. He initially took on "dangerous dog" cases and has, according to the *Los Angeles Times,* personally saved over 150 dogs that would have otherwise been euthanized (Kaufman, 2016). Soon, however, Wise reported that fighting for canines was not satisfying enough:

> I thought I wanted to begin changing the legal structure itself, not operating within the legal structure, because it was so biased. It was like representing a black slave in the early 1800s: Everything was stacked against them, and they're property. Animals

are in the exact same position that black slaves were before the Civil War. (qtd. in Kaufman, 2016, para. 18)

Since that realization, Wise has authored four books popular inside and outside of the academy: *Rattling the Cage: Toward Legal Rights for Animals*; *Drawing the Line: Science and the Case for Animal Rights*; *Though the Heavens May Fall: The Landmark Trial That Led to the End of Human Slavery*; and *An American Trilogy—Death, Slavery, and Dominion along the Banks of the Cape Fear River*. His writings have been lauded as "original and thoughtful work that marks what could become one of the groundbreaking civil rights battles of the next generation" (Verchick, 2001, p. 208). At the 2016 Sundance Film Festival, he premiered a documentary entitled *Unlocking the Cage*, following his many years of animal advocacy. In academia proper, Wise has served as a lecturer at Harvard University and has taught animal rights law at law schools nationwide. He is an active academic publisher, with over twenty highly cited, single-author publications, and has coauthored manuscripts with the acclaimed primatologist Jane Goodall. And, in 2007, he founded the Center for the Expansion of Fundamental Rights, which would officially become the NhRP in 2012.

The NhRP uses litigation, advocacy, and education to support its five central objectives: First, it seeks to change the legal status of great apes, elephants, dolphins, and whales from "mere things" to "legal persons." Second, it draws upon and integrates principles of common law, morality, scientific discovery, and human phenomenology to consider qualities sufficient for the recognition of nonhuman personhood. Third, the NhRP aims to develop grassroots campaigns at the local, national, and global level to support animal rights, particularly the rights to be free from captivity, to participate in their species communities, and to have their habitats protected. Fourth, it hopes to build a broad-based coalition of individuals and organizations to secure legal personhood and subsequently rights for nonhuman animals. Finally, the NhRP promotes understanding of justice from larger social, historical, political, and legal perspectives as well as the scientific discovery of nonhuman animals' cognitive and emotional complexities (Nonhuman Rights Project, n.d.). The organization enjoys the support of acclaimed animal rights activists like Singer and Goodall, the latter of whom serves as a board member for the organization.

At the core of Wise's theory of animal rights litigation is the concept of "legal personhood," specifically the notion that nonhuman animals ought to count as persons under the law and therefore should have both legal standing and "rights" in the American court system. According to Wise (1999),

> For centuries, a Great Legal Wall has divided humans from every other species of animal in the West. On one side, every human is a person with legal rights; on the other, every non-human is a thing with no legal rights. Every animal rights lawyer knows that this barrier must be breached. (p. 61)

Legal rights, as described by Wise (1996), are claims recognized by the law as valid "with a legal obligation upon the addressee, and that the legal system renders likely that the benefit will in fact be enjoyed" (p. 179). The rights for which Wise fights, he has argued, are not "moral rights," as legal rights are the "real rights" capable of protecting the real material interests of animals. Moral rights "are of little use until and unless they assume the shape of the law" (p. 179). In other words, Wise believes that top-down legal approaches necessarily determine morality at the layman's level. Bottom-up advocacy is of little relevance without official court rulings reifying certain visions of rights and justice.

Neither legal nor moral rights can be procured until one's legal "thinghood" is replaced with legal "personhood." Legal things are at once alive and inanimate, existing merely as means to ends of those called persons by the court. Those condemned to thinghood are "invisible to civil judges in their own rights," for "only legal persons count in courtrooms, or can be legally seen, for they exist in law for their own benefits" (Wise, 2010, p. 1). As legalized nonpersons, animals cannot have others file lawsuits directly on their behalf:

> Their interests can be protected only indirectly . . . when a legal person, who has legal rights . . . files a lawsuit in order to stop an illegal act or seek compensation for injuries already inflicted. . . . Not just any legal person can sue to protect animals . . . Judges, federal and state, usually restrict those who are able to obtain a judicial decision to plaintiffs with a sufficient large stake in the outcome of the controversy. (Wise, 2003, p. 100)

Achieving personhood status is a difficult and multistep process, but it is the legal baseline for having one's legal rights defended in court. Plaintiffs must be "Level 1" legal persons to possess "Level 2" legal rights to either sue or have a third party sue on their behalf. If the plaintiffs hold "Level 3" private rights of action, courts grant them "Level 4" standing. Standing, if granted to animals, would assure that "the question of whether a nonhuman animal plaintiff suffered a redressable injury caused by the defendant should rarely pose an obstacle," after all, "a chimpanzee confined to a tiny cage or injected with a deadly microbe . . . has a clear stake in the controversy" (Wise, 2010, p. 4). The task of the NhRP is to continue pressing for Level 1 legal personhood and Level 2 legal rights "for every appropriate nonhuman animal" (p. 11). Notably, however, this chapter seeks to question exactly what Wise's vision of *appropriateness* means compared to what, under a vision of total liberation, it *ought* to mean.

Wise correctly asserts that current "protections" for nonhuman animals are woefully inadequate. Legal *protection,* after all, is not the same as legal *personhood.* Although there are animal welfare laws seemingly in place to prevent cruelty, the violation of such a law *may,* although it rarely *does,* result in criminal conviction. Furthermore, punishment of the convicted hardly equates to the acquisition of legal rights for the victim. On the contrary, the legal procedure for convicting someone for torturing and killing a puppy is little different than prosecuting for damages to a shrub or a car (Wise, 2003). Mere "welfare" statutes must be replaced with legal rights for animals, as rights are "the least porous barrier against oppression and abuse that humans have ever devised" (Wise, 2000, p. 236). Personhood is essential.

True, one could argue that an animal's overall inability to directly sue another party might disqualify them the legal community, and thus personhood. That argument, however, purposefully misunderstands the workings of the legal system, wherein an individual's ability to sue or countersue is not indicative of their personhood. For instance, in criminal investigations district attorneys choose to file charges against defendants, not the laypersons affected by the crime. Such is the reason that parties without the individual ability to sue—such as young children or the deceased—can "have their day in court."

Furthermore, Wise has correctly critiqued some of the colonial roots of U.S. American legal theory, particularly because coloniality invokes unfortunate principles ripped from the annals of Western origin stories—or, more specifically, the literature of the ancient Greeks. He has frequently claimed that the largest challenge to procuring legal rights for animals is that such litigation "will necessarily implicate the law's deepest and most cherished principles and values, along with some of our widest, and most often contradictory, public policies" (Wise, 1999, p. 62). Among these contradictory policies is the broad legal understanding that animals are property, a rule which is "anachronistic as human slavery" (p. 62). And yet, the rule persists because of a warped historical narrative that says "because the ancient Romans did it, the biblical Israelites did it, and the ancient Greeks did it" (Wise, 1996, p. 180). He asserted that contemporary society adheres to classical conceptions of a "Great Chain of Being" that places humanity as the moral pinnacle of living organisms and all others below it. This Great Chain has transformed itself into the Great Legal Wall that prevents nonhuman beings from procuring satisfactory legal protections (Wise, 1999). However, Wise (2003) and the NhRP seek to amend such speciesist legal logics, as "an animal's species is irrelevant to his or her entitlement to liberty rights" (p. 103). "A species," after all, "is just a population of genetically similar individuals naturally able to interbreed, and no one suggests that it is the human ability to interbreed that justifies our legal personhood" (Wise, 2000, p. 241).

Of course, to attribute *all* animal exploitation to Greek moral and legal thought would present a thin, abstract understanding of environmental history. One need not read "the Greeks" to understand the millennia-long histories of humans' hunting, domestication, and consumption of nonhuman animals and animal products. Capitalist systems of property ownership and proprietary individualism—just the most recent form of this long relationship—are clear merely from existing in day-to-day life. Wise, however, is not suggesting that there was a singularly causal relationship between a Greek "Great Chain" ideology and animal exploitation. Rather, he probes the jurisprudential roots of anthropocentric U.S. American legal systems, as any law student will explain in their studies, that proudly attribute their roots to the "democratic" systems of ancient Greece. To argue for the legal rights of animals *without* knowing the active anthropocentrism undergirding the law's historical roots is to argue toothlessly.

Among the "most important rights" for which Wise and the NhRP fight are bodily integrity and liberty. Such rights "act like a suit of legal armor, shielding the bodies and personalities of natural persons from invasion and injury. These rights are so important that they are enshrined in the bill of rights of state and federal constitutions" (Wise, 2003, p. 103). Despite the wrongful Western assumption that only humans are due legal rights and moral consideration, "any who possesses practical autonomy has what is sufficient for basic rights as a matter of liberty" (p. 103). American courts have already granted personhood to "artificial" human beings like corporations. What is more, even certain humans who do not demonstrate Enlightenment-influenced qualities such as "rationality" have been awarded legal personhood and rights; using what is called the argument from marginal cases, Wise has asserted that "as long as society awards personhood to non-autonomous humans, such as the very young, the severely mentally retarded, and the persistently vegetative," then it must, as a matter of equality, award basic rights to "animals with *practical autonomy*" (p. 103, emphasis mine). Practical autonomy, for Wise's purposes, refers to "highly advanced cognitive abilities as consciousness, perhaps even self-consciousness; a sense of self; and the abilities to desire and act intentionally," which is sufficient (although not necessarily obligatory) for basic legal rights (p. 103).

Wise is hyper-aware of the difficulty of his and the NhRP's task. He has long warned animal advocates:

> The necessary foundation for the legal rights of nonhuman animals does not yet exist. Do not expect a judge to appreciate the merits of arguments in favor of the legal personhood of any non-human animal the first time, or even the fifth time, she encounters them. While a sympathetic judge might be found here and there, no appellate bench will seize the lead until the issue has been thoroughly aired in law journals, books, and conferences. (Wise, 1999, p. 66)

As such, he guides the NhRP by ensuring that it will only file suits in those jurisdictions most hospitable to arguments regarding the legal rights of animals, a method Wise has down to a science given his efforts to compose "a hierarchy of common law American state jurisdictions according to their perceived hostility to certain key legal arguments" (Wise, 2010, p. 10). Such attention to detail is of the utmost importance to securing fundamental rights to bodily liberty and integrity, for "if these early cases are brought at the wrong time, in the wrong place, or before the wrong judges, they may strengthen the Great Legal Wall" (Wise, 1999, p. 68). Nonetheless, Wise has consistently assured his audiences that the NhRP can and will secure victory for its clients, ultimately producing "a legal earthquake, a piercing trumpet that would shake the legal wall that was erected thousands of years ago between humans and all other beings and cause it finally to come tumbling down" (Wise, 1996, p. 186). In doing so, future generations of animal rights lawyers will have a solid legal foundation from which to fight for the rights of all species.

Discourses About and Surrounding Wise and the NhRP

Ideological rhetorical criticism necessitates investigating the contested discourses surrounding a rhetor like Wise and his organization. And, in the case of the NhRP, there are indeed many differential opinions regarding the group's judicial drive toward chimp, cetacean, and elephant personhood. Many big-name animal rights organizations such as PETA support Wise and the NhRP—although that support is not necessarily reciprocal on Wise's end (Wise, 2011). Multiple academics have come out in support of nonhuman personhood. Philosophers such as Michigan Tech's L. Syd M. Johnson, Dalhousie University's Andrew Fenton and Letitia Maynell, and fourteen others even helped Wise compose and file an amicus curiae brief for use at the New York Court of Appeals. The brief, informally dubbed "Chimpanzee Personhood: A Philosophers' Brief," asserted that U.S. American court systems were "using a number of incompatible conceptions of 'person' which, when properly understood, are either philosophically inadequate or in fact compatible with Kiko and Tommy's personhood" (qtd. in Berman, 2018, para. 13). Ultimately, these Wise-aligned philosophers fully agree with the powerful statement in "Philosophers' Brief" that "any attempt to specify the essential features of 'human nature' either leaves out a considerable number of humans—often the most vulnerable in our society—or includes members of other species" (qtd. in Berman, 2018, para. 15). In making their case, the brief asserted as its overarching thesis:

> We submit this brief in our shared interest in ensuring a more just co-existence with other animals who live in our communities. . . . We strongly urge this Court, in keeping with the best philosophical standards of rational judgment and ethical standards of justice, to recognize that, as nonhuman persons, Kiko and Tommy should be granted a writ of *habeas corpus* and their detainers should have the burden of showing the lawful justification of their current confinement. (qtd. in Choplin, 2018, para. 4)

Members of the scientific community also find value in Wise's assertions, particularly with regard to chimpanzee personhood. Jane Goodall has submitted affidavits on behalf of the NhRP's ape clients to argue that, at least in their natural communities, chimps have both duties and responsibilities, thus canceling out any court's claim that they cannot participate in a moral community (Berman, 2018). For Goodall, "surely, there can be no good reason to prolong their lives of servitude. So please, I beg of you, do the right thing" (qtd. in Cotroneo, 2016, para. 5). Mary Lee Jensvold, an environmental psychologist and former director of the Chimpanzee and Human Communication Institute, and Tetsuro Matsuzawa of the

International Primatological Society also supported Wise's cases on the grounds that a chimpanzee's communicative abilities were rich enough, advanced enough, and similar enough to *Homo sapiens* to merit personhood (Keim, 2013). Biological anthropologist Barbara King agreed, "I find [Wise's] definition of self-determination, which recognizes the reality of different levels of capability across species . . . to be persuasive . . . it's time now to be bold, to throw open our imagination and envision a different future for chimpanzees like Tommy" (King, 2014, para. 10). Even the National Institute of Health, while not specifically endorsing Wise or the NhRP, nonetheless has expressed indirect sympathy for chimpanzee personhood, retiring chimps at biomedical research facilities and refusing to fund research on the animals in the future. According to NIH director Francis Collins, "chimpanzees are special creatures" with "similarities to ourselves that are quite breathtaking" (qtd. in Berdik, 2013, para. 16).

Writers and journalists have also articulated their full support of Wise. In a detailed account of Tommy and Kiko's 2017 failed appellate trial, *Big Think*'s contributing writer Robby Berman offered insight into what he deemed the absurdity of anthropomorphic court decisions denying the chimpanzees personhood on the grounds of their inability to participate in some dubious "John Lockean" social contract:

> This has the relationship backward: One must *first* be seen as a person to be *able* to enter into such a social contract. . . . To say an individual isn't a person because he can't enter into a social contract that proves he's a person is mind-bogglingly circular. (Berman, 2018, para. 18)

Some technology-oriented outlets such as *Gizmodo* believe there is something to Wise's arguments, particularly with regard to the possibility of setting legal precedent for considering multiple nonhuman bodies as persons—even if those bodies are digital. According to *Gizmodo's* George Dvorsky,

> Clearly, this isn't an issue that's going away anytime soon. In addition to recognizing the personhood of qualifying nonhuman animals, our technologies may eventually get to the point when we'll have to start recognizing the moral worth of artificial intelligence and robots. It would be incumbent upon us to get this figured out before we take the monumental step of imbuing sentience into a machine. (Dvorsky, 2017b, para. 18)

Dvorsky (2017a) further purported that "the court's reasons for refusing to recognize chimps as persons was flawed; this decision won't stand the test of time" (para. 4).

For all Wise's support among differential communities, he also has his share of naysayers. Many of these detractors are lawyers themselves, who argue against Wise's personhood rhetoric on that grounds that animals cannot participate in reciprocal duties toward humans and that, should personhood status be granted, too many nonhumans might get too many protections. Among Wise's most vocal academic critics is the University of Chicago's law professor Richard Epstein. In a condemnation of Wise's *Drawing the Line,* Epstein upbraided the concept of "practical autonomy" (to be elaborated upon shortly) for being too malleable and thus applicable to far too many species to be legally useful: "Unless an animal has some sense of self, he cannot hunt, and he cannot either defend himself or flee when subject to attack" (qtd. in Berdik, 2013, para. 20). Achieving personhood for chimps might lead lawyers down a "slippery slope" of granting personhood to any species, a circumstance Epstein vehemently claims should not happen (Wise, however, claims it should happen). After all, explained Epstein, "We kill millions of animals a day for food. . . . If they have the right to bodily liberty, it's basically a holocaust" (qtd. in Monyak, 2018, para. 11). Pepperdine University's law professor Richard L. Cupp (2016) similarly critiques the consequences of nonhuman personhood as "fundamentally flawed and dangerous for society" (para. 4). Cupp fears not only that might too many nonhumans be granted legal personhood and rights but also that certain *humans* might lose their personhood status by virtue of a comparison to animals:

> The most vulnerable humans, those with significant cognitive limitations, would face the greatest risks in a shift to considering individual cognitive capacities as a basis for legal personhood. Although the legal personhood paradigm we assign to them would not immediately collapse, over time thinking of personhood in terms of individual abilities could erode their protections. (Cupp, 2014, para. 19)

Rather, says Cupp, "our focus needs to be on demanding appropriate responsibility from morally accountable humans and human institutions, rather than on the dangerous pretense of nonhuman animal personhood" (para. 26). Assistant New York state attorney general Christopher Coulston concurred, arguing that for all of "personhood's" legal vagaries, that the concept in some way refers to humanity should be obvious: "The reality is these are fundamentally different species. I worry about the diminishment of these rights in some way if we expand them beyond human beings" (qtd. in Rosenblatt, 2017, para. 25). Personhood, "whether it's a corporation, whether it's a ship that is treated as a legal person, we think that is the principle that has governed the assignment of legal personhood" (para. 26–27).

Many scientists are also, perhaps unsurprisingly, critical of Wise's efforts. The *Boston Globe's* Chris Berdik summed up biologists' arguments: "Legal personhood for animals is misguided, and even dangerous. They foresee a slippery slope in which a tightening web of rights starts to cripple scientific progress not just on lifesaving medical research, but also on such goals as species conservation" (Berdik, 2013, para. 5). Steve Feldman, a spokesman for the Association of Zoos and Aquariums, argued that personhood for animals might thwart important research for both humans and animals. After all, keeping animals in captivity and breeding them safeguard endangered species, and opponents of such captivity merely ignore the dangers of the outside world such as habitat loss, hunting, and poachers: "We need to study these animals to help them. . . . There are some people who believe that animals should be free, including free to become extinct" (qtd. in Berdik, 2013, para 17.)

Some disagree with Wise on a less extreme level. One party insists that Wise's ideology is only a *bit* too extreme, needing only moderate revisions. For instance, David Favre, a professor of animal law at Michigan State, argues that nonhuman personhood is a step too far, but the idea of nonhumans as mere chattel is also wrong. Instead, the law ought to establish a category of "living property" that might give nonhuman animals limited rights through legislation, such as requiring that for-profit sales of certain species be outlawed.

On the other hand, another party believes that Wise and the NhRP are to an extent correct about nonhuman personhood but do not go far *enough.* For example, the animal rights group Animal Charity Evaluator expressed mixed feelings as to the NhRP, at once calling it a promising effort to achieve the proper consideration of nonhuman personhood in society while simultaneously questioning if Wise's hyper-emphasis on cognitive prowess was really the "best" avenue to achieve animal rights writ large:

> We're excited about the possibility of legal personhood and rights for animals, though we have substantial uncertainty as to whether the NhRP's work will bring about this end for relatively large numbers of animals. We are also skeptical about ACE's ability to improve the rate of progress toward such a long-term goal with our

recommendation. We think that the best way to increase the likelihood of legal personhood and rights might not be to directly support legal work, but to support social change on behalf of animals that makes people more likely to support legal change. (ACE, 2017, para. 5)

This book takes seriously the concerns of this second party, the party that questions the supposed radicalness of the NhRP's suits. It is, in fact, critiques like ACE's that should give liberationists cause for concern. Wise's tactics are certainly *a* way to achieve animal personhood, but are they the *best* way? Does Wise's way really set a *favorable* sociolegal precedent for the future? The rest of this chapter will expand upon critiques of Wise and the NhRP on the basis that their arguments are shallow, exclusionary, and ultimately toothless. And, ironically, it will do so using the very reason that legal experts such as Richard Epstein have argued against Wise, specifically Epstein's fear of a "slippery slope" of granting personhood to animals. Whereas Epstein and other NhRP detractors dislike Wise's approach for his rejection of human exceptionalism, this chapter argues that the legal rhetorics in play in cases like Tommy's and Kiko's actually *reify* such exceptionalism. A slippery slope toward universal animal personhood is very much desirable. As ACE insisted, social change necessarily impacts support of legal change, and the legal change necessary for nonhuman animal personhood must be the *decentering* of the human body as ideal. Thus, in order to *achieve* the slippery slope, arguments such as Wise's, Goodall's, and others' purporting that cognitive prowess ought to be the necessary legal "proof" in favor of personhood must be seriously reconsidered as a premier legal tactic.

Are Similar Minds the Best Minds?

As mentioned previously, Wise has enjoyed a long career and ample media attention for his detailed animal rights philosophy and intensely persistent litigation tactics, some positive and some negative. At stake in this chapter, however, is the mode of praise espoused by legal adherents such as Robert R. M. Verchick, the Gauthier–St. Martin Chair of Environmental Law at Loyola University. In a highly cited review of *Rattling the Cage,* Verchick praised Wise for his ability "to know the [critical legal studies] playbook by heart and deftly [use] it to attack over 2,000 years of philosophy and law" (Verchick, 2001, p. 216). More specifically, Verchick echoed the sentiment of Wise's adherents: that Wise and the NhRP offer the most fruitful plan to promote a radical animal rights agenda in the U.S. court system with a set of practical, realistic guidelines for doing so. Thus, Wise has taken critical legal studies and other modes of critical theory to heart, then kept only those parts of the philosophy most suitable (in Wise's mind, at least) to achieving court victories for Tommy, Kiko, etc. In the words of Verchick (2001),

> By clipping the wings of critical theory, Wise is able to preserve more concrete principles for action than does the animal welfare movement. Feminists and critical race theorists have set the precedent here by insisting on rights in the midst of their deconstructive projects. If this is what it takes for critical tools to achieve results in the real world, the strategy appears worth it. (p. 228)

If Wise's tactics are indeed both radical and pragmatic enough to achieve an overarching goal of animal liberation, then Verchick's assessment would be valid. However, this chapter argues that Wise goes too far in "clipping the wings" of critical thought, so much so that he embraces colonial and highly speciesist strategies and tactics at odds with the animal rights ideology he claims to love. Specifically, by overemphasizing the moral value of animals holding cognitive similarities to humans, he recenters a humanist philosophy that places *Homo sapiens* at the center of the moral universe. In doing so, he devalues difference and risks drawing new lines between "us" and "them" that continues to exclude most living beings from legal personhood—an exclusion with potentially devastating environmental consequences. Such litigation tactics not only contradict Wise's radical status and purported anti–Great Chain strategy but also demonstrate the problems with an ultrarational approach to animal rights teeming with the legacies of colonial "Great Chain" thought.

Personhood, Wise has claimed, is first and foremost located in *practical autonomy,* a quality that makes animals much more like people than they are like things. This esoteric "quality" includes a being's ability to "desire," to "act intentionally," and to have a "sense of self" (Kleiner, 2002). Proof of this autonomy is evidenced especially in animal cognition, particularly through examination of characteristics and capabilities such as language-using, tool-using, a sense of moral obligation to others, and a complex emotional range. Having practical autonomy entitles beings to basic rights. Such an argument is only slightly different from prior theories of animal rights. Singer (1975), for instance, emphasized "interests" as most important to moral consideration. His legal counterpart, Gary Francione (who will be emphasized in the following chapter) has preferred locating rights in sentience alone (Francione, 2010). The animals most important to Wise and the NhRP, both strategically and (seemingly) morally, are bonobos and chimpanzees on the grounds that they are "exceedingly complex beings" (Wise, 1996, p. 184).

Since his writings in the 1990s, Wise had already concluded that chimps and bonobos ought to secure legal personhood due to their superior levels of practical autonomy. He particularly praised their possession of primary consciousness (which allows them to experience pain and suffering and hold an awareness of the present) and, more significantly, secondary consciousness. This more complex mode of consciousness allows the animals to "derive sophisticated cognitive, emotional, and social capabilities; immense and powerful intellects; and an ability to anticipate the future that qualitatively differs little from the capabilities of human beings" (Wise, 1996, p. 184). Chimpanzees and bonobos are so cognitively advanced that they have "wishes and desires and a complex family-based structure" (p. 184). They have their own cultures passed on from one generation to the next. Their mental abilities are so advanced that, with training, the animals can learn sign language and arithmetic. These attributes contribute to the apes' "profound sense of self" (Verchick, 2001, p. 214). Thus,

> to forcibly remove chimpanzees and bonobos from their natural environment or to maintain them in artificial environments for human purposes is usually to deny them their culture and their ability to form important and social relationships. This deprives them of a substantial portion of what gives meaning to their lives, as slavery would deprive us of a substantial portion of what gives meaning to our lives. (Wise, 1996, p. 185)

Over time, Wise has extended his possible clientele to include other cognitively "advanced" species such as dolphins, whales, gorillas, and elephants. His rationale for doing so, however, is little different from his reasons for asserting the biological superiority of chimpanzees and bonobos. Dolphins and whales, for instance, express linguistic capabilities that, while not as advanced as chimpanzees and bonobos, suggests substantial intelligence. Their brains are extraordinarily large for species of their size and possess neurological structures linked in humans to high-level social and intellectual capabilities (Keim, 2016). According to a report by *Wired* that drew heavily from Wise, "It's even possible to imagine that cetaceans, some of whom live as long as humans and spend their entire lives with a single family, have social sensitivities as pronounced as our own" (Keim, 2012, para. 16). For similar reasons, the NhRP filed a 2018 suit on behalf of two elephants, the first nonchimpanzees the organization has represented. Per Wise, "We're looking at any nonhuman animal for whom we think we have sufficiently powerful data that shows they are autonomous beings" (para. 22). When pressed by his interviewer about his endgame, specifically if a cat or a dog might qualify as a legal person under the law, he answered, "I don't know [about a cat]. There's my personal opinion, but no judge cares about that. The issue is, what facts can we prove in court, if we're claiming that autonomy is a sufficient condition for personhood?" (para. 25). And as for farmed animals, he scoffed, "Somehow, critics say, if you can't keep a chimpanzee in a cage it means that everybody has to be a vegan. Those two are far apart" (para. 29).

Thus, in a strikingly Orwellian manner, Wise's legal strategy not-so-subtly argues that all animals matter, but some matter more than others. One might assert that Wise's strategy is not necessarily in keeping with his personal beliefs about animal liberation. However, even on an unconscious level, this may not be the case. Wise's "starting point" in animal liberation is neither in a Singerian consideration of interests nor a Reganite concern for species' inherent value. Rather, his vision of animal liberation appears to come from a rejection of animal alterity—a desire to protect those particular species in which he sees himself. Indeed, in an interview with the *Los Angeles Times,* Wise asserted that "when I look into the eyes of an alligator, I don't get anything except I'm lunch. . . . When I look at them, I get a very different feeling than I do looking at a chimp" (qtd. in Kaufman, 2016, para. 13). As opposed to an almost-human chimp so clearly deserving of legal personhood, when it comes to an alligator, "we're very far apart from each other" (para. 13). Far from decrying the Great Chain of Being, Wise seems to, at some level, embrace it. The beings (that is to say, the charismatic megafauna) that matter are those Wise can argue are most like himself—an argument that appears not to be a short-term legal strategy or a strategic essentialism but rather a long-term vision of the "animal" that matters most in animal liberation.

Wise's easiest rebuttal to the claim that he favors certain forms of life over others is to emphasize the incremental possibilities of securing animal rights through litigation. An all-or-nothing approach to animal rights is laudable in theory but impractical in reality. This approach to animal rights has a vast and dedicated audience. In his ingratiating review of Wise's *Rattling the Cage,* Verchick (2001) praised Wise's incrementalism, specifically his willingness to concede that animals' property status will not vanish overnight. Rather, "the courts can work case by case, species by species, to determine when the 'thinghood' for animals clearly does not make sense" (p. 224). Although some might find Wise's clear omission of other species "disappointing or frustrating," here, Verchick praised, is where Wise "shows the pragmatism and timing of the seasoned civil rights litigator" (p. 229, 224). Wise's words are to be taken as "but one lawyer's opening argument, not a philosophical meditation" and "should not be faulted for searching his surroundings and choosing only sharp stones" (p. 229). After all, Verchick reflected, "Perhaps we need not comprehend the whole of justice to know, in one case, what justice is not" (p. 229).

It is here that I take serious issue with Wise and his followers' legal strategies and animal liberation discourse. Indeed, his decision to value the "autonomy" expressed most clearly in bonobos, apes, and a select few other species is rather shocking given his claim that "drawing the line" between persons and nonpersons on the basis of species is, in the current legal realm, irrational. After all, "no one can make a rational argument that you draw the line at that place. I don't know where you draw the line. But where it's drawn now is completely arbitrary, and it's not scientifically valid" (Wise qtd. in Kaufman, 2016, para. 9). Wise's legal strategy, however, seems to merely extend this vexingly important "line" to include a few prize species at the expense of the millions of other forms of life on the planet. And, following in his humanist predecessors' footsteps, his rationale for doing so is fundamentally anthropocentric.

Wise's legal counterpart in the animal rights arena, Francione, has named the discourse so central to the NhRP's legal cases the "similar minds approach" to animal rights. He has disparaged this strategy as speciesist nonsense: "To the extent that we link the moral status of animals with cognitive characteristics beyond sentience, we continue the humanocentric arrogance that *is* speciesism" (Francione, 2012c, para. 2). After all, "being 'smart' may matter for some purposes, such as whether we give someone a scholarship, but it is completely irrelevant to whether we use someone . . . as a nonconsenting subject in a biomedical experiment" (para. 5). The similar minds approach to animal rights may seem to be a daring legal strategy to procure rights for animals, but as Francione warns, it privileges a select few species over others only to the extent that those species are sufficiently similar to human beings. Yet again, the human is emphasized as the normative being to which rights are due, with animals forced to "prove their worth" to the extent to which they are biologically twin to *Homo sapiens*. And, as Francione rightly warned, a similar minds approach invokes "a game that animals can never win. They'll never be enough 'like us'" (para. 7). And, given Wise's lack of legal success thus far, Francione appears to be exactly correct.

The similar minds approach further diminishes the liberatory potential of animal rights to the extent that it devalues, even disparages, difference. To this point, I invoke the work of deconstructionist Jacques Derrida, who critiqued the category of "animal" as a whole in that it reductively includes "all the living things that man does not recognize as his fellows, his neighbors, or his brothers. And this is so in spite of the infinite space that separates the lizard from the dog, the protozoon from the dolphin" and so on and so forth, trapping them within a "strict enclosure" of animality that is merely "an appellation that men have instituted, a name they have given themselves the right and authority to give to another living creature" (Derrida, 2002, pp. 402, 392). Wise merely reifies the "us" / "not us" binary while adding a couple of token creatures to the elite list of beings grouped as "us." Thus, the crucial challenge to animal rights advocates ought to be "to avoid the trap of saying that other beings deserve moral consideration only to the extent that they are 'just like us'" (White, 2013, p. 86). Specifically, antispeciesists must condemned the tendency to claim that certain animals hold valuable affective and cognitive abilities "only if they demonstrate them in the *same way* that humans do" (p. 86, emphasis mine). Wise is a prime example of this nefarious tendency as evidenced by his explanations of apes' cognitive abilities in *Drawing the Line,* which primarily uses how well three primates performed on human intelligence tests to "prove" the moral worth of the animals.

Wise's rhetorical framework not only privileges human characteristics, but it conveniently erases the evolutionary processes explaining not why differences exist but why those differences are a *beneficial* thing for the animal bodies in question. Take, for example, the problem of language. As White (2013) explained, "If dolphins lack language, it may very well be because it is not a particularly helpful tool in the oceans, not because dolphins lacked the intellectual capacity" (p. 91). By talking of language almost exclusively in terms of conscious mouth manipulation or signed alphabets, Wise and his adherents forget that the problem of language is *not* that it must merely be "given back" to animals. Like "animality" and "humanity," language too is an arbitrary construct. Indeed, "if one reinscribes language in a network of possibilities that do not merely encompass it but mark it irreducibly from the inside, everything changes . . . does not allow us to 'cut' once and for all where we would in general like to cut" (Derrida, 1992, p. 117). An alternative approach to language could include nonvocal forms of communication such as a bee's dance to define the coordinates of a plant as a legitimately linguistic skillset. Similar communicative phenomena can occur across species lines to the extent that, when taken and studied as a "legitimate" form of discourse, they are dubbed "internatural communication" (Plec, 2013). Wise's dismissal of such a fact demonstrates a lack of "fluency in the philosophical (and especially, ethical) implications of the process of evolution and the mechanism of adaptation" (White, 2013, p. 91). "Intelligence," linguistic or otherwise, is relative when seen from an evolutionary standpoint and is best articulated not as a universal set of skills, but as a "species-specific trait" (p. 91). Thus, in a well-intentioned attempt to open the realm of personhood to animals, Wise and his NhRP *rejustifies* those same Cartesian categories and their operational definitions that were crafted to deny animals legal personhood in the first place. And, instead of doing away with speciesism altogether, similar minds rhetoric creates new speciesist hierarchies, grouping certain nonhumans into a preferred, "mostly human" group and leaving others to be exploited until and unless science "catches up" and willing lawyers pounce upon the case.

Philosophy aside, the long-term consequences of the similar minds approach on animal rights litigation could prove dire. Further embracing the slippery slope of Cartesian criteria for animal subjectivity, even if done in the name of strategic essentialism, risks reifying human superiority further. History, after all, "teaches that once a legal right is won, the specter of political retrenchment is always near . . . rights theory is not as bulletproof as [Wise] would like" (Verchick, 2001, pp. 226–227). By anthropocentric, humanist logic, once the chimpanzee no longer met the "necessary" criteria for autonomy, then it would logically be excluded once again from the moral and legal communities, leaving activists right back where they started. Tommy and Kiko are "autonomous" because they are self-aware and emotionally intelligent, yet they have not developed writing tools and cannot serve on jury duty. Wise claims they do not need to in order to be granted personhood, but if the facets of a proper Cartesian "subject" are truly so arbitrary, then those facets are easily alterable via rhetorical twists and turns. As Freeman (2010) cogently critiqued, "it is always humans (and certain groups more than others) who maintain the power to redefine mental traits in ways that could just continue to serve instrumental interests and maintain human privilege" (p. 17). Endless definitional arguments demanding that animal subjectivity ought to mean meeting Western Enlightenment-style standards forces all species to endlessly "exist under accusation," forced to prove "justification for every movement that emanates from one's body" (Lingis, 2003, p. 180). Wise's tactics backfire upon themselves through the establishment of even more legal precedents favoring human characteristics as the basis of legal obligations and, subsequently, legal personhood. Even if Tommy and Kiko *were* to be granted legal personhood on the grounds that they are similar to humans, it is likely that, in the long run, only Tommy, Kiko, and their lookalikes would benefit. Achieving rights for an animal *in*sufficiently similar to a human body, such as the alligator dismissed by Wise, would be even harder to try in court. Wise and the NhRP have essentially removed the grease from the slippery slope toward full animal rights under the law, rendering the slope benign.

In *Rattling the Cage,* Wise scoffs that "no one but a professor or a deep ecologist thinks that a language using animal is not a bigger deal than island-building coal" (Wise, 2000, p. 237). I argue that academics, ecologists, activists, and lawyers alike should care intensely about the moral processes of "ranking" forms of life. In primarily basing criteria for legal personhood on animals' humanlike cognitive qualities, Wise and his NhRP ultimately advocate an ideology at odds with the liberatory goals for which he purportedly fights. He ultimately premises personhood and deservedness of legal rights on scientific discoveries providing evidence of sameness, which limit the moral sphere to only a few specific species. The "dividing line" separating humans from nonhumans is just barely altered, thus furthering the Cartesian, humanistic paradigm that has allowed for speciesism to flourish over the years. Instead of insisting that animals must be "like us" to earn respect, "scholars and advocates should begin to ask how all species are unified and in what ways primary differences can be viewed as strengths" (Freeman, 2010, p. 16). Indeed, acknowledging differences between humans, bonobos, dogs, crickets, and trees "*does not have to equate with an admission of inferiority*" (p. 27, emphasis mine). At stake in Wise's court cases is not only the fate of individual animals like Tommy and Kiko but also the reification of "a pecking order of animal cognition" that can determine a being's moral worth and deservingness of humane treatment (Verchick, 2001, p. 215). Recommending a "standard based on scientific data and levels of animal consciousness" that will, hopefully, "evolve along with the rest of the common law" might help a few species in a few cases, but ultimately it places millions more at risk of drifting further from moral consideration (p. 214). If estimates are correct, and there are over 7.77 million members of kingdom *Animalia* existing in the world today, of which only 1 to 2 million have even been catalogued (California Academy of Sciences, 2011), then establishing personhood standards benefitting great apes, cetaceans, and elephants hardly seems like a "winning" outcome for animal life. A positive outcome for Tommy and Kiko might ultimately be a loss for animal rights.

Despite the many legal barriers standing in his way, Wise and his followers at the NhRP will continue to fight for the freedom of Tommy, Kiko, and (purportedly) all other animals. In this chapter, I articulated concerns that, should Wise succeed, he would set a concerning legal precedent that could ultimately harm an animal rights agenda more than help it. By insisting that legal personhood, and subsequently legal rights, should be granted to animals only when scientific evidence definitively shows that a being has "personal autonomy" (perhaps best defined as humanlike cognitive capacities), Wise perpetuates the speciesist notion that *human* traits are the most important traits by which to judge who is worthy of moral concern. As Freeman (2010) cogently claimed, such a strategy is ultimately deadly to liberatory praxis, for "in thinking long-term, if animal activists fail to convince humans to respect their animality instead of despite it, humans may never treat animals with appropriate respect" (p. 25). This chapter asserted that, good intentions aside, Wise's and the NhRP's continual privileging of the human at the expense of all that is "Other" ultimately contradicts the principles and potentials of animal liberation theory and praxis.

In summary, for all the good intentions of Wise and the NhRP, their call for what is by all accounts a humanistic "rationality test" dramatically restricts which nonhuman beings are owed legal personhood and legal rights. The "radicalness" of Wise's agenda is far from radical at all. Instead it relies on the same principles of rationality, universality, and human supremacy that have allowed for the oppression of animals for centuries. A mix of critical legal and ecofeminist thought demonstrates the detriments of Wise's agenda, not only by pinpointing its anthropocentrism but also by questioning how "good" the future would be for animals if he and the NhRP succeeded in setting such legal precedents. As Albright (2002) so wisely stated, genuinely liberatory thought ought not to impose a "particular cut-off point at which humans' moral obligations end, other than perhaps to comply with Jeremy Bentham's oft-quoted standard: 'The question is not, Can they reason? nor, can they talk? but, Can they suffer?" (p. 936). Wise and the NhRP are simply not "critical" *enough,* as he remains interested in scientific proof of humanlike qualities in animals.

This chapter does not argue that speaking of "rights" and "personhood" is a pointless endeavor. On the contrary, it celebrates animal law's ability to bring such concepts to the forefront of legal rhetorics of animal rights. That every being has "rights to be recognized and revered" is ultimately a useful starting point for promoting larger cultural understandings of bilateral legal relations between the human and nonhuman worlds. When "relations" are established as the "context for interaction" between humanity and those historically "Othered" by this concept, new duties will be placed upon human beings ultimately more beneficial to an animal rights agenda (Burdon, 2010). Times are changing, and despite the ever-worsening threats of climate change, mass extinctions, brutal agricultural practices, and rainforest depletion, there is still hope that global legal systems might reimagine and slowly replace current destructive, anthropocentric ideologies. However, the question for legal practitioners like Wise must not merely be, "What is the most efficient way to achieve animal rights in the courtroom?" We must broaden our scope of thought to ask "Which legal approach will promote a long-term ideological shift away from anthropocentrism and promote differential conceptions of humanity's duty to nonhuman life?" Viewed through the lens of ecofeminist legal theory, and working under a paradigm of total liberation, the NhRP ultimately ends up going in the wrong direction.

CHAPTER 3

For the Good of the Species

Species Essentialisms and Eugenics in Gary Francione's "Vegan Abolitionism"

Beings do not preexist their relatings. "Prehensions" have consequences. The world is a knot in motion. Biological and cultural determinism are both instances of misplaced concreteness—i.e., the mistake of, first, taking provisional and local category abstractions like "nature" and "culture" for the world and, second, mistaking potent consequences to be preexisting foundations.

—Donna Haraway, "The Companion Species Manifesto"

n 1993, environmental philosopher Paola Cavalieri and acclaimed animal rights theorist Peter Singer released an anthology entitled *The Great Ape Project: Equality beyond Humanity.* In line with the future legal work of Steven Wise and the NhRP, Cavalieri and Singer collected a series of essays from an amalgam of big-name environmental philosophers to argue, at least in the philosophical realm, in favor of the possibility of great ape personhood. Within the collection was a "Declaration on Great Apes," supported by all contributors, which vehemently insisted upon "person" status for chimpanzees, gorillas, and orangutans. Contributors included classical rights theorist Tom Regan, future Wise supporter Jane Goodall, and other "big" academic names such as Richard Dawkins and Jared Diamond. Among these contributors was a lesser-known name, lawyer

Gary Francione, whose essay "Personhood, Property, and Legal Competence" echoed arguments later seen in the NhRP, namely that in cases of legal person versus legal property, the legal person would always come out on top. Thus, any possibility of animal rights must, in the legal sphere, necessitate legal personhood be given to animal species. For Francione:

> The Declaration on Great Apes requires that we extend the community of equals to include all great apes: human beings, chimpanzees, gorillas and orangutans. Specifically, the Declaration requires the recognition of certain moral principles applicable to all great apes—the right to life, the protection of individual liberty, and the prohibition of torture. If these principles are going to have any meaning beyond being statements of aspiration, then they must be translated into legal rights that are accorded to the members of the community of equals and that can be enforced in courts of law. Indeed, the Declaration itself suggests that moral principles would be enforceable in courts of law. (Francione, 1993, p. 248)

Francione, a young lawyer seemingly eager to "get his feet wet" in the world of academic publishing, appeared to, at least tacitly, adhere to arguments similar to those of Singer, Cavalieri, and later Wise and the NhRP: to grant personhood to great apes, legally and extralegally, on the basis of their exceptional characteristics. One could hardly predict what Francione would write thirteen years later.

On December 20, 2006, Francione, now an accomplished legal scholar, author, and animal rights activist, released a blog post entitled "The Great Ape Project: Not so Great." In it, he reflected upon recent attempts by the New England Anti-Vivisection Society to raise money in support of the release and restitution of all chimpanzees from U.S. laboratories. NEAVS's campaign prompted Francione to reflect on the publication of *The Great Ape Project* so many years ago. So disgusted was Francione with the book, he panned the Declaration on Great Apes, particularly its argument that personhood was merited on the basis that primates "are the closest relatives of our species" and that they "have mental capacities and an emotional life sufficient to justify inclusion within the community of equals" (qtd. in Francione, 2006a, para. 3). The Francione of the twenty-first century had little to compliment about this assertion. Condemning past-Francione's contribution to the work, he explained:

I was a contributor to GAP and an original signatory to the Declaration on Great Apes. Nevertheless, in my 1993 essay in the GAP book, and at greater length in my subsequent writing, I have expressed the view that only sentience is necessary for personhood. But I now see that the entire GAP project was ill-conceived and I regret my participation. (Francione, 2006a, para. 6)

In many ways, his condemnation of *The Great Ape Project* mirrored the previous chapter's critique of Steven Wise and the NhRP. Francione, who used the term "sufficient similarity," the very basis of the previous chapter's critique, in relation to arguments about animal rights, had much to say about restricting personhood to primates alone:

Some animal advocates argue that a campaign that links moral significance with human characteristics is acceptable because the recognition of the personhood of great apes may well lead to recognizing the personhood of other nonhumans. But focusing on the humanlike cognitive characteristics of some nonhumans who are declared to be "special" is like having a human rights campaign that focuses on giving rights to the "smarter" humans first in the hope that we will extend rights to less intelligent ones later on, or treating those with only one black parent as better because they are more like whites. We would certainly reject that elitism where humans are concerned. We should similarly reject it where nonhumans are concerned. (Francione, 2006a, para. 15)

While, at the time of writing, it is difficult to find a text from Francione directly critiquing Steven Wise and the NhRP, his forceful condemnations of similar rhetoric suggest that he, like me, would have little to compliment about legal tactics for animal rights based solely off of cognitive sophistication.

An ecofeminist legal framework makes clear that rights-focused animal activists who understand those rights from the perspective of Enlightenment philosophy ironically use the same emotionless, objective, and rational discourses they simultaneously denounce for their prevalence in animal exploitation. Such discourses consistently manifest in the U.S. American legal sphere. Such was the case in the last chapter's analysis of Steven Wise and the NhRP. However, even among those activists who more or less embrace liberal ontologies, particular approaches to strategies and tactics in pursuit of animal liberation can be different in both kind and degree. For this reason, this chapter thus turns to the man that much of the animal rights movement considers the "most radical of the radical," the father of "vegan abolitionism," legal theorist Gary Francione.

Despite assertions inside and outside of academia that Francione has created the most "revolutionary" animal rights theories to date, this chapter asks: are his rhetorical tactics really that groundbreaking? The answer: not entirely. This chapter once again uses ideological rhetorical criticism to explore a Western rights-based theorist who *claims* to be fundamentally different from the "mainstream" rights theorists like Singer and from toothless groups like Steven Wise's NhRP, via the strategies and tactics of vegan abolitionism. However, unlike Francione and his followers, this chapter does *not* take vegan abolitionism as an animal rights anomaly. In line with Steven Wise and the NhRP, I reimagine Francione as a representative of a larger, vexing strain of animal activist discourse that assumes a patriarchal, colonial, Enlightenment-style application of rights—legal *or* inherent—and personhood is the *singular* panacea to ending animal exploitation and pursuing total liberation. In other words, while Francione goes further than Wise in pursuit of legal justice for animals, his discourse does not align with my vision of a critical vegan rhetoric.

In the following sections, this chapter accomplishes a series of tasks. First, it introduces Francione and his vegan abolitionist stance. Second, it takes note of varying discourses surrounding Francione's philosophy, strategies, and tactics. Third, this chapter homes in on two strands of anti-abolitionist discourse that merit further consideration in line with my principles of a critical vegan rhetoric, both of which reveal Francione's heavy reliance upon a binary construction of a tainted human culture versus a necessarily separate nature. I briefly attend to and extend a critique of Francione's essentialist construction of the *human* condition, particularly with regard to racial identity politics, vis-à-vis a rhetoric of "species essentialism." Then I offer a deconstruction of Francione's essentialist discourse regarding the *animal,* particularly his disdain for more-than-humans existing in the realm of the liminal—better termed the "domestic," the "companion," or the "pet." Ultimately, this chapter concludes that for all of Francione's valuable insights into personhood, sentience, and bottom-up tactics of ethical veganism, his vehement essentialisms ultimately align with a mode of legal and moral positivism that prohibit total liberation.

Gary Francione and the Abolitionist Approach

Francione is a relatively recent addition to the animal rights canon. Unlike other popular theorists such as Singer and Regan, who are philosophers by trade, he is a legal scholar. From 1990 to 2000, Francione ran the Rutgers Animal Rights Law Clinic, making Rutgers the first university in the United States to have animal rights law as part of the regular academic curriculum. He currently serves as a Board of Governors Distinguished Professor of Law and a Nicholas DeB. Katzenbach Scholar of Law and Philosophy. Francione's groundbreaking books include *Animals, Property, and the Law* (1995), *Rain without Thunder: The Ideology of the Animal Rights Movement* (1996), *Animals as Persons: Essays on the Abolition of Animal Exploitation* (2008), *Introduction to Animal Rights: Your Child or the Dog?* (2010b), and the coauthored works *The Animal Rights Debate: Abolition or Regulation?* (Francione & Garner, 2010) and *Eat Like You Care: An Examination of the Morality of Eating Animals* (Francione & Charlton, 2015). Francione also publishes in academic journals (Francione, 1997, 2006c, 2007a, 2010a, among multiple others) and maintains a frequently updated Facebook and Twitter presence. His most obvious public presence is via his personal website, titled "Animal Rights: The Abolitionist Approach," on which he keeps an active blog to address contemporary animal rights–related news stories and to argue against his dissenters.

Francione grounds all of his works on a fundamental legal assumption: animals, by virtue of their legal status as chattel property, are inherently doomed to ill-treatment at the hands of humans. Thus, without attaining legal personhood, in situations in which human pleasure conflicts with animal welfare, the former will always win (Francione, 1995). By using this principle as a basis for his writing, Francione argues against the "humane treatment principle," which purports to establish humane treatment as a legal standard but in practice does the opposite by virtue of favoring humans' interests over animals' by default (Francione, 2010b). Thus, he is adamantly opposed to the mere regulation of animal welfare or the advancement of more humane animal welfare policies. Such policies merely constitute "happy slavery" (Francione, 2012a).

For Francione, that so many big-name philosophers and organizations have come to support welfare-based policies that merely lessen animal suffering while continuing animal exploitation spits in the face of a true animal rights philosophy. These people and groups are not animal rights advocates but rather New Welfarists (Francione, 1996). New Welfarism encompasses the now traditional approach to animal ethics as promoted by large animal advocacy worldwide. It holds that the abolition of animal use is the long-term goal of animal advocacy but that welfarist regulation of the treatment of animals is the most efficient short-term way of moving (incrementally) toward that goal (Francione & Charlton, 2010). Francione, then, is no welfarist; he is an abolitionist.

Francione argues that such a dearth of abolitionist content in scholarly work is understandable. How could scholars, so often obsessed with performing toothless philosophical thought experiments about animal rights, be any more reliable than the "big names" in animal activism ignoring abolitionist content? Per Francione:

> The abolitionist movement, currently developing as an international phenomenon, is one that has emerged largely as a grassroots endeavor of advocates who have little or no connection to any of the large animal organizations. Abolitionists are often part of Internet communities that provide social support and discussion of theoretical and practical issues. (Francione & Charlton, 2010, p. 1)

Abolitionism, then, represents an uninstitutionalized, uncorporatized approach to animal rights. Among animal rights theories and tactics, it is the most radical of the radical—so radical that the mainstream pretends it does not exist. Abolitionism is a pure and untainted vision of animal rights that fight for animals alone. Of course, as the following analysis shows, this purity is not always so pure.

Francione lays out his general philosophy and corresponding tactics, or the abolitionist approach, in six parts. First, this approach rejects all animal use—for food, fur, entertainment, sport, or any other means. This rejection is grounded in the rights-based doctrine that all "people" regardless of their particularities, maintain a fundamental, prelegal moral right not to be treated exclusively as the resources of others (Francione, 2013). Second, given his rejection of animal use, Francione's abolitionist approach demands that activists should not support campaigns supporting the mere reform of animal exploitation. Reformist campaigns are not only inadequate but harmful, as "welfare reform makes the public feel more comfortable about using animal products, and perpetuates rather than discourages animal exploitation" (Francione & Charlton, 2010, p. 3). For example, abolitionists would not support a U.S. Department of Agriculture policy to increase the size of battery cages for hens. Rather, they would only accept the complete erasure of battery cages. Third, Francione's approach regards veganism as the "moral baseline" for activists, arguing "we cannot draw a morally coherent distinction between flesh and other animal products, such as dairy or eggs, or between animal foods and the use of animals for clothing or other products" (Francione, 2013, para. 14). Advocates who claim to love animals but still wear, use, or consume them are hypocritical, as they are no different from those who claimed to be in favor of human rights but continued to own slaves (Francione & Charlton, 2010, p. 3). Fourth, Francione explicitly links the moral status of nonhumans with sentience alone. All animals qualify as sentient beings, and these beings, "by virtue of their sentience, have an interest in remaining alive. . . . Therefore, to say that a sentient being is not harmed by death denies that the being has the very interest that sentience serves to perpetuate" (Francione & Charlton, 2010, p. 2). This emphasis on sentience is in direct opposition to other big-name activists like Singer, who values interests, and Regan, who considers inherent value in deciding which animals are worthy of moral consideration. Fifth, Francione's approach explicitly rejects violence and ecoterrorism as appropriate activist tactics. And finally, the abolitionist approach equates speciesism with other isms: "Like racism, sexism, heterosexism, and classism, it uses a morally irrelevant criterion (species) to discount and devalue the interests of sentient beings" (Francione, 2013, para. 20). Thus, antispeciesists must subsequently reject all other forms of discrimination and vice versa. (This final principle, while intersectional at first glance, will be deconstructed and diminished as this chapter progresses.)

Although Francione rejects nearly all current forms of traditional, welfare-oriented animal activism, he very frequently expresses disdain for two parties: PETA and Singer. He once scoffed as PETA's founder, Ingrid Newkirk, for saying that an all-or-nothing approach to animal rights was unrealistic (Francione, 1996). Francione runs in direct opposition to PETA's support of incremental changes to animal welfare policies, which, though not ideal, are thought to be a step in the right direction for animal rights. In other words, "although PETA espouses an abolitionist end, it maintains that at least some welfarist means are both causally efficacious and morally acceptable" (Francione, 1996, p. 35). Examples of these flawed tactics include collaborating with humane slaughter advocates and PETA's online claim that personal purity ought not to be a huge factor in an effective vegan lifestyle. Furthermore, mainstream organizations like PETA frequently run single-issue campaigns that highlight one form of animal exploitation while ignoring others. Francione explicitly rejects these types of campaigns. For instance, opposing the killing of dogs for meat in Asian countries while not opposing the slaughter of domestic chickens highlights the savagery of the Asian "other" while actively ignoring the critical self-reflection required to eschew all forms of animal exploitation, not merely those that are foreign (Francione & Charlton, 2010). PETA, in Francione's mind, ought not to be conceived of as a radical organization at all.

Francione's primary problem with Singer and his adherents is that, despite *Animal Liberation*'s reputation as the animal rights "bible" (Maltby & Mountford, 2012), Singer does not argue for animal liberation via a coherent rhetoric of rights. Rather, because Singer's utilitarianism calls for moral decisions to be made via an equal consideration of interests, Francione accuses him of consistently giving animal lives lesser moral value than human lives. For instance, Singer admitted that in certain instances, animal experimentation might be justifiable and identified instances in which not living as a vegan might be morally justifiable (Francione, 1996). To Francione, Singer's tactics encapsulate welfarist thinking by reflecting the troubling notion that human exploitation of animals is not necessarily a moral problem because, according to act-utilitarianism principles, animals do not have an interest in their lives. Francione denounces such a position (a position twin to Steven Wise's) as speciesist: "The cognition of nonhumans is most likely very different from human cognition. . . . But that certainly does not mean that nonhumans do not have equivalent cognitive phenomena" (Francione, 2009, para. 8). Furthermore, Singer's tactics are impractical for securing ethical short-term advances in animal welfare. An act-utilitarian would happily endorse reformist measures like larger battery cages or humane slaughter because, within an ideology that does not rely on innate rights, such policies would be acceptable. Singer "clearly, explicitly, and repeatedly rejects the concept of animal rights despite his claim . . . that he sought 'to create an animal-rights movement'" (Francione, 2009, para. 11). Therefore, to name Singer as the father of the contemporary animal rights movement is flawed at best, wicked at worst.

Ultimately, Francione's main argument against mainstream animal rights theorists and groups is their willingness to support and even partner with institutions that favor the humane exploitation of animals. For Francione, "animals, like humans, have an interest in not suffering at all from use as resources, however 'humane' that use may be. A more 'humane' form of human slavery is not less morally objectionable than a less 'humane' form" (Francione, 2010b, p. 146). Because good persons agree that any form of human exploitation is fundamentally wrong, to claim that animals can be satisfied with a happier form of slavery is speciesist. If animal rights practitioners really think that the exploitation of nonhumans is analogous to the exploitation of humans, "then we should not regard it as any more acceptable to give an award to someone who exploits nonhumans 'humanely' than we would to give an award to a 'humane' rapist, pedophile, or murderer" (Francione, 2006b, para. 32). Thus, any fundamental right afforded to humans to prevent them from being treated as chattel must likewise be afforded to animals.

On the surface, Francione appears to advocate for a particularly radical conception of animal rights. However, a close reading of his texts makes clear that Francione is not as distant from New Welfarists as he would like to think. When dealing with human difference, he invokes a disturbingly species-essentialist rhetoric. In arguing about domestication, his discourse lies the nexus of ableism and speciesism vis-à-vis a eugenical rhetoric supporting a firm, hierarchical nature/ culture divide. These arguments are neither radical nor in line with a principle of total liberation.

Conflicting Perceptions of Francione and Vegan Abolitionism

Again, to conduct a proper ideological rhetorical criticism, it is necessary to go beyond what Francione "says" or "does" and move to investigate how others interpret his sayings and doings. Scholars outside of communication have long grappled with Francione's radical rhetoric. Animal rights–inclined scholars sometimes take Francione's words as law, citing vegan abolitionism as an ideal means of helping animals if used appropriately. Bob Torres, for instance, admired Francione's writing as influential for his social anarchist theories, claiming that "animals are fortunate to have such an intelligent and eloquent defender on their side" (Torres, 2007, p. iv). He commented:

> As a direct protest against the commodity form and property relations that animals are subject to, it is a great refusal of the system itself, a no-compromise position that does not seek reform, but which seeks abolition. For anyone who wants to end animal exploitation, living as a vegan is living the end that we wish to see—no one will exploit animals for mere choices of taste and convenience. (Torres, 2007, p. 131)

Corey Wrenn has cited vegan abolitionism as a site for bottom-up, consumer-based social change—a necessary additive to top-down, courtroom-based approaches such as the Wise and the NhRP:

Vegan abolitionism is the most appropriate approach as it seriously considers our moral obligation to non-human animals and adopts an incremental, vegan consumption–based action towards ending non-human animal use altogether. . . . Here the consumer-citizen is engaged in merging economic action with political action in hopes of creating social change with certain choices in consumption. (Wrenn, 2011, pp. 11, 17)

Animal activists outside of academia also have positive things to say about Francione. His many, many followers within the vegan community, dubbed "Franciobots" by some critics, stand by him and insist on the validity of the abolitionist approach (Leenaert, 2015). Outside of academia, Francione is an online phenomenon. Discussions of and hyperlinks to his work frequently emerge in vegan forums, vegan blogs, and vegan social media. He has been invited to give talks and have debates on radio shows, and multiple vegan outlets, such as Vegan Voice, Vegan Freak, and Vegan Sanctuary, have interviewed him for online publications and podcasts. And, on occasion, non-vegan talk podcasts, talk shows, and magazines, such as the social justice–oriented outlets *The Believer* and *UTNE* and the philosophy podcast *Philosophy Bites,* have interviewed him as well (Edmonds & Warburton, 2012; Unferth, 2011). Some organizations, such as The Advocacy for Veganism Society (formerly called the Abolitionist Vegan Society), were premised on Francione's philosophies. According to the group's mission statement: "The mission of TAVS is to galvanize and facilitate an organized grassroots movement of abolitionist veganism around the world that reflects our recognition of the moral personhood of nonhuman animals. Creative nonviolent vegan education is the foundation of our movement" (Mission, n.d.). To date, Francione has nearly 80,000 Facebook followers and more than 10,000 Twitter followers.

Nonetheless, Francione's radicalism consistently has its critics. Criticisms of Francione generally focus most often either on the radicalism of his ideas or the divisiveness of his strategies and tactics. Among the most common critiques of abolitionism is its all-or-nothing approach to animal rights. Sztybel (2007), for instance, excoriated Francione as an animal rights fundamentalist lacking pragmatic solutions to real-time animal issues; Garner (2006) further critiqued that Francione has fallaciously conflated poor-quality animal welfare laws with the property status of animals, arguing that laws that are made for the benefit of humans can benefit animals as well, and that the main goal of animal liberation ought to be to reduce animal suffering in the here and now; and Twine (2010) worried that Francione's ignorance of regulatory developments in science and agriculture risked making animal activists ignorant of the scientific developments that make futuristic modes of exploitation possible.

Another critique of Francione's dissenters stems from his unapologetic villainization of other activists and academics as complicit in animal exploitation, as described in the previous section. Tobias Leenaert, author of *How to Create a Vegan World* and of the well-known animal rights blog *Vegan Strategist,* explained in a 2015 posting how, while he used to be a Francione fan, "Virtually no organisation, in his eyes, seems to deliver a net benefit for the animals. One could wonder: where is the appeal in this kind of message?" (Leenaert, 2015, para. 1). Indeed, Francione and his Franciobots "are raging against all kinds of groups, uncritically taking Francione's words for true, believing that PETA, FARM, Mercy For Animals, the Vegan Society in the UK . . . have all sold out" (para. 4). Tired of Francione's "divisive" rhetoric, Leenaert concluded his incisive critique of vegan abolitionist discourse with a series of questions:

> Is it credible that those who put their lives in the service of the animals, some of whom started decades ago, and who have not eaten animal products for ages, and who have had a huge impact in creating awareness about veganism and animal rights . . . is it credible that those people have actually sold out? Is it credible that all of a sudden they have all become reformists or welfarists? Is it credible that they're actually not thinking about strategy? Is it credible that they're all less intelligent than you and Gary Francione? (Leenaert, 2015, para. 5)

In summary, Francione's abolitionist discourse is at once famous, infamous, renowned, reviled, incisive, and divisive. He has fans and detractors in arenas ranging from academia to Facebook. This chapter ultimately agrees with vegan abolitionist adherents that, compared with people like Steven Wise, vegan abolitionism offers a much more fruitful approach to creating an antispeciesist cultural shift that, through bottom-up layperson activism employing veganism as a moral baseline, would influence top-down legal decisions in favor of animal liberation. Furthermore, Francione's commitment to sentience, not practical autonomy or sufficient similarity, as the basis of legal personhood offers a much broader array of perspective clientele should legal rights and personhood for animals be pursued through the courts. Francione's tactics, in other words, offer a far more morally consistent and pragmatically possible version of animal liberation.

However, the rest of this chapter is dedicated to two necessary critiques of Francione that, when investigated seriously, reveal the most pernicious flaws of vegan abolitionism from a strategic perspective. If strategies represent "what we want," then in point of fact, what Francione "wants" is dangerously at odds with his purported commitment to the dissolution of the human/animal binary that has for so long allowed for animal exploitation. For someone who is seemingly opposed to the moral separation of humans and animals, Francione's articulated strategies actually appear to embrace such binaries through essentialist genres of discourse. First, he simplifies the category of the *human* through a species-essentialist rhetoric of normative Whiteness. And second, he essentializes the *animal* by advocating for the extinction of any animal body tainted by extended human contact—specifically, domesticated species. And, in doing so, he makes visible the intersections of ableist thoughts and speciesist praxis.

Francione's Species-Essentialist Approach to the Human Condition

Among the most important critiques of Francione and the abolitionist approach to animal rights have come from vegans of color and feminist vegans. Namely, this critique states that vegan abolitionism, despite its sixth principle stating Francione's disgust with racism, classism, and other such isms, does not work hard enough to negate animal activists' complicity in Whiteness-bound, neoliberal frameworks of consumption. Francione ultimately relies upon conceptualizations of the human condition that flatten inequality and render oppressive systems into the realm of individual choice. This denial of difference, this lumping together of humanity into a species of seemingly equal opportunity (if only the disenfranchised might try a little bit harder to embrace veganism), represents a strain of postracial rhetoric that extends to *Homo sapiens* writ large. Francione's advocacy is, in other words, reliant upon a rhetoric of what Corey Wrenn has called "species-blindness" (Wrenn, 2017). To avoid the potentially ableist connotations of the previous term, I will refer to this concept as "species essentialism," a phrase most typically used by philosophers of science to denote the arbitrariness and (often pure wrongheadedness) involved in naming members of a taxonomic species as coherent, unified wholes lacking meaningful individual/group differences within that same *taxon* (see Ereshefky, 1998). Here I use the term to describe differences in humans' lived realities and material conditions that require serious interrogation in the pursuit of multispecies justice. In this section, I explain the many accusations of normative Whiteness that have been and, if Francione's defensive retorts remain the same, will continue to be lobbed against him and vegan abolitionism. Using my ecofeminist legal framework as a guide, I further extend these accusations to explicate how species-essentialist veganism does not mesh with a politic of total liberation.

Scholar-activists like Amie Breeze Harper, author of the much-acclaimed book *Sistah Vegan: Black Female Vegans Speak on Food, Identity Health, and Society,* fear that Francione's insistence on a postracial legal theory is yet another example of "the taken for granted lineage of 'Eurocentric cisgender men's canon of morality' that philosophy in the USA (Academe, at least) is rooted in as 'common sense'" (Harper, 2015b, para. 18). In other words, Francione's simultaneous reliance on legal positivism and grassroots consumerism *sounds* like flawless approaches to animal liberation but is, in actuality, a convenient way to essentialize the human condition in a manner that forgets how material inequalities and intercultural conflicts necessarily influence individual choices. Or, to put it in terms of intersectionality, rhetors like Francione engage in a sort of faux-intersectional veganism wherein a total liberation ethic is defined as "merely wanting justice for all" (Martendill, 2015, para. 20). Rhetoric emerging from Francione's purportedly intersectional fifth principle, then, uses a Whiteness-centered framework as "a method for rank ordering the form of oppression that most needs to be addressed" where animal rights is the most important and all other oppressions are legitimate, but subordinate (para. 5). Such a stance can be defined as an "Oppression Olympics" paradigm (Dhamoon, 2015), wherein material and experiential differences of degree and kind are not engaged with in any serious, coalition-building manner, but rather put into competition with one another to see which group has suffered the most, and thus must be given the most attention at any given moment. Thus, in line with women-of-color feminist critiques that the "mainstreaming" of intersectionality risks reaffirming and recentering Whiteness at the expense of the concept's antiracist roots, "the whiteness of the abolitionist vegan movement isn't an illusion . . . the whiteness of the movement happens *because* vegans are known for their appropriation [of intersectionality]" (Martendill, 2015). Such appropriation, for instance, can be seen in the name "vegan abolitionism," which recalls the antislavery movement of the twentieth century.

Again, to suggest that vegan abolitionism is somehow wrong to point out the tens of billions of animal bodies exploited, abused, and slaughtered each year is not at all this chapter's intent. Rather, the point here is to explain how particular rhetorical *tactics* of doing so not only exclude diverse subjectivities from the vegan moral universe, thus prohibiting coalition-building among social justice–oriented groups, but also perpetuate the unfortunate and inaccurate notion that animal rights is, at its core, an animal *Whites* movement (Wise, 2005). There is, of course, plenty to be critiqued about the seeming connection between veganism and "privilege." Many of these critiques have been launched against animal liberation activists by speciesist rhetorics to somehow "prove" animal rights are, in fact, human wrongs. For instance, as some anonymous online personas have argued through the creation and spreading of creative memes, if "there is no ethical consumption under capitalism," then attempts by animal liberationists to eschew cruelty by boycotting animal products is both pointless and hypocritical. After all, vegans must not care very much about the plight of, say, produce workers placed in unethical, inhumane working conditions.

I *fundamentally disagree* with the premise that a critique of privilege in animal liberation discourse, particularly in the form of normative Whiteness, necessitates the complete abandonment of ethical veganism or animal liberation writ large. Rather, my approach to ecofeminist theories of law and critical rhetorical analysis investigates and critique animal liberation discourse not to *divide* the U.S. American animal rights movement, but to make it *stronger* and *more inclusive*. In critical rhetorical terms, while animal rights rhetors make clear the necessity of antispeciesism through much-needed "critiques of domination," it is equally important to evaluate those moments when those critiques, and the prescriptive formulas for justice embedded within those critiques, reify oppressive practices rather than dismantle them. This second mode of critique is not an attempt at fomenting dissent and divisions among the vegan rank and file, but rather a "critique of freedom" (McKerrow, 1989).

The necessity of critiquing Francione's rhetoric of freedom is best exemplified in his recent online "bloggers' battle" with Harper and vegan activist Ruby Hamad, who both critiqued Francione's fundamentalist approach to animal rights as postracial and patriarchal. Hamad initially penned an editorial for the *Sydney Morning Herald* entitled "When Is Being Vegan No Longer about Ethical Living?" The piece was initially directed at a "celebrity" vegan activist's misogynistic response to a victim of domestic violence, which she lambasted as one of many examples of "ill-informed and outright dangerous attitudes prevalent amongst vegans" (Hamad, 2015, para. 4). Hamad continued:

Mainstream veganism is not always a safe space for people of colour, feminist women, the disabled, and those who don't fit the conventional model of attractiveness. . . . I found myself endlessly frustrated with a movement that readily appropriates the struggles of other groups by comparing factory farms to slavery, but ignores the voices of people of colour when they object to white vegans. (Hamad, 2015, paras. 12–13, 15)

However, what most likely drew the ire of Francione was Hamad's annoyance at his many quotes on feminism, including but not limited to: "If you consider yourself a feminist and you are not a vegan, you need to think more clearly" (Francione, n.d.). For all Francione's good points about the relationship between feminism, the unnecessary attempts to control women's bodies, and the exploitation of female animals' reproductive systems, his many publicized thoughts on the subject were, for Hamad, representative of how a "movement that is comprised mostly of women nonetheless elevates white men to most leadership positions," positions wherein men such as Francione deemed it appropriate to "lecture women on whether or not they can call themselves feminists" (Hamad, 2015, para. 16).

Francione, never one to take public criticism lying down, posted an unusually lengthy and unsurprisingly unapologetic response to Hamad's critiques in a blog post called "Sexism and Racism in the Animal Rights Movement: A Reply to Ruby Hamad." He initially responded in agreement: "The modern animal movement as a general matter has failed to see the inextricable connection between human rights and animal rights. It has failed to see that the 'otherization' of nonhumans is no different from the 'otherization' of humans" (Francione, 2015, para. 6). However, his tone quickly took a turn toward the negative upon evaluating Hamad's critique of his work. He accused Hamad of a reverse-racist double-standard: "I suspect that you may actually want to promote a position that allows for animal exploitation and then claim that the problem with those who disagree is that they are white males or women who are automatons" (Francione, 2015, para. 42). He then went on an unusually lengthy tirade:

Abolitionist vegan advocates are not only engaging in creative, nonviolent vegan education all over the world, but they are promoting veganism as part of a broad vision of human rights that rejects *all* discrimination and calls it out *whenever* it is seen in various animal campaigns. But these people—these women—apparently don't count in your view. And why is that? Do you think they are merely automatons who can't think critically? If that is what you are saying, your position is completely dismissive and disrespectful of all of those women, including women of color, who embrace the idea that veganism is a moral baseline and a moral imperative, and who agree with the other aspects of my work, including the human rights–animal rights connection that is far more encompassing and inclusive than are many other supposedly progressive approaches. The Abolitionist Approach focuses on *all* discrimination. (Francione, 2015, paras. 36–39, 41)

Particularly annoyed with Hamad's insistence that women, particularly women of color, ought to get more attention from the vegan mainstream, Francione turned his attention to the highly publicized scholarly and vernacular writings of Harper, and quickly dismissed them:

Harper characterizes promoting veganism as a moral imperative as a matter of "preaching veganism or vegan fundamentalism." That is *exactly* the way in which corporate welfarists characterize promoting veganism as a moral baseline. Putting aside that veganism is more than just a diet, this is nothing more than the "veganism is a sort of an okay default but it is subject to convenience, individual idiosyncrasy, etc." position. But let's be clear: it explicitly rejects veganism as a moral baseline and makes veganism a matter of the particular situation—the "who you are space." Is veganism a matter of the "who you are space"? It is most certainly not, any more than observing the fundamental rights of humans is a matter of the "who you are space." (Francione, 2015, paras. 50–52)

Surprised by her sudden involvement in a debate she never started, Harper responded on her own Facebook page and on her well-publicized blog, "The Sistah Vegan Project," that Francione would do best to look at her academic profile as a Black Marxist scholar with a PhD in critical food geographies rather than as an uninformed woman of color deigning to question veganism as an ethic as opposed to a diet:

You know you are getting "popular" when Gary Francione responds to an article (not written by me) about the problem of lack of intersectionality by white vegan men by taking something you said out of a lecture and using it to prove the author (Ruby Hamad) has a "weak" analysis. . . . I think it would be best to draw from my book work rather than a short talk I gave. (Harper, 2015a, para. 1)

Francione, undeterred, nonetheless continued his disdain for critiques of vegan Whiteness in a new post entitled "Essentialism, Intersectionality, and Veganism as a Moral Baseline: Black Vegans Rock and the Humane Society of the United States." In an attack on one of the largest vegan organizations run by persons of color, Francione complained how Black Vegans Rock, composed of "so-called 'intersectional vegans,'" ultimately "embrace speciesism in that, like the welfarists/new welfarists, they reject veganism as a moral baseline" (Francione, 2016, para. 27). Indeed, any vegan ethic based off of moral contextualism, even based on racial inequality, should not be considered liberatory:

> Instead of being unequivocal in support of the rights of all, they equivocate and negotiate on the rights and well-being of everybody, replacing a firm commitment to social justice with "journeys" and "spaces," in which violence and oppression are excused rather than excoriated. And instead of eliminating the essentialism of discrimination, they substitute a new essentialism that says that the rightness or wrongness of a position is dependent on *who* the speaker is and not *what* the speaker says. (Francione, 2016, paras. 28–29)

In what was, at the time of writing, by far the single longest post on Francione's twelve-year-old blog, he inexplicably felt it apropos to offer the proper definitions of "essentialism" and "intersectionality" to his feminist and critical race critics. He then continued in what ultimately became a tirade against accusations of normative Whiteness in his abolitionist movement:

> So we won't look at *what* I am saying. We won't discuss my position that someone who is a feminist but is not a vegan is arbitrarily ignoring the commodification of female nonhumans. We won't discuss whether intersectionality analysis militates in favor recognizing the particular ways in which misogyny as a general matter informs the use of female animals. We can just dismiss my position because I am a white male. (para. 86)

Francione is not alone in his insistence that vegan abolitionism could not possibly be essentialist (or even strategically essentialist) of the human condition. In a recent publication in the *Journal of Agricultural and Environmental Ethics*, animal ethics philosopher Bob Fischer took direct issue with Harper (and even the author of this book) by claiming that Francione might, in some way, perpetuate discourses of normative Whiteness in animal liberation discourse. In a critique of such irrational and illogical rhetoric put forth by vegan (or, by Fischer's assessment, antivegan) critics such as myself, he decried identity politics in animal ethics:

> Although moral obligations place different burdens on different groups, this isn't a reason to think that those obligations aren't real. . . . After all, abolitionism is the extreme case: Francione is the least flexible when it comes to accommodating burdens on human beings. So, if the objections fail here, they are likely to fail across the board. I grant, then, that abolitionism has problems. However, it doesn't seem to me that racism is one of them. Nor, I submit, is racism likely to be a problem for other defenses of veganism. (Fischer, 2018, p. 10)

The issue at stake in this apparent rhetorical cage match ultimately becomes a matter of who is allowed to speak about veganism and identity, when, and about what. This conclusion is evident in Francione's ultimate discursive turnabout, wherein he renames intersectional vegans into "essentialist vegans" (Francione, 2016). To do so, he continually defines essentialism for the academically uniniti-ated (presumably, his critics) as well as defining—even "teaching"?—the origins, meaning, and *proper* application of Kimberlé Crenshaw's (a woman-of-color feminist) concept of intersectionality. An ecofeminist legal theorist can easily see the irony in Francione's discursive tactic: instead of engaging in an act of critical listening, he decides to embark on a journey to teach women-of-color feminists about the most famous names and concepts in their field. Such a tactic not only recenters himself as the only legitimate authority on vegan ethics but also exemplifies the pattern of liberal humanist–oriented animal rights rhetors of dismissing context, relationships, and diverse subject positions if those factors risk coming into conflict with unflinching moral universalist rules regarding animal liberation. And, while I do not deny that the desire for universalisms is *understandable* given the depth and breadth of animal exploitation, engaging in such dismissive tactics does little to dissuade worries of social justice activists regarding the animal rights movement's feigned concern for human inequality *only* insofar as such concerns might be utilized, in a "missionary" sense, to "convert" the disenfranchised groups to veganism and stop at that. This missionary style is neither intersectional nor colonial—on the contrary, it is patriarchal and steeped in rhetorics of consumption dependent on keeping possessive investments in Whiteness invisible.

Ultimately, and perhaps most importantly, by arguing against "essentialist vegans," Francione engages in dramatic essentialisms himself. Francione's insists that people like Hamad, Harper, and groups like Black Vegans Rock essentialize individuals into coherent wholes, systematically excluding apparently "many" women, people of color, and sexual minorities on board with vegan abolitionism while falsely accusing them of being mere tokens or race traitors. Although Francione is absolutely correct that "cultural groups" do not exist as coherent wholes with impenetrable "cultural borders" (Chang, 1999), he ironically argues *against* individual humans being usurped into an essentialist cultural category (such as race) by arguing *for* the premier importance of animal liberation against an essentialist *species* category (*Homo sapiens*). For all Francione's insistence that human inequality is an inherently bad thing, he and his adherents seem little concerned with how racialized consciousness might be related to consumption habits integral to vegan abolitionist principles. As Harper (2016) explained:

> We are all racialized subjects with racialized consciousnesses that have been born out of a white supremacist racial caste system; the way we are socially and geographically located in that system affects how we *frame, perceive, experience,* everything. This includes ethical consumption. This isn't about me saying individuals are *bad vs. good. (para. 5)*

Francione's self-labeled moral purity ends up as a "spiritual bypass" that masks "new forms of White supremacist racist 'logic' that is then labeled as 'post-human' or 'beyond the human' condition"—meaning, in other words, that "humans need to only focus on the suffering of non-human animals and not human 'identity politics'" (Harper, 2017, para. 1).

Identity politics, however, frequently manifest in the animal rights movement during the many moments in which campaigns and texts "punch down" marginalized *Homo sapiens* groups in order to "lift up" marginalized more-than-human beings. Antiblackness has been central to many of these unfortunate moments. Some instances occupy the realm of "micro-aggressions," and some are macrolevel, unapologetic racism. Black Vegans Rock's founder Aph Ko, for instance, critiqued the visual rhetoric of PETA and its choice to make "campaigns about going vegan to 'get skinny' or 'be sexy,'" and therefore to put forth a sexist, sizeist norm that "has absolutely nothing to do with the racialized history of meat consumption in the US. . . . Furthermore, it perpetuates a very *white standard of beauty and body acceptability* that has a horrendous history of *maligning the bodies of black women* (Ko, 2015, paras. 25–26, emphasis mine). Another example includes the best-selling vegan cookbook *Thug Kitchen,* in which white authors Matt Holloway and Michelle Davis provide admittedly delicious plant-based recipes to get readers to "eat like you give a fuck." Their use of "gangsta" language throughout the text is used for comedic effect. However, it has attracted mass criticism and even boycotts from communities of color. The word "thug" carries rhetorical weight and racial connotations. It "can illicit such pain and suffering amongst a significant number of Black Americans who fear that their husbands, brothers, fathers, and sons will be perceived as 'thugs' by the White American imagination ensconced in centuries of *negrophobia*" (Harper, 2014, para. 4). As Harper explained:

> *Thug Kitchen* and vegans of color protest is a microcosm that reflects the current racial climate in the USA. The book's support and "post-racial" comments by a significant number of mostly white people says a lot: it says *"I don't have the trauma of racialized and state violence against my body that Black people do and other racial minorities do*)." (Harper, 2014, para. 5)

Thug Kitchen is one small example of what Ko has identified as a general trend of the animal rights movement appropriating the experiences of Black oppression to gain sympathy for animals. According to Ko, mainstream animal rights groups focus only on "the animals" but "without context" (Ko, 2015, para. 24). Examples of this trend include visual rhetorical displays used by organizations such as PETA in which images of farmed animals are juxtaposed to images of enslaved Black bodies. While the affective response of such sights can be severe, critical analysis of those images shows that the creators appeal to *white* sensibilities, calling upon a perceived collective guilt that says "we realized slavery was wrong, so this is wrong too!" This rhetorical trope conveniently ignores the agonizing effect on those not only impacted by their enslaved ancestors' plights but also struggling under a racial caste system. Or, as Ko summarized: "constantly comparing animal oppression to slavery or lynching seems to suggest that the only way racism figures into the conversation is by its usefulness in producing analogies for the benefit of animals alone" (Ko, 2015, para. 51). This unidirectional activism merely reifies the notion that "the white animal rights movement hasn't explicitly expressed a desire to take anti-racist work seriously" since "it seems as though they are using our struggles for their own gain" (paras. 52–53). Ultimately, "if you're going to make a campaign to try to get black folks to become vegan or animal rights activists, you have to speak to our unique history—not attack it" (para. 23).

However, attempts to speak to this "unique history" are often not enough for vegan abolitionists *too* committed to Francione's conception of a "moral baseline." What I mean here is the erroneous assumption that a vegan ethic must start and end with the more-than human world: animals come first, humans come afterward. Getting "into" veganism for the sake of one's own health is not abolitionist. While there is some merit to this assumption (after all, veganism is *not* a diet, it is an ethic, and discourses of diet and health are raced/classed/gendered in damaging and biologically distorted ways), Harper's construction of the Sistah Vegan Project in 2005 suggests that health, veganism, and liberation are not mutually exclusive phenomena. After all, "one's racialized experience influences how one writes, teaches, and engages in vegan praxis" (Harper, 2012, p. 156). Therefore, Harper's project explores the Black American female vegan experience, paying close attention to how race, legacies of colonialism, sexism, and classism manifest in U.S. American veganism. It also was the subject of Harper's first book, *Sistah Vegan,* which incorporated her and other Black women's unique narratives of their journeys toward and rationales for maintaining a vegan lifestyle. Per Harper:

> I have found that Sistah Vegans collectively know that understanding optimal health (for themselves and the planet) and liberation must be achieved through a) decolonization of the diet b) careful scrutiny of mainstream Westernized-industrialized based food and health industry and/or c) embracing the food, nutrition and healing systems that have a more Afrikan and Afro-centric basis to them. ("Sistah Vegan Anthology," 2012, para. 3)

In other words, rather than assuming that once animals are free from speciesism, freedom from racism will necessarily follow, "recognizing racism as *foundational* in today's capitalist food system helps explain why people of color suffer disproportionately from its environmental externalities, labor abuses, resource inequities and diet related diseases" (Holt-Gimenez & Harper, 2016, p. 4, emphasis mine).

Therefore, while Francione may accuse feminist vegans and vegans of color of engaging in "essentialist veganism," it is perhaps more appropriate to accuse Francione of engaging in species essentialism. This vegan narrative assumes "that all people in the USA start from a *universal* social location/consciousness; however, *universal* is simply a coded term for assumed white middle-class experience"

(Harper, 2012, p. 156). There are many possible names for this mode of rhetoric, particularly when strategic discursive choices by vegan abolitionists aggressively target marginalized rhetors for bringing up material and experiential inequalities in relation to the pursuit of a vegan ideal. Colloquially, one might accuse Francione and his Franciobots of "mansplaining" or "whitesplaining." The former term is drawn from Rebecca Solnit's famous book *Men Explain Things to Me,* where she describes her many experiences of having her own research explained to her by other people, usually men, often in antagonistic or condescending ways; and the latter from sociologist Catriona Elder's mass disseminated editorial "Whitesplaining: What it is and How it Works," which continued on Solnit's path by emphasizing moments where persons of color have their racialized subject positions explained to them by persons steeped in White privilege. Both terms seem to match Harper's own experiences, particularly her quip that "if I had a dime for every time my critical race feminist scholarship was called 'racist' or 'white-hating,' the *Sistah Vegan Project* would be fully funded!" (Harper, 2016, para. 4).

Cordeiro-Rodrigues (2017) explained vegan abolitionist discourse as a manifestation of "racism without racists," a concept drawn from critical race theory to explain an insidious, even if unintentional, rhetorical trope in a "postracial" U.S. American discursive sphere. Harper, however, coined a different phrase to explain Francione's tactless tactics: the "return of the n*gger breakers" (Harper, 2017, para. 2). This act of "breaking," often accomplished in tandem with "strategic trolling," manifests in discourse that "ranges from DIRECT aggressive attacks to subtle and subversive attacks in order to TEAR YOU DOWN" (para. 2). Harper drew upon her own many experiences of being targeted to be "broken," not-so-subtly noting the work of "snarky white male professors who have tried to tear down my scholarship as unviable or ridiculous" (para. 4). Summing up her experience with challenging normative Whiteness in vegan abolitionism's species-essentialist rhetoric, Harper recalled:

> The mere fact I mentioned race was enough to try to *break* me and prevent me from crossing the epistemological borders of 'white vegan [postracial] logic and methods' that *pathologize Blackness* without ever *pathologizing* or *problematizing* the inherent injustice, violence, and inequities of *normative whiteness.* (Harper, 2017, para. 6)

Francione's vegan abolitionism is intensely powerful from a strategic and tactical standpoint because it encourages bottom-up approaches, particularly ethical veganism, in addition to top-down judicial decisions as necessary steps toward the procurement of animal liberation. After all, if the legal system and its corresponding legal decisions stem not from objective, scientific rules but rather from cultural patterns of the time, animal rights activists must practice justice-from-below via grassroots activism, particularly through the boycotting of animal products, to create cultural conditions conducive to positive legal decisions for animals. However, when dealing with questions of consumption, it is important to grapple with issues of material inequality in the United States. And, in relation to such material inequalities, liberationists must explore how issues of identity, particularly of race, necessarily influence patterns of consumption. These explorations must not be done purely through "missionary" work (trying to "recruit" more people of color into vegan abolitionism by demonstrating the connection between racism and speciesism). Stopping there manifests little more than racial tokenization. A blog post explicating, for instance, the historical, ideological, and material ties between the transatlantic slave trade and contemporary animal labor can be true enough but is in practice little more than offensive when the blogger has no interest in reciprocal and restorative justice for both animal and Black bodies (bodies historically and contemporarily relegated to less-than-human, and thus disposable, status in the eyes of the law).

Rather, if vegan abolitionism is to be "radical" enough to pursue total liberation, it must seriously contend with how species essentialism offers activists a disingenuous "out" that, rather than demonstrating a reciprocal commitment to both veganism and racial justice, discursively presents veganism as the cure to racism. Francione, for all his insistence that his abolitionist stance is intersectional and anti-essentialist, ultimately engages in anti-intersectional and essentialist rhetoric by cloaking a commitment to normative Whiteness. Harper summed up the challenge facing Francione, should he ever choose to accept it:

> Giving up possessive investment in whiteness is HARDER than giving up speciesist privilege—particularly since going vegan is primarily enacted through *objects of consumption.* Going vegan *replaces* cow milk with soy milk and leather jackets with PVC. . . . But giving up possessive investment in whiteness? Oh, I don't think there are any *cute* and *yummy* replacements for that. (Harper, 2017, para. 8)

In other words, both veganism *and* the possessive investment in Whiteness are about more than ideological frames of mind. Materially, they manifest in access to things and patterns of consumption. And although ideology and materiality are often set in opposition to one another, they are in fact mutually constitutive phenomena. Such is the case when dealing with a species-essentialist (read: Whiteness-bound) vegan abolitionism.

Abolitionist Extinctionism as Essentialist Eugenics

Francione, for all his critique of the moral distinction between humans and animals, nonetheless enjoys reifying such binaries through rampant essentialist rhetoric. As noted above, he lumps humanity into a coherent whole vis-à-vis a species-essentialist rhetoric that negates, even deplores, differences in subjectivity and material reality. However, he also essentializes the animal side of the human/animal binary—more specifically, he deplores any mode of animality that functions in the realm of the liminal, any being that does not cleanly fit into the categorization of "human" or "animal." Such an essentialist opposition to animal "hybridity" (Bhabha, 2006) manifests in a decidedly eugenical rhetoric surrounding the extinction of domesticated animals "for their own good" under a vegan abolitionist philosophy. This rhetoric ultimately drives Francione into a state of strategic contradiction, wherein he simultaneously purports the exact moral equality between *Homo sapiens* and all other members of kingdom *Animalia* while advocating for certain beings' destruction with a distinctly speciesist-ableist discourse that would not, at least according to vegan abolitionism's own anti-oppression principles, be acceptable to use on human beings. Thus, for all the rhetoric of radical purity espoused by Francione and his Franciobots, vegan abolitionism must either admit that humans and animals are *not* equal or that, under principles of human/animal equality, ableism and eugenics are justifiable practices. Either way, Francione's heavy reliance on essentialism places him firmly in the camp of liberal humanist ontologies so intent on universality that they eschew difference to their own detriment.

To clarify, "eugenics" is often understood to be a discourse confined to racist, reactionary conservatives of the past. However, it constitutes many different discourses throughout many different historical moments. Eugenics was, and is, "an ambiguous term that allowed many respectable Anglo-Americans to voice their concerns on a number of social issues" (Hasian, 1996, p. 14). One might argue that this definition is so broad as to be meaningless, but eugenics scholars like Hasian would argue the reverse—that overly specific definitions of eugenics, its targets, its time frames, its geographies, and its ideological adherents purposefully misunderstand the concept and even cloak it in narratives of "times now passed." Understanding eugenics' ambiguities requires an understanding of how invocations of choice and necessity are reassembled and reappropriated to fit particular agendas—for instance, the defective measurements of inherent societal deviance to defend discriminatory quotas in the United States' Immigration Act of 1924; the slaughter of the disabled in Nazi death camps during World War II; or even the contemporaneous Human Genome Project (Hasian, 1996; Twine, 2010). Much of the concept's broad definitional roots are attributed to nineteenth-century British eugenicist Francis Galton, who perceived eugenics as a socially acceptable practice of making people noble in heredity or good in birth. Galton's contemporaries strategically used this broad definition to define societal boundaries of moral delinquency. By doing so, authorities could defend policies to have societal deviants institutionalized, forcibly sterilized, or exterminated.

Animals have been inextricably linked with eugenic practices for millennia, particularly via practices such as selective breeding, forced sterilization, and institutionalization. As genetic and agricultural science advanced and people learned about the inheritance of traits, animals were (and continue to be) bred for very specific characteristics, such as the size and color of dogs or the growth rate and breast size of chickens. In the nineteenth century, as Charles Darwin became more and more interested in theories of natural selection in plants and animals, Herbert Spencer coopted Darwinist rhetoric into Social Darwinism, which theorized that human society ought to model itself over the adaptability of species. Galton, Darwin's eugenicist cousin, proposed that civilizations engage in positive eugenics to encourage the proliferation of good genes as well as negative eugenics (via institutionalization, sterilization, and antimiscegenation) to discourage breeding among the unfit. Selective breeding practices in the agricultural industry directly influenced the U.S. American human eugenics movement by the early twentieth century. Indeed, in 1903, U.S. agriculturalists founded the American Breeders Association to serve as "a conduit for the exchange of ideas between animal breeders, plant breeders and human geneticists," which proved crucial for advancing genetic science and launching the U.S. American eugenics movement (Lockwood, 2010, p. 159). Harry Laughlin, the face of U.S. American eugenics, translated ideas about livestock breeding into human breeding in an effort to influence Congress's decisions on immigration quotas, demonstrating via pedigree charts which races were fit to enter the country.

Less often mentioned is how eugenic rhetoric functions with respect to animals themselves—for better and for worse. Twine (2010) claimed that within our "anthropocentric cultural context, one cannot by definition be performing eugenics on animals" (p. 87). Nonetheless, even those who claim to work on behalf of animals (many vegans included) directly support reproductive control of some, if not all, animals to prevent an "unwanted surplus of 'unwanted' animals" (p. 88). For animal advocates, the word eugenics is most often replaced by various incarnations of more benign terms, such as "selective breeding" and "population control," which are, for all intents and purposes, "methodologically the same science" of biopolitics (p. 88). For example, to deal with problems of animal overpopulation, policies advocating forced sterilization are reproduced via benign terms like "spay-and-neuter" and "contraception." For some, controlling animal reproduction is critical to keeping domestic pets and saving wild animals. The utilitarian case for such practices is that from "the animal's perspective, foregoing reproduction is preferable to death and the suffering that may be associated with death" (Rutberg, 2010, p. 612). Animal organizations thus sponsor a slew of benevolent sterilization campaigns every year in the name of preventing the births of unwanted cats and dogs. Some animal proponents advocate for wildlife contraception as a humane alternative to population control methods like hunting and/or culling of animals like free-roaming deer (Lockwood, 2010). And, perhaps most notably for this chapter, Dinesh Wadiwel offered a dark assessment of eugenic-adjacent practices upon companion animals:

> They involve compulsory body modification, regimes of surveillance, and controls over movement and bodily function. . . . These apparatuses of control are designed to enable a tolerated "companionship" . . . by using coercive restraint methods to control for any unintended effects that might arise from an unregulated friendship between humans and animals, particularly that which might exceed the bounds of human utility. (Wadiwel, 2015, p. 203)

Contemporarily, animal rights activists have been criticized for invocations of ableist, even eugenical, rhetoric with respect to humans. Singer in particular is famous for his argument from marginal cases, which demands that if humans with low cognitive abilities (such as infants and the mentally disabled) have the right to equal moral consideration, there is no reason to deny such consideration to animals on the grounds of mental deficiencies (Singer, 1975). Although

Singer's argument makes sense to those familiar with the rhetoric of speciesism, his argument is troubling to those who worry about the rhetoric of ableism. O'Brien (2013) critiqued Singer's proposition that intellectually disabled humans, technically, have a lesser claim to moral consideration than apes because of the apes' higher cognitive abilities. The critique is due to the longstanding history of eugenicists comparing who they called the "feeble-minded" to animals to justify discriminatory practices. Indeed, this so-called animal metaphor was, and is, a common argumentative trope among eugenicists who "often include a 'scale of humanity' where various gradations of humans can be gauged. . . . Some may be denied certain rights or opportunities on the basis of their placement on such a scale" (O'Brien, 2013, p. 25). Luckily, Francione abhors Singer, and thus should be free of the taint of ableism via the moral purity of vegan abolitionism. Unfortunately, this is far from the case.

A large reason why Francione is considered so extreme in comparison to Singerites and Reganites is because of his views on domestication and pet-keeping. Neither Singer's nor Regan's canonical texts devote much time to critiquing companion animal–keeping as a practice. Of those animal rights theorists who do talk about pets, many do so in the affirmative. Leahy (1991) noted that well-fed, well-treated dogs gave no indication of wanting to escape their guardians; DeGrazia (1996) maintained that, compared to zoo animals, pet confinement constitutes a decidedly good life; Petrinovich (1999) argued that "anyone who has seen a trained dog . . . would be hard-pressed to conclude the animal is working contrary to its nature and that it is not experiencing pleasure" (pp. 388–389); and Donaldson and Kymlicka (2016) insisted that:

> if we don't view dependency as intrinsically undignified, we will see the dog as a capable individual who knows what he wants and how to communicate in order to get it—as someone who has the potential for agency, preferences, and choice. (p. 84)

For Francione, however, domestication is wholly unnatural because of the forced intermingling of humans and nature to create forced conditions of a very pitiable state of dependence. Through "selective breeding and confinement," humans have created a sort of hybridized, quasi-animal that belongs neither in civilization nor in the wilderness (Francione & Charlton, 2016, para. 32). Domesticated animals "exist forever in a netherworld of vulnerability, dependent on us for everything and at risk of harm from an environment that they do not really understand" (Francione, 2012b, para. 5). Furthermore, "domestication itself raises serious moral issues irrespective of how the non-humans involved are treated" (Francione & Charlton, 2016, para. 29). The entire malicious point of domestication is that "we want domesticated animals to depend on us . . . for everything that is of relevance to them" (para. 29). Therefore, despite how "humanely" humans may treat them, these unfortunate creatures simply "do not belong in our world" (para. 5). His solution is a simple one: "Care for all those domestic animals that are presently alive, but we should not continue to bring more animals into existence so that we may own them" (Francione, 2010b, p. 170).

Although Francione's critique of domestication also applies to livestock, he particularly emphasizes the ethical challenges of animals groomed as pets. For him, pet ownership is just another means by which humans exert bodily control over animals and thus deprive them of their fundamental rights. Pets are to be pitied, for they "are dependent on us for everything that is important in their lives: when and whether they eat or drink, when and where they sleep or relieve themselves, whether they get any affection or exercise, etc." (Francione, 2012b, para. 4). They have been groomed to contain traits that are pleasing to humans but inadequate for existence in the wild. Pets are the very worst form of quasi-animals, for they cannot exist without human intervention: "We might make them happy in one sense, but the relationship can never be 'natural' or 'normal' . . . irrespective of how well we treat them. This is more or less true of all domesticated non-humans" (Francione & Charlton, 2016, para. 29).

Indeed, Francione consistently critiques the very existence of dogs and cats. He guided his *Introduction to Animal Rights* by deconstructing the burning house scenario that is so often used against animal rights activists. In this scenario, a person is trapped within a burning building with his child and his dog and must choose which to save. Other theorists, he contends, would say that it is most ethical to choose the child, regardless of one's views on animal rights. Francione's tactic, however, was to reject the choice entirely, arguing that the dilemma is merely a manufactured conflict of human design. A purer vision of animal rights would make such a decision impossible to make, for the dog in question would not exist:

If we recognize that animals have a basic right not to be treated as our resources . . . we will stop producing animals for human purposes . . . We will stop dragging animals into the burning house, and then ask whether we should save the human or the animal. (Francione, 2010b, p. 153)

This is not to say that Francione favors euthanasia. He has explicitly stated that euthanizing animals in overpopulated animal shelters is killing, regardless of how painless the death supposedly is. He has used this distaste for euthanasia as a means of critiquing welfarist organizations like the American Society for the Prevention of Cruelty to Animals, which he has called a pro-euthanasia organization (Francione, 1996). Although care should be taken to ensure that no more animals are born to overpopulate existing shelters, the animals currently there ought not to be killed in the name of saving space. He also defends his seemingly extreme views by describing his five rescue dogs. Despite his love for his pets, "were there only two dogs remaining in the world, [he] would not be in favor of breeding them so that we could have more 'pets'" (Francione, 2010b, p. 170). Morally speaking, humans have a duty to care for the overwhelming numbers of cats and dogs in existence now. Euthanasia ought not to be favored over adopting and fostering, and spay-and-neuter policies must be enforced. To Francione and his wife, their five dogs are not his pets but rather "refugees of sorts" (Francione, 2012b, para. 9). And, "although we love them very much, we strongly believe that they should not have existed in the first place" (Francione & Charlton, 2016, para. 1).

Oddly enough, it is in Francione's departure from mainstream arguments about domestication that he ends up giving us more of the same eugenic underpinnings used in traditional animal rights arguments. Whereas some animal rights activists either do not give much attention to pet ownership or believe it to be alright under certain circumstances, Francione adamantly states that not only can pet ownership *never* be justified, but domesticated animals ought to be bred out of existence entirely, a viewpoint that Sue Donaldson and William Kymlicka's (2016) acclaimed *Zoopolis* decried as not "abolitionist" but "extinctionist" (p. 88). According to them, Francione's and other similar positions hold that companion species' dependence on and neotenization by humans are not only unnatural (and therefore wrong) but undignified, thus eliminating the possibility that domesticated species might live a fulfilling life. However, "the abolitionist approach is multiply flawed; it wrongly treats states of dependency as inherently undignified, and wrongly treats human-animal interaction as somehow unnatural" (p. 88).

This chapter agrees with Donaldson and Kymlicka's (2016) assessment that "the abolitionist/extinctionist position supports a massive intervention and makes no attempt to justify it in relation to the individuals whose liberty is being restricted" (p. 81). Indeed, Francione's views on domestication may be vastly different from his peers,' but the radical Francione turns to uncomfortably familiar eugenic tactics to make his case. Although Francione claims that people should never do to animals what they would never do to a human being, his eugenic ideas about pets suggest that his logic is not wholly consistent with his rhetoric. When it comes to cats and dogs, Francione's tactics become less than merciful. Unlike "genuine" animals, domesticated animals are not so much in need of legal personhood as incremental extermination. Animal rights does not mean that nonhumans have "some sort of right to reproduce" (Francione, 2007b, para. 20). There are some animal rights advocates who oppose the sterilization of nonhumans, including domesticated cats and dogs. Such a view, to Francione, is a logical fallacy: "If that view is correct, then we would be morally committed to allowing all domesticated species to continue to reproduce indefinitely. We cannot limit this 'right of reproduction' to dogs and cats alone" (para. 20). Furthermore:

> it makes no sense to say that we have acted immorally in domesticating nonhuman animals but we are now committed to allowing them to continue to breed. We made a moral mistake by domesticating nonhumans in the first place; what sense does it make to perpetuate it? (para. 20)

The only rational solution to solving pet overpopulation is to eschew any moral quandaries about sterilization, care for the pets currently in existence, and (for their own good) sterilize them to ensure that no others are brought into existence. After all, "our cities are full of stray cats and dogs who live miserable lives and starve or freeze, succumb to disease, or are tormented by humans"—why continue the epidemic any further? (Francione, 2010b, p. 169).

Francione's ideas for kindhearted, incremental extermination of certain people (since, for Francione, animals *are* people!) are far from novel. Such paternalistic arguments about reproduction can be traced back to early eugenicists' justifications for sterilizing the mentally disabled. As O'Brien (2013) explained, "Even the most drastic form of social control, large-scale extermination, has been supported by arguing that the action largely results from humanistic regard for the victims" (p. 107). Eugenics supporters frequently lobbied for policies that would protect future children from suffering by being born with a disabling condition. Indeed, "for those 'future children' . . . the issue was not a choice between living without a 'hereditary illness' and living with one, but whether it was better to live with such a condition or not live at all" (p. 123). Much like Francione's demand for the compulsory sterilization of pets for their own benefit, the 1927 Supreme Court case of *Buck v. Bell* (1927) defined the benefits of the compulsory sterilization of the intellectually disabled due to its societal benefits. Some state laws even prohibited the disabled from marrying.

Indeed, Francione's depiction of pet ownership merely represents an ableist-speciesist hybrid of what O'Brien (2013) dubbed the "altruistic metaphor," a common argumentative trope historically used by eugenicists. Authorities who use this metaphor point to their spiritual and moral "duty to provide for and protect such unfortunates who could not live on their own and were constantly threatened by the dangers of their environment" (p. 117). To "save the children" (or in this case, the puppies), Francione too seeks the slow extermination of those animals with what one might call a "species-induced" disability, a medicalized understanding of animality and disability wherein the animals' inability to exist in the wild precludes it from living a "good life." In this case, Francione points to the poor cats and dogs who are abandoned and miserable on city streets or euthanized in shelters. In addition, adherents to this metaphor envision themselves as "missionaries" sacrificing themselves for the "public good" (p. 105). Again, Francione meets this standard by housing refugees despite believing that they should not exist. Much like the institutional caregivers and other authorities in the late nineteenth and early twentieth centuries, Francione strategically presents himself as one of many "benevolent care-givers who were sacrificing their time to protect morons and provide them with a higher quality of life than they otherwise could be expected to have" (p. 117). Despite Francione's benevolent intentions, the paternalistic rhetoric he uses when describing sterilization and incremental extermination draw on old eugenic arguments that, if applied to human beings, would likely not be well received by disability activists (or, really, any decent person) today.

His well-meaning exterminism represents an ultimately damaging aim "to make animals independent of human society in a way that precludes the very idea of positive relational duties" (Donaldson & Kymlicka, 2016, p. 7). Indeed, such rhetoric is hauntingly similar to Francis Galton's claim that "what Nature does blindly, slowly, and ruthlessly, man can do providently, quickly, and kindly" (MacKenzie, 1976, p. 503). John Sanbonmatsu's existential critique of speciesism is thus ironically applicable to Francione's antispeciesist ethic, for "dismissing in advance every fact that might unseat my concept of the other beings as being *unworthy of life,* I avoid having to reflect on the moral implications of my participation in an *exterminationist* way of life" (Sanbonmatsu, 2011, p. 40).

Furthermore, Francione uses a disturbing amount of ableist rhetoric reminiscent of early eugenic conversations regarding the disabled. To echo Taylor (2017), "The ableist assumption that it is inherently bad, even unnatural, to be a dependent human being is here played out across the species divide" (p. 214). Francione denies any responsibility to "'liberate' animals and let them wander freely in the streets" (Francione, 2007b, para. 5). The rationale for this, however, is somewhat troubling: "To allow animals free reign in human spaces would be as irresponsible as allowing small children to wander around" (para. 5). Even if pets were, by some miracle, legally given the same rights as human children, this would still be fundamentally opposed to a vegan abolitionist philosophy, for "the overwhelming number of human children mature to become autonomous, independent beings" (Francione, 2012b, para. 4). Comparing dogs and cats to children is troublingly familiar to how early eugenicists described the mentally ill while defending discriminatory policies against them. O'Brien (2013) pointed out how the disabled were described using a perpetual child metaphor so as to rationalize placing reproductive restrictions on intellectually disabled persons. Eugenicists "considered the feeble-minded to have the mentality of children, and that their rights could thus be controlled in the same way as a child's rights are" (p. 118). By consistently using ableist rhetoric to explain his rationale on pet ownership, Francione not only exerts biopolitical control over animals but fails to understand that very rhetoric's roots in institutionalized discrimination against disabled persons.

Francione's paternalism and ableism are further perpetuated through dualistic discourse. As Cassidy and Mills (2012) explained, "Human/animal boundaries are drawn by humans, and in doing so they exert power/control over spaces and resources: when those assigned to the 'outside' come in, the response is stark" (p. 500). Francione seems to see pets as a breach of these manmade boundaries that differentiate humans from animals. Like mainstream environmental thinkers, he "constructs 'wild' spaces as ones in which humans are absent, and 'human' spaces as ones which 'wild' animals should never enter" (p. 507). He denounces the presence of animals in human spaces, seemingly upset by direct human relationships with animals. Dogs, cats, and other domesticated animals blur the lines between human and animal, between civilization and wilderness, representing a hybridized entity that threatens Francione's traditional, boundary-laden explication of the animal world.

Whereas the "mere welfarists" deplored by vegan abolitionists see few problems with pet-keeping and domestication, Francione differs by arguing that the domestication process is fundamentally immoral and unnatural. However, it is in this ethical departure that Francione reveals his adherence to the troubling hyper-naturalistic, eugenic rhetoric almost inherent in a liberal humanist paradigm of animal rights. No matter how hard Francione tries, he remains stuck in a traditional hegemonic worldview that separates nature from culture. This cross-species worldview functions "in a parallel of the 'better off dead' narrative of disability" wherein domesticated animals are viewed as 'better off extinct' (Taylor, 2017, p. 215). And, within this ableist-speciesist conception of life, humans are obligated to grant rights only to those who fit within these arbitrary boundaries while exterminating those that do not.

This book does not argue that there are no issues with pet-keeping under an ethic of total liberation. Perhaps, just perhaps, it *is* immoral and unjust to keep companion species. As Dinesh Wadiwel notes, many practices of pet-keeping engage a "violent relationality that is founded upon a sovereign prerogative" (p. 220). However, to justify the extinction of companions on the grounds that they are "wrong bodies" represents a troubling intersection of speciesism and ableism. The dissolution of speciesist practices requires a more serious engagement with liminalities, with those bodies that do not "belong" to an arbitrarily constructed ideological binary between human and animal, wild and domestic, free and unfree. So perhaps, just perhaps, companion species are not *necessarily* antithetical to animal liberation, for just because something *has been* violent does not necessarily mean it *is always and will always* be so. Like Wadiwel (2015), I argue that a more nuanced, less eugenic exploration of companion species "does not *preclude* innovations in friendship or developing intimacy and connection in resistance to enveloping systems of domination" (Wadiwel, 2015, p. 220, emphasis mine). The *Homo sapiens* tendency to "act in ways that deny animals a dignified existence" is indeed "morally wrong in a special way" (Cao, 2014, p. 185). However, perceptions of existence-as-dignified must cease being tied to depictions of a proper body free of dependence upon other human beings. Such a stance, guided as it is by liberal humanist understandings of freedom and individuality, not only ignores the inherent interdependence of all species but also portrays the "dependent" body as the "disabled" body, and the disabled body as "life unworthy of life" (Sanbonmatsu, 2011).

———————

Gary Francione's vegan abolitionist stance offers a potential alternative to Wise and the NhRP. Vegan abolitionism not only counters Wise's overemphasis on cognitive prowess in favor of sentience, thus advocating for rights and personhood for a much broader array of beings, but also invokes a multidirectional mode of advocacy that is both top-down and bottom-up. In doing so, he offers a compelling counterargument to Wise's claim that court decisions will necessarily influence public perception, instead asserting that laypersons' adoption of animal rights ethics via a vegan moral baseline offers a more fruitful way to direct future legal policy. In other words, in terms of strategic and tactical consistency, Francione appears considerably more successful than Wise.

However, for all the benefits Francione brings to the vegan table, his seemingly liberatory praxis belies discriminatory ideologies based in a liberal humanist reliance on universalisms and essentialisms. Francione's articulation of a vegan abolitionist's duties ultimately relies on a human/animal binary that essentializes both categories and decries any being relegated to the realm of the liminal. In doing so, his seemingly intersectional, antispeciesist lens crumbles into an aggressive, but ultimately toothless, rhetoric based in oppressive ideologies of normative Whiteness and eugenics. In assuming that humanity can be conceived as a unified whole, in arguing that "talking about race" in animal rights arenas is ultimately distracting and/or divisive, and in vehemently criticizing people of color who attempt to challenge his rhetorical choices, Francione perpetuates a species-essentialist stance. This stance *appears* to be intersectional, particularly in its ability to draw connections between the treatment of animals and the treatment of historically marginalized groups via invocations of, say, chattel slavery or holocausts. However, by denying diverse subjectivities and differences in material existence that affect a person's, a family's, or an entire cultural community's ability to adopt veganism as a moral baseline with as much speed and ease as Francione would prefer, he ultimately utilizes intersectional rhetoric in a manner that *re*centers normative Whiteness. This is not to say that Francione is incorrect to advocate for ethical veganism, but rather that his indifference to the complexities of issues like race in comparison to the "most important" issue of speciesism demonstrates a lack of engagement with how the dark cloud of coloniality necessarily impacts all living beings, albeit in ways that are different in degree and in kind.

I further expressed concern that the radical vegan abolitionist framework understands which lives are worth living through a vexingly essentialized, binary, and ableist lens. Francione's insistence that legal personhood and a vegan diet would constitute a just world for animals only holds for those animals that exist separately from human contamination. For those animals tainted by human presence, such as cats and dogs, the merciful solution is to do away with them for good. However practical or altruistic his tactics may be, they mimic a troubling eugenic rhetoric that has been and is often still used to describe what to do with dependent bodies, specifically the intellectually disabled—wherein the "best" solution is to "cure" them by preventing their existence altogether. Whereas Francione insists that New Welfarists happily subject animals to harm they would never subject humans to, his plan for cats and dogs has frequently been applied to disabled humans in a morally controversial way (see, for instance, contemporary debates over prenatal testing for disabled fetuses). Despite his assertions that animals ought to have legal personhood, Francione restricts personhood to wild animals only—suggesting a decidedly moral compromise not so dissimilar from the New Welfarists he so abhors.

This book advocates for an ecofeminist legal theory which opposes either/ or binary thought in favor of a more complex both/and approach to moral decision-making and associated actions. This theoretical framework deconstructs the erroneous divides between human/animal, nature/culture, and wilderness/ civilization. As an alternative to abolitionism/extinctionism, an animal rights perspective focused on compassion over purity, in contextualization over universalization, could understand caring for humans and for domesticated animals as "listening to what animals are telling us about the care they are receiving and the care they would like to receive" (Taylor, 2017, p. 217). Thus, if there is indeed a way to abolish the companion animal industrial complex without abolishing the companion animals themselves, vegans should want to find it. No body (and *nobody*) embodies the *wrong* body. Thus, critical listening is essential to liberatory praxis, and unfortunately, in this instance, Francione appears unwilling to listen to anyone but himself.

CHAPTER 4

Radical Environmentalism as Animal Rights Law?

Ecological Ambivalences and the Rhetoric of Earth Jurisprudence

> Many environmental thinkers are torn in two opposing directions at once. For good reasons we are appalled by the damage that has been done to the earth by the ethos of heedless anthropocentric individualism. . . . But also for good reasons we are repelled, at the other extreme, by the environmentally correct image of mindless biocentric collectivisms in which precious personal values are overridden for the good of some healthy beehive "whole."
>
> —Frederick Ferre, "Personalistic Organicism: Paradox or Paradigm?"

I n April 2001, the Gaia Foundation invited an elite group of individuals from around the world to congregate at a conference center just outside Washington, DC. The London-based foundation collected participants from diverse backgrounds, including but not limited to university professors, environmental lawyers, community developers, environmental educators, wilderness experience leaders, and Indigenous activists. This mishmashed party had a common goal: to discuss the feasibility of developing a form of environmental legal thought in line with the aims of the Gaia Foundation, which were "creating international networks of individuals and groups concerned about the survival of the planet, its species, and its indigenous cultures" (Bell, 2003, p. 71). Guided by the acclaimed cultural historian Thomas Berry, the group concluded that the development of an "Earth Justice System" required a baseline assumption that all species on planet Earth, and even the planet itself, have (and have always had) prelegal rights, and that those rights ought to be respected in larger legal systems by virtue of natural beings' membership in a singular "Earth Community" (Bell, 2003).

Then, in 2006, Sister Patricia Siemen, JD, utilized her Marie V. Gendron Grant to create the Center for Earth Jurisprudence (CEJ) at Barry Law School in Orlando, Florida. By 2007, the CEJ was offering seminars on this unique mode of environmental legal thought at both Barry and the St. Thomas University School of Law in Minneapolis. Hundreds of law students have enrolled in coursework offered by the CEJ. Outside of the classroom, the organization has engaged in local, national, and international advocacy efforts ranging from authoring the Florida Springs and Aquifer Protection Act in 2013 to composing an amicus curiae brief on behalf of the Global Climate Change Movement and Leadership Council of Women Religious in support of a constitutional climate change lawsuit filed by twenty-one plaintiffs across the United States (Center for Earth Jurisprudence, n.d.). And, each year, the CEJ invites scholars worldwide to attend its Future Generations Conference, an annual gathering intended to

> shift human consciousness to understand humanity's basic interdependence with the wider natural world; to provide a legal critique of current assumptions, values, and structures of law that are blind to this reality; and to develop alternatives building on current legal tools. (Center for Earth Jurisprudence, n.d., para. 6)

In 2008, the country of Ecuador broke environmentalist ground by writing the rights of the planet Earth into its official constitution. Among the multiple provisions relating to the rights of nature was Article 1, which stated:

> Nature or Pachamama, where life is reproduced and exists, has the right to exist, persist, maintain and regenerate its vital cycles, structure, functions and its processes in evolution. Every person, people, community or nationality, will be able to demand the recognitions of rights for nature before the public organisms. The application and interpretation of these rights will follow the related principles established in the Constitution. (qtd. in Burdon, 2011, p. 9)

Following this was Article 2, which read that nature, broadly conceived, maintained the right to "an integral restoration" to be promoted by the "most efficient mechanisms" of the state, which according to Article 3 must "promote respect towards all the elements that form an ecosystem" (qtd. in Burdon, 2011, p. 10). These constitutional provisions would be tested a few years later during a constitutional injunction against the Provincial Government of Loja in favor of the Vilcabamba River, finding that the defendants had violated nature's right to be fully respected in its existence and its maintenance of vital functions due to corporations' unlawful endeavors to widen the Vilcabamba-Quinara road.

It followed that in 2009, sixty-three legal professionals from each state and territory in Australia gathered for the continent's first conference on "Wild Law." The participants ended their time together by summarizing the themes and outcomes of the conference into a declaration which stated, among other things, that the "participants of Wild Law declare that the separation between nature and human beings is a fundamental cause of the current environmental crisis," and thus "the law needs to transition from an exclusive focus on human beings and recognise that we exist as part of a broader earth community" (Burdon, 2010a, p. 62). Given that "the universe is composed of subjects to be communed with, not objects to be used," legal professionals and by extension governmental judiciaries had a moral responsibility to "commit to evolving law so that it protects that natural world from destruction" (p. 62).

And finally, in 2010, Evo Morales, the president of Bolivia, convened the World Conference of Peoples on Climate Change and Mother Earth Rights in Cochabamba. This conference, attended by over 35,000 people, resulted in the composition of a "Universal Declaration on the Rights of Mother Earth," which demanded that humanity, in its entirety, engage in a moral paradigm shift and make a conscious effort to amend global patterns of environmental degradation and consumption. Drawing from texts such as the Universal Declaration of Human Rights, the declaration proclaimed that a living being—*any* living being—was entitled to the right to exist, to habitat, to participate in accordance with its nature, to maintain its identity and integrity, to self-regulate, to be free from pollution, and the to participate in communities of beings (Burdon, 2011; Schillmoller & Pelizzon, 2013).

This decade-long sampling of jurisprudential philosophy and legal decision-making offers a tiny glimpse into the "Western Hemisphere's" growing interest in developing a type of environmental law that goes beyond the instrumental regulation of land use. Called "Wild Law" in some venues and "Earth jurisprudence" in most others, this mode of ecological legal thinking requires legal practitioners at the local, national, and international levels to expand their visions of the moral community to include "sentient" beings such as *Homo sapiens* and kingdom *Animalia* as well as those ecological bodies like stones, plants, and rivers erroneously deemed, to use the Cartesian terminology, mere automata. Under visions of Earth jurisprudence, environmental law would undergo a dramatic paradigmatic shift from an exclusive focus on management and regulation to a central mission to secure personhood, legal rights, and human guardianship for any and all members of a broader Earth community. Central to this legal philosophy and its guiding rhetorical tropes are difficult questions such as:

> What if there were an Earth Justice System with its corresponding jurisprudence based on the concept that the planet and all of its species have rights—and that they have those rights by virtue of their existence as component members of a single Earth community? And what if we could build a consensus within and among communities, regions, and nations to recognize these rights and reflect them within our human justice systems? (Bell, 2003, p. 70)

This book has, up until this point, focused exclusively on "animal law," more specifically "animal rights law," as its legal genre of consideration. While at first glance the study of Earth jurisprudence may seem to deviate from notions of animal rights litigation, I argue that radical environmental law based in principles of ecological holism has much to offer parties interested in animals as bearers of legal rights. Earth jurisprudence, with its focus on legal justice for all of Earth's beings, necessarily includes legal rights for animals—subsumed, of course, under a broader notion of a "biotic community" (Leopold, 1949) in need of legal intervention and protection. It is a holistic, communitarian stance on animal law that sees humans, animals, plants, and even rivers and rocks as persons deserving of legal protections. What is more, it insists on a broader reconceptualization of the nature/culture binary that has proved so damaging to animal-oriented litigation by designating nonhuman beings as objects devoid of subjectivity or agency. In essence, while Earth jurisprudence does not advertise itself as animal law per se, its tenets necessitate its inclusion in the "canon" of animal rights litigation. It is a vision of animal liberation that includes, as much as possible, the lives of *everyone*—even those beings that prototypical animal rights rhetoric often casts aside as less morally relevant than, or even too distracting from, animal subjects—from insects to plants to rivers to stones.

This chapter accomplishes the following tasks: First, it investigates competing interpretations of how "environmentalism," broadly conceived, might fit or conflict with notions of "animal rights" writ large. The chapter then explains the origins and general tenets of Earth jurisprudence and examines how the radical, deep ecological stance of Earth jurisprudence offers a unique vision of animal liberation that those offered by lawyers such as Francione and Wise have not yet been able to articulate. Finally, it conceptualizes the theoretical and practical incoherence of Earth jurisprudence as a result of two factors: its expansion of the moral community to the legally impractical realm of the infinite, and its strategic rhetorical absences regarding liminal legal situations, such as the legality of keeping and/or slaughtering livestock and "invasive" species. Unfortunately, for all the necessary insights Earth jurisprudence provides to the animal rights canon, its ultimate downfall lies in its subtle reification of nature as "pristine wilderness."

Competing Voices: Can Environmentalists "Do" Animal Rights?

To reiterate, an ideological rhetorical criticism necessarily requires an analysis of competing discourses surrounding the artifact of analysis. This chapter, however, posits that the most important discursive conflict does not lie in competing interpretations of Earth jurisprudence among different strains of environmental law—for example, how someone working in a conservation-oriented litigation arena focused on instrumentalist/profit-oriented environmental policy, perhaps at the U.S. Department of the Interior—might have agreed and/or disagreed with legal strategies premised upon ecological holism. Rather, in this book's analysis of the varying rhetorics of *animal rights* law, it is more useful to investigate contested discourses regarding whether or not "environmentalism" and "animal rights" can truly coexist on philosophical and legal levels. While neither of the two concepts should be considered ideological monoliths, public discourse surrounding the similarities and differences between the two concepts/movements are nonetheless important when distinguishing the apparent rhetorical gaps and ethical contradictions between "animal" law and "environmental" law.

By and large, the terms "environmentalism" and "environmentalists" are not used synonymously with "animal rights" or "animal rights activists." Certainly, there are some similarities in overarching philosophies, strategies, and tactics. The many strands of environmentalist thought and the many variations of animal rights thought have in common an overarching critique of how the *Homo sapiens* species "uses" the more-than-human world. Both parties generally agree that more-than-human exploitation for human ends has led to undesirable consequences (including but not limited to mass extinctions and global climate change), and that interpersonal and systemic changes are needed to combat the degradation of the more-than-human world. Both agree that such change must occur, at some level, through the U.S. American legal system, be it through stricter enforcement of food safety laws by the Food and Drug Administration's investigators or through the securement of animal personhood. And, perhaps most importantly, both agree that the more-than-human world ought to be given more attention than it gets at the moment—and ultimately moral consideration.

Because of these similarities, some parties believe that animal rights and environmentalism are two sides of what is ultimately the same ecologically engaged coin. Indeed, many vegetarians and vegans acknowledge that their reason for avoiding animal products was not initially due to ethics, but rather out of a concern for animal agriculture's effect on the environment (Fox & Ward, 2008). Environmental scholars and activists consistently insist that eating less meat is an important step to lessening ecological devastation and global climate change. *Scientific American*'s recurrent *EarthTalk* column explained that "red meat such as beef and lamb is responsible for 10 to 40 times as many greenhouse gas emissions as common vegetables and grains," meaning that "our meat consumption habits take a serious toll on the environment" (Scheer & Moss, n.d., para. 1). A 2016 study by the Oxford Martin School saw scientists advocating mass meat reduction, insisting that widespread adoption of vegetarianism would reduce food-related carbon emissions by 63 percent, and veganism by 70 percent (Harvey, 2016). The study's lead author, Dr. Marco Springmann, explained the initial rationale for completing the study: "The food system is responsible [currently] for more than a quarter of all greenhouse gas emissions, and therefore a major driver of climate change" (qtd. in Harvey, 2016, para. 9). The popular environmentalist website *Reducetarian* argued that while "unplugging the TV, taking shorter showers, and using refillable water bottles" are good steps to take to reduce one's carbon footprint, "simply eating less meat can save water, land, energy, and other vital resources" (Puckett, 2017, paras. 1, 6). High-profile documentaries such as *Cowspiracy* and *Forks over*

Knives also emphasize industrial agriculture's impact on broader ecological health, particularly with regard to the U.S. American cattle industry. And Greenpeace (a group whose radical, visually provocative tactics make it, in many ways, the PETA of the environmentalist world) insisted that

> with a rising global middle class, societies are becoming meat obsessed. Nowhere else is this more prevalent than rich nations whose appetite for beef, pork and processed chicken have reached a tipping point. . . . We're not advocating that everyone adopt a "meatless" diet tomorrow. But we all must develop "meat consciousness" and reduce the level of meat in our diets. Shifting to more plant-based foods is essential to combatting climate change, soil, air and water pollution, ocean dead zones, and myriad other problems caused by industrial livestock production. (n.d., paras. 1, 3)

What is more, given environmentalism's emphasis on biodiversity for sustaining a healthy planet, saving "wild" animals from extinction is considered a vitally important task to most environmentalists. The National Resources Defense Council (NRDC), one of the most influential environmental law organizations in the United States, recently joined with the Oregon-based Xerxes Society for Invertebrate Conservation to sue the U.S. government in an attempt to have honeybees declared an endangered species and thus subject to more attention and protection by U.S. governmental entities (Rosenberg, n.d.). Acclaimed environmental organizations like the Sierra Club frequently organize campaigns on behalf of species deemed endangered. After the death of the last male white rhino in March of 2018, the Sierra Club's publication *Sierra* composed a mournful editorial decrying how the "northern white's end is wholly the result of human depredation" (Rauber, 2019, para. 2) and calling for an attempt at the in vitro fertilization of the remaining females to save the species from extinction. *National Geographic* even published a thought-provoking 2013 article that complicated notions of "saving" endangered species by moving from questions of *how* to do so toward critiques of *why* people gravitate toward helping certain species over others, especially when those species are large megafauna—an analysis very much in line with antispeciesist sentiments articulated by animal rights organizations (Dell'Amore, 2013).

Environmental organizations often join animal rights advocates in opposing animal cruelty for cruelty's sake, particularly with regard to the use of animals for human entertainment (notably, however, entertainment does not always constitute sport hunting for environmentalist rhetors). The Sierra Club has advocated for nonendangered "nuisance" species such as rattlesnakes in an effort to avoid the animals being used for cruelty-based entertainment, as demonstrated in their 2018 campaign against rattlesnake "roundups" and "ritual decapitations" in western Texas "coliseums" (Schipani, 2018). Environmentalists worldwide—governmental, legal, and layperson—have consistently argued against the international trade in elephant ivory to create cutlery, musical instruments, jewelry, and other material extravagances (see Kahumbu & Halliday, 2016; WWF, 2016).

The above examples are but a few of many instances of apparent common-alities between two "movements"—environmentalism and animal rights. The two movements definitely overlap, both in people and in ideas. Indeed, one would think, given the surface-level similarities between environmentalist and animal rights stances on animality, particularly with regard to their critical stances on heavy meat consumption, species extinctions, and exploitation/killing for entertainment purposes, the two movements would have little difficulty building ideological coalitions. However, the reality is far more complicated. Again, to speak of "environmentalism" as a coherent, singular ideological whole is too simplistic. However, much like the varying strains of "animal rights" theory and praxis, which are all at some level united in their critique of speciesism, various environmentalist theories and practices have a few premises in common. These premises, while useful in uniting different threads of environmentalist thought, are oftentimes at the root of the seemingly unsolvable conflicts between environmentalism and animal rights.

At the root of the apparent contradictions between an environmentalist ethic and an animal rights ethic is, according to some voices, a conflict between individ-ualism and communitarianism (Varner, 2002). That is to say, animal rights theory and praxis emphasizes the moral worth and rights of each being as an individual subject, whereas environmentalist theory and praxis prefers a systems approach that emphasizes the health of broader ecosystems over individual animal subjects. Therefore, in cases where an individual animal body's life or needs might run into conflict with, say, the health of a forest or swampland as a whole, an animal rights activist might advocate for very different tactics than an environmentalist. Such divisions are best exemplified in varying debates over hunting and culling. As the previous chapters have explained, an animal rights approach—be it utilitarian, abolitionist, ecofeminist, or something else—does not believe in killing animals to suit an ecologist's interpretation of how a particular geographic area ought to look or which species ought to be there and in what numbers. Francione, for instance, pointedly critiqued the deer hunters in his neighborhood:

> I know some of these hunters would not hesitate to spend hours trying to rescue a deer "out of season" from some hazard. But they have no problem with shooting an arrow that has four razor points that open on contact and literally "lock" onto the organs or muscle of the victim, into that same deer a month later, when it is legal to kill her. (Francione, 2007, para. 10)

For Francione and other animal rights practitioners, these hunters' "relationship" with the animals they stalk, based on a tenuous definition of love or admiration for "nature" writ large, is nothing but a mere exemplar of the incoherent (and dubiously nicknamed) "moral schizophrenia" (Francione, 2007) surrounding pseudo-environmentalist stances on animal lives. For environmentalists that hunt "in season" animals, however, an animal rights stance appears morally incoherent itself. According to Tovar Cerulli, author of the controversial book *The Mindful Carnivore: A Vegetarian's Hunt for Sustenance,* hunting and environmentalism have a deep historical and moral connection that is, at the core, founded on a commitment to conservation:

> I understand that caring for animals and their ecosystems is not incompatible with participating in those systems as a predator. . . . The most avid hunters I know—including ecologists, educators, and birdwatchers—are committed to environmental causes. The most passionate environmentalists I know—whether they hunt or not—respect the roles played by all predators, including humans. (Cerulli, 2014, paras. 2, 6)

In other words, while not all environmentalists are hunters, *no* animal rights activists hunt. While environmentalism considers hunting to be a controversial, but ultimately morally gray issue, animal rights sees hunting as a clear-cut, black-and-white one. (Well, other than instances of Indigenous tribes hunting for sustenance, of which there is still an active debate regarding what constitutes an "acceptable" instance of killing—debates that are, admittedly, often dominated by Whiteness-bound rhetors as opposed to culturally fluent Indigenous voices.) Yet again, the issue is one of individualism versus communitarianism. Which matters more: the life of the deer killed for sport, or the health of the deer's home that (presumably) would wither away should the deer and its friends be allowed to overpopulate (since, ironically, the deer's natural predators, wolves, were already hunted away for being "menaces" to human populations)? Obviously, the animal rights position generally argues for the former, and environmentalism generally for the latter.

And, while environmentalists have consistently agreed with animal rights activists that excessive meat-eating takes a damaging toll on the environment, they are rarely so quick to advocate for the total abolition of animal exploitation for food, clothing, entertainment, etc. According to Freeman (2010), while many animal rights organizations are eager to present themselves as environmentalists, the reverse is rarely true:

> It seems on the surface as if environmentalists can more easily justify prioritizing a reformist option such as reduction or replacement of harmful products. *Moderation* seems to be consistent with EO [environmental organizations'] rationales that privilege ecological sustainability, human health and wellbeing, and, sometimes, welfare for farmed animals and marine mammals. . . . EOs *only* [*tend*] *to protect the rights of individual animals if they* [*are*] *human, endangered, or charismatic megafauna* (particularly marine mammals or key predators), most of whom are not animals Americans typically eat. (Freeman, 2010, p. 271, emphasis mine)

Freeman's critiques seem particularly accurate given the many publications in journalistic outlets insist that an omnivorous diet is not only consistent with, but essential to, an environmentalist ethic. For instance, environmental law student Isabel Cowles published an article in the *Huffington Post* entitled "Real Environmentalists Eat Meat," insisting through naturalistic argumentation that

> it's true that eating animals is not necessary for the average adult where survival is concerned. But the plain truth is that no person, not Einstein, not Gandhi, not Safran Foer can change the fact that most people long to eat meat, and will eat meat. The argument to turn everyone into a vegetarian is creating a polarization that is not helping the effort to move away from factory farming. Therefore, the argument against meat could actually keep our food system in a rut. (Cowles, 2011, para. 9)

Rather, environmentalists ought to focus on creating *sustainable, local* food systems wherein "animals are slaughtered and butchered by locals who share a sense of pride and reverence for the work they do. I can think of no better cause to support" (para. 10). Her rationale for this statement included an argumentative trope common among environmental rhetors, condemning industrial agriculture while simultaneously promoting small-scale, organic operations:

> Perhaps those of us who have the time, energy and means to get twisted up about it should make a point to support local meat producers—believe me, good ones are out there—in hopes that they can take some of the market share away from factory farms and create an ever-widening circle of sustainable meat suppliers. (para. 11)

This stance is, obviously, condemned by staunch antispeciesists, who take statements like the above as manifestations of mere welfarism. The animal rights group Mercy for Animals published a counterpoint to articles likes Cowles's on its website, arguing:

> Lots of people call themselves environmentalists, and we don't doubt for a second that most really do care about the well-being of our planet. But the truth is, if you eat meat, you're contributing to one of the worst causes of environmental destruction. . . . There is no such thing as "sustainable" meat, and plant-based alternatives to meat, dairy, and eggs take a mere fraction of the resources to produce as their animal-based counterparts. . . . If you really want to save the world, don't just drive a Prius, cut meat out of your diet. (Loria, 2017, paras. 1, 11, 13)

The documentary *Cowspiracy* made similar arguments, so much so that PETA, an ardent supporter of ethical veganism, exclaimed "*Cowspiracy* makes a lot of the environmental groups' reps squirm in their seats . . . and calls on environmental organizations to walk the walk, not just talk the talk" (Moore, 2014, para. 8). While one could conceivably make the argument that vegetarianism and veganism are necessary to environmentalist practices *without* a distinctly antispeciesist ethic (e.g., preserving the environment for its aesthetics or so "future children" can enjoy it recreationally), these animal rights groups maintain that to purport to "care" about the more-than-human world while exploiting animals for pleasure and profit is always and already inconsistent with someone trying to be "green."

Hunting and diet are two of many moral disagreements between those who claim to practice environmentalism versus adherents to animal rights. There is hardly enough space in this chapter to cover all of them, but the aforementioned two exemplify a fundamental ideological disagreement between the rights of an individual animal subject and the rights of entire environmental systems. Earth jurisprudence, however, offers a particularly interesting stance on environmental ethics that, through the legal system, would afford legal rights and personhood to all members of the "environment," from the largest forest to the smallest ant. The rest of this chapter will argue that Earth jurisprudence is among the most ideologically radical modes of environmental law to emerge in U.S. American legal discourse. It has much to offer theorizations of animal rights, particularly in terms of expanding the larger moral community to its broadest possible extent. However, these lawyers' ultimately fall into the similar ideological divisions mentioned above, so much so that their tactics become pragmatically impossible and their strategies ideologically incoherent—and ultimately, reliant on notions of a welfarist vision of pristine nature.

A Deep Ecology of Law: Articulating Earth Jurisprudence

Long before the 2001 meeting by the Gaia Foundation, Professor Christopher Stone was conceptualizing a primordial vision of Earth jurisprudence. In 1972, Stone published a book entitled *Should Trees Have Standing?* In it, he argued that, yes, in fact, they should. At the time, his commentary was the subject of much derision. His assertion that "the world of the lawyer is peopled with inanimate right-holders: trusts, corporations, joint ventures, municipalities, Subchapter R partnerships, and nation-states" (Stone, 1972, p. 5) set a clear precedent for society to give "legal rights to forests, oceans, rivers and other so-called 'natural objects' in the environment—indeed, to the natural environment as a whole" (p. 9) seemed simply absurd. Nonetheless, Stone was steadfast in his claim that "natural objects" like trees and rivers should be able to seek redress on their own behalf. After all, "It is no answer to say that streams and forests cannot have standing because streams and forests cannot speak. Corporations cannot speak either; nor can states, estates, infants, incompetents, municipalities or universities. Lawyers speak for them" (p. 7). Based upon the legal precedents set by cases granting personhood and rights to nonindividuals, Stone advocated for a system in which "when a friend of a natural object perceives it to be endangered, he can apply to a court for the creation of a guardianship" (p. 10). This approach would "secure an effective voice" (p. 23) for the natural world in a much broader array of cases, even those where federally implicated public lands were not involved.

Stone further addressed the particularities of the rights of "natural objects," immediately dismissing the notion that legal rights for rivers might necessitate calling the water for jury duty or demanding that anyone throwing stones into it needed to be tried for assault. Indeed, "to say that the environment should have rights is not to say that it should have every right we can imagine, or even the same body of rights as human beings have" (p. 10). Natural objects, he reasoned, "can communicate their wants (needs) to us, and in ways that are not terribly ambiguous" (p. 24). Every particular object thus needed particular types of protection (rights) specific to their species, protections that "guardians" would be capable of defending in court:

> There is no reason not to allow the lake to prove damages to them as the *prima facie* measure of damages to it. By doing so, we in effect make the natural object, through its guardian, a jural entity competent to gather up these fragmented and otherwise unrepresented damage claims, and press them before the court even where, for legal or practical reasons, they are not going to be pressed by traditional class action plaintiffs. . . . All burdens of proof should reflect common experience; our experience in environmental matters has been a continual discovery that our acts have caused more long-range damage than we were able to appreciate at the outset. (Stone, 1972, pp. 28, 32)

The application of *particular* rights for *particular* beings protected through legal guardianship would, according to Stone, encourage judges to refer unabashedly to the legal rights of the environment as "socio-psychic" rather than "legal operational," which is to say preexisting in nature rather than invented in a court of law. Understanding nature's rights as inherent and encouraging the repetition of such discourse in the courtroom would encourage court rulings to "develop a viable body of law—in part simply through the availability and force of the expression" (p. 42).

Thomas Berry would continue where Stone left off. His 1988 book *The Dream of the Earth* and his 1999 book *The Great Work: Our Way into the Future* sought to outline a new understanding of humanity that translated recent work in ecology into narrative form in order to expand the moral community and compose an "ecocentric cosmology" of human ethics (De Lucia, 2013, p. 173). Berry's "new story," a "cosmological ecology" (Bell, 2003, p. 78), was based in a three-pronged conceptual framework that asserted a new understanding of the nature of the planet. These tenets were summarized by Bell (2003) as follows:

1. The Earth is a single integral community composed of multiple and diverse modes of being. It received its life from the universe, which propelled it into existence.

2. The Earth expresses itself in various species and components, and shares its life with its various species and components. These species and components enter into a relationship with one another to form a mutually enhancing web of life. Because they share life, the Earth and its species are not a collection of objects but are rather a communion of subjects.

3. As an integrated Earth community, the Earth provides an energizing and supportive environment for its species and components. It does this through its ecosystems—its life-support systems—and manifests this support most visibly in its bioregions. As a community of subjects, the Earth community has a capacity for self-propagation, self-nourishment, self-education, self-governance, self-healing, and self-fulfillment. (p. 79)

And, in line with Stone's past thesis, Berry asserted that nature had rights preexisting the courtroom. The environment is governed by the "Great Law," a set of "timeless as unified principles, or laws, 'manifest in the universe itself'" that ought to "serve as a standards against which human laws are to be assessed" (De Lucia, 2013, p. 174). Legal reform calls upon courtrooms to understand and recognize nature's *primordial rights* to flourish.

Since Stone's and Berry's seminal works, Earth jurisprudence has developed and expanded. Within all of the work is a shared commitment to securing "a healthy planet" by recognizing "the earth as the center of the moral community" (Koons, 2008, p. 265). Cormac Cullinan, for instance, who often names Earth jurisprudence "Wild Law" in his work, has engaged with critical legal frameworks upon suggesting that the legal order is necessarily constrained by the judicial systems' dominant master frames that are implicit in prevailing social structures (De Lucia, 2003). Despite the canon of Western law, which is dominated by property frameworks relegating the environment to "object" instead of "subject," Cullinan explained how

the time has come to rephrase Stone's famous question, "should trees have standing?" The key issue is not whether or not humans should magnanimously decide to grant legal standing to trees. The real question is whether or not we will be able to correct the distortions inherent in contemporary legal systems that prevent the law from seeing the reality that members of the Earth community already have what we humans term "rights." (Cullinan, 2008, p. 20)

Cullinan emphasized the primordial rights of the Earth, noting how "in the real down-to-Earth world, trees already have standing . . . our ancient elder cousins that have fed us, sheltered us, provided us with clean air to breathe, water, wood, fodder, and food, and delighted us with their beauty and majesty" (p. 20). As such, humanity ought to conceive of itself as "fellow earth citizens" morally obligated to take their place in the "community of life." Indeed, the present environmental crises are merely "the failure of our legal and political systems to recognize the rights of Nature." In addressing this failure, "the fate of our societies will, to a large extent, be determined by the speed with which we are able to develop and adopt an ecocentric approach to law and governance" (p. 12).

Earth jurisprudence articulates a systems approach to law and governance. In other words, it aims to pivot from "reductionist, mechanistic" approaches to human-nature relationships in favor of incorporating environmental science into moral, ethical, and legal thought (Cullinan, 2008). Koons (2008) argued that moral and legal responses to environmental degradation ought to align with scientific data, for instance, by using data on extinction rates to expand moral consideration to other species or, in the case of climate change, "requiring a reduction in emissions to the level that accords with the natural capacity of Earth to remove them from the atmosphere" (p. 283). "Science" is easily reclaimed in the name of Earth jurisprudence:

> Oddly, the "scientific method" which, in its infancy, consigned nature to the status of object, to be used mechanically, now may be seen as giving birth to theories which re-animate nature and bring it into the moral community. Scientific disciplines such as quantum physics, evolution biology, and ecology have unearthed data and offered insights that challenge a mechanistic, objectified view of nature. (Koons, 2008, p. 287)

In detailing the "primordial" rights of nature, Earth jurisprudence understands that such rights are best discovered through scientific inquiry wherein scientists main task is "discovering the governing principles of nature and the fundamental norms of human-Earth relationships," a task in which "Earth has the dual role of teacher and lawgiver" (De Lucia, 2013, p. 174). Modern science, then, grants Earth jurisprudence valuable insights from such areas as relativity theory, quantum physics, Heisenberg's uncertainty principle, living systems theory, cosmology, evolution, ecology, chaos, and complexity theories (Bell, 2003). In doing so, it utilizes ecological thought and contemporary scientific discoveries to articulate a healthy systems-based approach to legal philosophy and praxis.

Earth jurisprudence is, at its essence, a call for a "deep ecology of law" (Alexander, 2010, p. 131) that demands legal practices based in ecocentrism. A major paradigm shift from an anthropocentric to an ecocentric legal system is the only way to secure lasting and positive ecological change. As Bell (2003) aptly discerned, "trying to use a human jurisprudence system to recognize and protect the rights of other species is a bit like sending the fox to guard the chickens" (p. 70). Bell articulated that a lawyer's natural instinct to start environmental legal thought at a normative anthropocentric baseline and then try to expand it outward to embrace nonhuman beings is not, in fact, a valid starting point for four reasons: First, human jurisprudence is necessarily designed to recognize the preeminence of the human species. Second, Western jurisprudence is like Western science and politics in that its colonial roots make it reductionist in nature, responding solely to the needs of individuals (including corporations) and the individual ownership of property. Third, normative legal frameworks are adversarial, not communitarian, thus working against the delicate balance of ecology since the "victory" of one species corresponds to the "defeat" of all others. And finally, Western jurisprudence may be a *legal* system, but it is hardly a *justice* system—in other words, the courts are easily manipulated by the whims of the rich and powerful, thus rendering it unlikely that the voices of the poor, the disenfranchised, and the "voiceless" will be granted the justice they are due (Bell, 2003).

Ultimately, a legal framework based in deep ecology requires that judicial systems understand humanity not as the center of the moral universe, but as a "species in relationship" (Bell, 2003, p. 80). This relationality is due to humanity's place in a broader Earth community, one which requires something of Aldo Leopold's "land ethic" to prosper, one which "necessarily limits some of our individual rights in the best interests of the rights of the Earth community as a whole" (p. 89). The ultimate goal of Earth jurisprudence is to end the devastation of the planet for the shortsighted economic gains of an anthropocentric human species. After all,

unlike previous devastations of our planet which were natural, the present devastation is man-made. The Earth can no longer re-balance the environmental
destruction that we are causing. Only we can do that. . . . Our challenge as a human
species is to recognize the present situation and take steps to stop the damage,
heal the planet and ensure its future survival and development, and ours along
with it. (Bell, 2003, p. 81)

By acknowledging humanity as a species in relationship with a broader Earth
community, by decentering *Homo sapiens* as the center of the moral universe, by
rearticulating the rights of nature as primordial and always-already, and by nor-
malizing judicial discourse that articulates these novel values, Earth jurisprudence
combines deep ecology with legal philosophy in an attempt to save a dying planet.

Holistic Praxis: The Benefits of Earth Jurisprudence

The radical environmentalism of Earth jurisprudence offers certain ideological and
practical benefits that prototypical animal law and purportedly radical animal rights
law does not. Specifically, Earth jurisprudence expands the moral community to
its theoretical limits, including not only those beings with instrumental value to
humans, not only large megafauna with elite cognitive skills, and not only beings
that are sufficiently sentient, but also "natural objects" considered to be part of a
larger Earth community. In doing so, it integrates non-Western, Indigenous-style
thinking into its tenets; it offers a valid critique of capitalist property and economic
development laws; it expands the temporal jurisdiction of legal decisions; and
it offers a situated, relational understanding of "rights." For these reasons, Earth
jurisprudence ought to be considered an important member of the canon of animal
rights thinking, even though animals are, in the deep ecological sense, understood
as a part of a larger environment to be protected.

As I explained in depth in the previous section, the most apparent, most unique,
and perhaps most important difference between Earth jurisprudence and other
forms of animal law is that it does not end its focus at kingdom *Animalia*. Rather,
using the tenets of deep ecology, these legal minds "draw the moral line" somewhere
very different than people like Francione or Wise, conceiving of all members of
"nature" as worthy of legal consideration, personhood, and rights. In this way,
Earth jurisprudence pivots from some of the problems inherent in animal rights

law, wherein determining which species are worthy of personhood, and how that personhood ought to be measured, is a subject of heated debate. The line in question is drawn at "natural objects," those beings that are "of the earth," those beings that are "alive," even without a beating heart, and those beings that, should they vanish from the world, would wreak horrific consequences on the larger Earth community. It is in this expansion of the moral community that Earth jurisprudence opens its ontological foundations and its praxis to opportunities outside of traditional, liberal humanist modes of animal rights law.

Earth jurisprudence further differs from Western-style animal rights thought in that it attempts to counter colonial thinking through the integration of Indigenous epistemologies. Admittedly, these deep ecologists could do a better job of articulating *which* epistemologies they are drawing upon and from *whom* they owe their ideas instead of lumping "Indigenous" into a singular, essentialized group. As Black (2011) explained on jurisprudential writing writ large, "there is a dearth of books and articles *on* Indigenous jurisprudence and a glut of texts on Indigenous peoples *and* Western jurisprudence" (p. 9). Nonetheless, they certainly make more of an attempt than Francione and Wise to include non-Western voices into their legal praxis. While there is room for improvement, I argue that this attempt is at the very least worthy of acknowledgment. As Bell (2003) explains:

> We learn from indigenous jurisprudences that a change of heart in the offenders is essential for the survival of the group. The same is true when it comes to the survival of the planet, except that the change of heart must occur on an individual, local, national, and international level. (p. 86)

This "change of heart" ought to come from new understanding of humanity's relationship to nature, and these understandings can also come from "the Indigenous stream" and the "traditions of Aboriginal peoples" such as:

> the concepts of the sacredness of the land, the kinship relationship between humans and animals, the dependence of the human on the munificence of the earth, the spirituality of living in harmony with the land and its species, and an ethic of appropriate use of resources. (p. 78)

Or, as Indigenous legal expert Christine Black would put it, "the true source of the law is the land" (Black, 2011, p. 9).

Integrating "Indigenous" (and I acknowledge that is an overly broad term) epistemologies into environmental thought allows for animal rights thought to more easily integrate itself into other social justice arenas, such as environmental justice, thus better enabling the possibility of coalition-building and cross-species kinship (Koons, 2011). Settler-colonialist morality is, after all, a primary source of contemporary environmental thought and, consequently, mass extinction (Armstrong, 2002; Belcourt, 2014). While Earth jurisprudence must move away from allowing White rhetors to *translate* native voices into White people-speak, its tenets do more than a Francione- or Wise-style approach in considering decoloniality's importance to ending speciesist exploitation. For example, Bell's cosmological "rules" for Earth jurisprudence mirror Black's assertion that, in taking Indigenous jurisprudence seriously, the individual is situated "in a cosmology in which balance is paramount" and in which that balancing force "comprises legality, rather than the governance of men" (Black, 2011, p. 27). In doing so, the world "moves from being a space subordinate to the human desires to one of a superior informant, of the human's need for survival—a survival based upon the interpenetration of the knowledge found in the seen and unseen" (p. 27).

And, like Francione and Wise, Earth jurisprudence extensively critiques Western notions of property and the objectification of nonhuman life-forms for purely instrumental ends. Rather than emphasizing veganism or personhood status for megafauna as the solution to this abject economy, however, deep eco-logical legal minds emphasize larger notions of ecological "degrowth" (Alexander, 2010). Degrowth comprises "a radical critique of economic growth" in times when "an economy has grown so large that it exceeds the regenerative and absorptive capacities of Earth's ecosystems," thus calling upon lawmakers to initiate a process of "planned economic contraction" (Alexander, 2010, p. 132). In a "growth model" of capitalist economics, *efficiency* is the "governing ethical norm," but *sufficiency,* or "how much of the economic pie is enough," is rarely questioned (pp. 135–136). Degrowth, by contrast, argues that certain countries *over*con-sume and certain countries *under*consume, resulting in stark global economic inequalities. The solution is not to encourage underconsuming countries to embrace capitalism and consumerism, but rather to encourage the purportedly "developed" countries to *de*grow. Such a process results in humanity "repaying their ecological debts to the Wild" (p. 132) as well as forcing overconsumptive "first-world" countries to change their behaviors in the name of human and nonhuman equity.

What is more, Earth jurisprudence offers practical solutions for an ecologically sustainable, social justice–oriented degrowth model for society. These solutions are not only based in individual behavioral change but also broader a legal reconceptualization of property and economic prosperity. Alexander (2010) proposed multiple reformations, including but not limited to: articulating communitarian, ecologically responsible corporate structures such as worker cooperatives; regulating banks, corporations, and mass media in accordance with *the common good;* devising land rules that are *socially beneficial* as opposed to individually enriching; increasing taxes for the purposes of corrective redistribution, the channeling of money toward socially and environmentally oriented causes, and better funding of public services; and establishing "green" taxes to better price the "true cost" of commodities. This model demonstrates an economic shift toward *compassion* as opposed to *consumption.*

Ideas like Alexander's fight against neoliberal perspectives "naively entrenched in an outdated context and dangerously informed by an outdated set of values" (Alexander, 2010, p. 144). They also fly in the face of capitalist perspectives on private property which, as De Lucia (2013) suggests, is "inscribed within a tacit cultural reference" (p. 174) that must be changed before alternative imaginings of legal property relations can come into fruition. Indeed, according to Berry, human property rights are far from absolute. Rather, "property rights are simply a special relationship between a particular 'owner' and a particular piece of 'property' for the *benefit of both*" (Berry, 2001, para. 7, emphasis mine). Burdon (2010b) supplemented this argument, proposing that "the greatest consequence from recognizing the rights of nature is that it contextualizes and places limits on human property rights. It is implicit in this framework that property owners *look to nature as the standard or measure* for their action" (p. 85, emphasis mine). Of course, whether or not such communitarian, even socialist, ideas can possibly come into fruition in countries dominated by capitalist kleptocracy remains to be seen.

Another beneficial component of Earth jurisprudence is its ability to extend the temporal focus of the law beyond "what is just and fair *now*" to "what will be just and fair *later.*" Koons (2011) helpfully articulated this farsighted commitment as one of *intergenerational justice.* That is to say, "as a matter of justice and ethics, it is indefensible for our present generation to bequeath an impoverished world to future generations. . . . This measure places responsibility on the present generation to live sustainably for itself and future generations" (Koons, 2011, pp. 120–121). Intergenerational justice not only considers the yet-unborn as members of the moral community but also necessitates including the more-than-human world in democratic deliberations on the basis of "fundamental fairness" (p. 129). After all, "the consequences of industrial development will not be borne by the extracting companies that have produced rampant environmental degradation. Instead, the full consequences will be assumed by generations in the future of human beings, other-than-human species, and ecosystems" (p. 129). Although basing environmental legal ethics upon the needs and wants of future *humans,* intergenerational justice is hardly instrumental or anthropocentric. Rather, it acts as an intersectional interchange between environmental and social justice, wherein the lives of future humans are dependent upon the lives of present-day ecosystems, thus solidifying the innate and intersectional connection between human, animal, and environmental rights.

Speaking of rights, Earth jurisprudence is particularly useful in that it reconceptualizes "rights" not as abstract and universal, but as concrete and contextual. They are "role specific . . . species specific, and limited" (Berry, 2006, pp. 149–150). In other words, Earth jurisprudence accepts a *relational view of rights* (Nedelsky, 1993). This view of rights understands that rights need not be understood as the clashing interests of individuals, but rather as a construction of interdependence wherein "what rights do and have always done is construct relationships—of power, of responsibility, of trust and obligation" (Nedelsky, 1993, p. 13). Rights, according to Earth jurisprudence, are fundamentally primordial, relational, and wholly species-specific. Berry (2001) articulated three rights granted to each member of the Earth community that must be eternally respected: "The right to be, the right to habitat, and the right to fulfill its role in the ever-renewing process of the Earth community" (para. 5). These rights are not liberal humanist and individualistic, but ecocentric and communitarian: "These rights as presented here establish the *relationships* that the various components of the Earth have toward each other. The planet Earth is us a *single community* bound together with *interdependent* relationships" (para. 9, emphasis mine).

This is not to say that Earth jurisprudence denies the rights of the individual altogether. Rather, individuals are considered as part of larger webs, wherein an individual is part of a flock, which is part of a species, which is part of an ecosystem, and which is part of an Earth community. The result of this conceptualization is the ability to acknowledge that the realization of Berry's three primordial rights will not be accomplished in the same manner by every species: "Rivers have river rights. Birds have bird rights. Insects have insect rights. Humans have human rights.

Difference of rights is *qualitative* not *quantitative*. The rights of an insect would be no use to a tree or a fish" (Berry, 2001, para. 6, emphasis mine). To gauge the needs of a species, humanity need not look to itself as a model, but rather toward "the nature of Earth itself, which confers a sense of purpose and direction" (Bell, 2003, p. 74). Understanding rights in this way ought to prevent the "ranking" of one species' rights over another's. Per Cullinan (2008), "Does it really make sense to debate at length whether a brain or a heart is more important in a body? They are interdependent, and both are essential to the health of the whole body" (p. 15). Rights-as-relational thus fights against the dangerous notion that "one moral language must be found that adjudicates all questions of life" (Koons, 2008, p. 266).

Burdon (2010b) offered a specific example of relational rights in practice. He examined an Australian legal case in which the South Australian government passed a law recognizing the River Murray and Lower Lakes' primordial right to a healthy flow of water. Plainly, argued Burdon, these new legal rights necessarily conflicted with the rights of landowners and townspeople to obtain and use the water for their individual purposes. A prototypical, individualistic view of rights would, in this circumstance, "focus on the adversarial clash of interests and a legal hierarchy would be established to settle the dispute" (Burdon, 2010b, p. 85). A relational view of the case, by contrast, forced the court to consider the social and environmental contexts of both the human and nonhuman parties. The environmentally responsible legal outcome to this case necessarily encumbered the irrigators' and other human parties' rights to draw water because, in this instance, the needs of the whole outweighed the needs of the few. Water could only be drawn to the extent that the vital functions of the river could be maintained. The decision "does not remove the irrigators' rights; it *contextualizes its use* . . . and places *limits* on human property rights" (p. 85).

Ironically, Earth jurisprudence advances animal rights law specifically in that it expands its focus beyond kingdom *Animalia*. Grouping "animal rights" under a broader understanding of the "legal rights of nature," it fights against notions that animal law must favor only those select species deemed valuable by particular humans in a particular moment. Turning primordial Earth rights into species-specific legal rights is a difficult task, but an ultimately beneficial one in which:

> the existence of a legal right means that the holder is entitled to call upon the courts, and ultimately the power of the state, to enforce that right in relation to others. In other words, rights are used as a means of defining those aspects of the

relationships between members of the community that the community considers important enough to enforce where necessary. (Cullinan, 2008, pp. 15–16)

By refusing anthropocentrism and embracing ecocentrism, deep ecological thinking complements legal theories and praxis by conceiving of the law as a reflection of Earth systems' natural processes. Earth jurisprudence is particularly suited to animal rights thinking in that it furthers Francione's and Wise's critiques of animals-as-property by opening up conversations about Western property doctrine writ large. It does away with the troubling extension of human rights to animals deemed sufficiently similar to human beings on the basis that, while each beings' primordial rights are the same, the enactment and protections of those rights are species-specific and contextual. "Wild" thinking not only embraces human, animal, and "natural object" conflicts as they occur in the present but also considers the needs of future unborn beings, conceiving of the law as necessarily intergenerational. And, in doing so, Earth jurisprudence opens up animal-oriented justice to broader arenas of social justice, both by the inclusion of Indigenous and ecocentric ontologies as well as an engagement with environmental justice.

At Once Everything and Nothing: Complicating Earth Jurisprudence

For all the good that a broad, morally inclusive, and morally contextual Earth jurisprudence brings to conceptualizations of animal rights law, it is hardly a panacea to speciesism. Rather, the deep ecological holism of Earth jurisprudence brings with it a series of vagaries and moral ambivalences that, when left uninterrogated, relegate "Wild" thought to, at best, the realm of the fanciful and ambivalent. In this section, I articulate the many issues with Earth jurisprudence, particularly as they apply to the lives of kingdom *Animalia* and, subsequently, to the pursuit of total liberation. Among these pernicious matters is the near-impossible attempt to appropriate individualist Enlightenment-oriented applications of rights for communitarian ends in the *actual*, not *ideal*, American legal sphere; the incoherent conceptualization of "nature" that pivots from discussing domestication; and, perhaps most significantly, the "holistic" (and morally ambivalent) utilitarianism of legal theorizations based in notions of nature as pristine.

The first issue with Earth jurisprudence is, ironically, one if its best surface features: the turn to ecocentric communitarianism. The problem arises not in the concept itself, but in its application in Western legal settings—specifically, in the courtroom. Animal and broader environmental law already face the massive challenge of an anthropocentric legal system. Earth jurisprudence adds a second layer of difficulty by trying to argue for the rights of "systems" in arenas specifically designed to account for the rights of singular entities. Granting legal personhood to humans, animals, and natural objects could easily dismantle the conceptual importance of "rights" at all, particularly as a legal "trump card" used to secure protection from parties seeking to cause harm to others. As De Lucia (2013) warned:

> The over-proliferation of subjective rights and of legal subjects that may result from a rights-of-nature approach carries the risk of a devalorization of both rights and rights-subjects, to the extent that they may either remain largely symbolic in an overcrowded legal space, or may remain trapped in a largely adversarial and contingent framework, disjointed from any comprehensive idea of a common good. (p. 187)

In other words, if *everyone* has rights, then in a sense *no one* has rights. The current structure of the U.S. American courtroom is simply not equipped to deal with a world in which nearly everything and everyone must be granted legal protections that are naturally unique depending on the subject. Deep ecologists often critique approaches like Francione's or Wise's for focusing too much on the individual at the expense of the community, but, when involved in a court case, this critique is easily turned on its head. In a court of law, an adversarial environment with competing claims, decentering the individual means losing the case. Unless and until courtrooms dramatically reform themselves and their most basic practices, Earth jurisprudence has little chance of large-scale success. Of course, one rebuttal might be that using the master's tools to destroy the master's house is inherently offensive. However, if Earth jurisprudence intends to achieve personhood through the courts, which it most clearly does, then its attempt to fit peaceful communitarianism into an adversarial system is in many ways a fruitless attempt to fit a square peg into a round hole. Philosophically, the ideas are wonderful. Tactically, they are fanciful.

Legal rights are claims that place a certain number of duties on *individuals*. They entail a series of *bilateral* jural relations. Earth jurisprudence and its goal to decenter the individual will necessarily come into conflict with this premise. Indeed, "the application of this concept to nature is potentially problematic. Indeed, it asks us to fragment an integrated system and impose an artificial system of competing interests" (Burdon, 2010b, p. 83). Alongside the rhetorical construction of nature's "interests," Earth jurisprudence must cope with the legal system's insistence that a legal subject must recognize the rights of others. While any form of animal law will cope with this issue, as the ability of animals to be "moral" is consistently disputed, Earth jurisprudence's extended moral community compounds the issue. As Burdon (2011) noted, "Even if a landslide kills human beings, it does not violate human rights. The mountain is not guilty of reprehensible behavior and one cannot bring it to be shamed in a court of law" (p. 6). Therefore, restricting the rights of nature to a juridical model inevitably sets it up to fail. The only possible way to reconcile nature's legal rights in this respect is to categorize them as "claim rights"—claims that correlate to the duties of others and thus "generate reasons for action for people who are in a position to help in the promoting or safeguarding of the underlying right" (p. 7). Relying solely upon the kindness of others to act as guardians is likely not enough to defend the rights of nature, for without substantial changes of heart outside the courtroom, those "others" will inevitably be in a moral minority.

There are, of course, potential solutions to this problem. In line with Francione's vision of vegan abolitionism, many adherents to Earth jurisprudence advocate for simultaneous top-down *and* bottom-up approaches to environmental liberation. These approaches include what Burdon (2011) dubbed the "recognition route," wherein there is not necessarily legislative or institutional enforcement of environmental behaviors but an acknowledgement of the necessity of nature's rights. An example of this would be the Universal Declaration of Mother Earth Rights, which could be conceived of as the environmental version of the UN Declaration of Human Rights. However, as we know well, under current systems of transnational economics, holding the largest polluters accountable for their actions, and even forcing them to *acknowledge* their actions, is often impossible. Recent evidence includes the Trump Administration's decision to leave the Paris Agreement, leaving it as the only nation in the world denying its complicity in climate change while simultaneously contributing to it more than almost any other nation on the planet. Burdon (2011) also noted the potential for "advocacy" in securing the rights of nature, particularly in the form of nongovernmental organizations and their capacity to use "organized agitation" to urge compliance with basic claims about Earth rights (p. 10). But again, the advocacy route works only insofar as the courtroom is willing to accept the advocates as legitimate spokespersons. And, in a world where massive corporations and their monetary billions consistently emerge victorious in legal cases and the environmental advocates are named ecoterrorists, we must seriously question the ability of advocates to maintain the rights of the environment. The question of "who speaks" for nature is always an important one, but in this case, it could potentially dismantle the whole field of Earth jurisprudence. In this way, Earth jurisprudence's understanding of a bottom-up approach to liberation does not seem to make up for its top-down incoherence.

Again, the problems of reciprocal justice, recognition, and advocacy in fights for animal rights are not restricted to Earth jurisprudence. However, this philosophy's extraordinarily broad definition of the moral community makes progress in traditional courtroom settings much more difficult than does a Francione or Wise approach to animal rights. And, without a solid case in a court of law, without a chance to establish legal precedents and legal personhood inscribed in court documents, recognition and advocacy do little to advance legal rights of the environment. Communitarianism and holism are fantastic notions, to be sure, but are quite incoherent in Western courts of law. This, combined with the problem of anthropocentrism as the legal norm, make Earth jurisprudence perhaps even more inconceivable than animal rights litigation such as that of Wise's NhRP.

A second issue with Earth jurisprudence, again ironically, is its conceptualization of "nature" in and of itself. Nature has never existed—at least, not in the pristine and pure state rhetorically constructed to further environmentalist causes (Cronon, 1996; DeLuca & Demo, 2000). In line with theories of deep ecology, environmental communication, ecofeminism, and multiple other schools of critical environmental thought, Earth jurisprudence is explicitly critical of a nature/culture binary that has allowed humanity to conceive of itself as "separate" from the more-than-human world. However, in delegitimizing the supposed superiority of the "culture" section of the binary, Earth jurisprudence falls into an all-too-familiar pattern among staunch, unflinching ecocentrists: elevating "nature" to such an extent that it actually *reifies* the binary under critique, "maintaining a one-sided 'centrism' at either pole of an oppositional anthropocentric-ecocentric binary" (DeLucia, 2013, p. 189). Within this binary is an assumed "eco" that can be centered, a clearly "nonhuman" that must be protected at all costs. And, when such a conceptualization proliferates, it risks emphasizing, not de-emphasizing, the notion that humanity and nature are two parties at odds with one another, not interspersed communities in need of cooperation. At its philosophical extreme, the only difference between anthropocentrism and ecocentrism is in the latter's misanthropy. Nature, to be considered natural, must be in some way "pristine" (Cronon, 1996)—awe-inspiring, aesthetically pleasing Not-Man, untouched by Man, separate from the unfortunate taint of industrialization.

While it is inaccurate to contend that all of Earth jurisprudence is fundamentally binary and misanthropic, it *is* important to point out the field's strategic rhetorical pivots from dealing with issues wherein living beings do not fit easily into "nature" or "culture"—in other words, those liminal domestic beings denounced by Francione for being neither human nor animal, for being too tainted by human touch to be pristine and deserving of protection. For example, essays on Earth jurisprudence consistently gloss over the plight of domestic animals, seemingly ambivalent as to where they might "fit" in a larger Earth community. As White (2011) has pointed out, these theorists and practitioners have a significant "lack of judicial clarity about whether farm animals can be [a] subject of 'environmental protection'" (slide 10). To date, one of the only scholars to grapple *in depth* with animal agriculture's role in Earth jurisprudence occurred at the 2011 Wild Law Conference, where Melissa Hamblin argued that an Earth jurisprudence approach would involve a reframing of regulations to include smaller operations, improved animal welfare standards, better consumer education, and a focus on the systemic environmental impacts of industrialized animal agriculture. The goal in this scenario would be to improve humans' relationships with other members of the Earth community. However, as Wright (2013) cogently critiqued, Hamblin makes zero mention of why, exactly, it is that Earth jurisprudence would not require the abolition of the killing of animals for meat if, in fact, every member of the Earth community has a primordial "right to be." Clearly, for all the rights afforded to rivers and rocks and other "natural objects," those beings which are for all intents and purposes *subjects* are not being given their due—at least according to the very tenets of Berry and Stone, who staunchly articulated every member of the Earth community's right to live fully.

Could it be that in this scenario, Earth jurisprudence has shoved domesticated animals from the realm of "nature" into the realm of human "culture"? Are cows, pigs, and sheep no longer "natural objects" in need of protection because they are, in a way, a product of capitalist culture? Or are domesticated animals simply so difficult to fit into a nature/culture binary of natural and unnatural objects that Earth jurisprudence would prefer not to deal with them at all? Perhaps it is all of these, or perhaps something more. Ultimately, however, an ideological rhetorical criticism deems rhetorical absences and silences to be just as important as presences and pronouncements (Cloud, 1999; McKerrow, 1989). In dealing with issues of meat consumption, authors like Cullinan often address "low-hanging fruit" legal cases instead of tackling morally ambiguous questions of killing. Wright (2013) mocked one of Cullinan's examples as "so extreme as to be almost comical" (p. 12), referring to one of Francione's dog-in-a-lifeboat circumstances in which a bushman has no option but to kill a zebra for its meat. The binary notion of a rural African bushman versus a colonial European caricature of a hunter who is "opportunistic and wasteful" (p. 12) is far from a realistic example of the choices needing to be made in countries where domesticated animal slaughter is the norm, but not necessarily the necessity. Or, in ecofeminist terms, the few times the Earth jurisprudence attempts to deal with domesticity invoke moral contextualism in decidedly shallow, uncomplicated ways.

Hamblin, like other members of the Earth jurisprudence camp, simply cannot (or will not) articulate whether "an animal's role in the Earth system includes a role as a resource for humans" (Wright, 2013, p. 14). To explore such an issue would risk these staunch ecocentrists venturing back into the other side of the anthropo-centric/ecocentric binary expressed above—after all, a Francione-like argument *could* be made that domesticated species are so intimately intertwined with human processes that their (un)natural state is always and already in subservience to human needs. Under such understandings of domesticity, Earth jurisprudence could argue that "it is now the [role] of these animals to provide the products they have been bred for: domesticated animals would not be in existence but for human use and would serve no function if transferred to their original habitats" (Wright, 2013, p. 13). But this assertion is laden with moral ambivalences, allowing for a fallacious reasoning that assumes that long-term exploitation of Others necessitates their continued exploitation so as to avoid confusion for the exploited. As Wright (2013) indicated, "although humans have *changed* the ability of domesticated animals in such a way as to prevent them from existing in the wild, the rights accorded to these animals should arguably be derived from their role *pre-human intervention*" (p. 13, emphasis mine). Here again is a moral ambivalence, wherein the primordial rights of the more-than-human world can only be articulated through humanity's perceived separation from abstract "nature."

Is domestication unnatural? Are primordial rights nullified upon human contamination? Perhaps it is this desire to avoid accusations of moral ambiguity that have led Earth jurisprudence adherents to have an extraordinarily vague, if not defective, conceptualization of animality. However, Earth jurisprudence does itself no favors by absenting from its writing such difficult issues purely because "it is difficult to determine what the natural function of domestic animals is" (p. 13).

If indeed this school of thought seeks to argue that domestic livestock should be killed for meat, eggs, and dairy, but should be killed in a humane manner, then it is very difficult for these practitioners to argue, as some do, that the field is not merely "welfarism gone wild" (Bekoff, 2013). I wholly agree with Wright (2013) that "this 'right to be' proposed by Earth jurisprudence is not the same as the absolute right to life sought for animals by animal lawyers" (p. 12). Under this system, whether stated explicitly or not, "animals can be exploited so long as the exploitation is conducted as a part of an ecologically sustainable relationship" (p. 12). How convenient that the ones who would ultimately be left in charge of determining such sustainability would be the hunters and the butchers, not the hunted and the butchered!

The moral ambivalence regarding domesticated livestock only furthers the issues of assuming that each member of the Earth community has a specific set of "rights" to be discovered and legally protected. While I do not deny that conceiving of rights as both primordial *and* contextual is a useful (and perhaps essential) insight, Earth jurisprudence says little of value about *who* has the moral authority to determine *which* rights must be protected for each individual species and *how* those rights might be reconciled when they come into conflict with one another in arenas not restricted to "greedy companies" versus "vulnerable ecosystems." Indeed, by casting rights as something to be discovered for each species, Earth jurisprudence puts its entire theoretical system at risk by giving too much power to purportedly unbiased human "authorities" tasked with determining what "the greater good" would mean in competing conflicts of interest.

If indeed "our moral response must match the scientific data that has been presented" (Koons, 2008, p. 283), then Earth jurisprudence would have little choice but to turn to scientific institutions to determine who needs what, and how to meet those needs. While on the surface this seems to be a better solution (particularly since a zoologist would conceivably have more knowledge of a zebra's needs than, say, a politician), we should be wary of granting ultimate moral authority to institutions consistently funded by outside sources with vested interests in maintaining an agricultural status quo. Furthermore, a quick glance at the history of Western science should remind deep ecologists that the "cold rationality" of scientific insight does not have a reputation for acting in the best interest of the more-than-human world, particularly with regard to lab animals or other situations where specifically human-on-animal interactions must be dealt with. Tasking any set of humans, restricted as they are by the ideologies of the institutions funding them and the paternalistic, anthropocentric models that formed the institutions in the first place, is a risky business. A major risk of Earth jurisprudence, then, is that the best-funded scientists would present the best-funded research to the best-funded lawyers, who would, only in an ideal world, present legal arguments in the animals' best interest. Here we must turn back to Francione's cogent warning that, when already objectified animals are placed into legal conflict with humans, the humans will always have the legal advantage (Francione, 1995). Unless and until these deep ecologists can convince the entirety of biology and academia that animal testing is not inherently right, that dairy science might be an unethical field in its entirety, or that accepting grants from corporate interests for the sake of tenure is a dangerous way to produce public knowledge, then Earth jurisprudence's goal of retooling scientific insight for the identification of rights for animals is questionable at best.

But let us pretend that deep ecologists *do* have a plan for recruiting morally good biologists, that scientific institutions *are* fundamentally good, and that animals *can* be protected once experts identify their species' individuated rights. This still does not sort out the problem of dealing with realistic, nonsimplistic interspecies conflicts. What exactly does Earth jurisprudence demand that conservationists do with "invasive" species? Is the "greater good" of a larger ecosystem contingent upon exterminating them, thus depriving them of their right to be? And even if such an argument could be justified, why should an invasive species like a wild boar be killed for encroaching upon territory that does not "belong" to it when, by that logic, *Homo sapiens* should have been exterminated a long, long time ago? Indeed, from an Indigenous American perspective, are not European colonizers the more pernicious invasive species that the Western hemisphere has ever seen? Was it not the invasive hunters who nearly exterminated native plants, animals, and peoples? Who destroyed native lands to make room for intensive agriculture? Who introduced many of these "invasive" species to foreign lands in the first place? To argue that the "greater good" must be achieved through some level of death takes on a distinctly anthropocentric tenor when Earth jurisprudence ignores humanity's own reputation as an invasive species. Thus, if Earth jurisprudence truly intends to use Indigenous perspectives in its praxis as opposed to providing a shallow lip service, it must embrace decoloniality in a more complicated manner, one best described by Katherine McKittrick, the colonization of the Americas was both "genocidal *and* ecocidal," both "interhuman *and* environmental" (McKittrick, 2006, p. 135, emphasis mine). Thus, as Billy-Ray Belcourt suggested, critical animal scholars such as vegan ecofeminists cannot talk about animal liberation "without naming settler colonialism and White supremacy as political mechanisms that require the simultaneous exploitation or destruction of animal and Indigenous bodies" (Belcourt, 2014, p. 3).

Now let us pretend that some deep ecologist *does* account for humanity's colonial reputation. Here comes an even more difficult question: how can we do the actual *math* that determines what legal decision would create the greatest good for the benefit of the Earth community? Apparently economic analysis is moot, so it appears that this task is once again left to scientists. But how exactly is "good" to be quantified when dealing with transcendental values? In this scenario, we see how Earth jurisprudence, for all its talk of primordial rights and the value of love and care, will inevitably need to turn to a strictly utilitarian ethic to make any legal decisions. While there is nothing inherently wrong with using cost/benefit analyses and pro/con lists to make moral and legal decisions, had Earth jurisprudence seriously engaged with the works of Peter Singer and his critics, they would understand why advocating for beings' rights through utilitarianism is a cold endeavor (see this book's introduction).

However, as animal rights practitioners such as Wise and Francione have complained, utilitarianism is hardly sufficient in its efforts to combat mere welfarism. Koons (2008) and other deep ecological thinkers have also critiqued the utilitarianism of the status quo, wherein "the utilitarian idea of the good has come to be identified with human welfare" (p. 279). According to Earth jurisprudence, "utilitarianism must be transformed. As a predicate, those endorsing utilitarian ends should consider broadening their sights to consider *the greatest good of the greatest number for the greatest length of time*" (p. 278, emphasis in original). Herein lies a mathematical impossibility in the task of calculating the impact of "forever" on an unidentifiable number of human, animal, plant, river subjects, etc., each with their own definition of "good." Koons has fallen into a common trap of utilitarian logic: not accounting for the vast number of parties potentially implicated in seemingly easy decisions regarding human and more-than-human conflict that, when taken into consideration, fall outside the confines of materialist mathematics. Note the complicatedness of legally battling industrialized agricultural operations identified by Greta Gaard and Raymond Frey:

> This list includes negative consequences that would befall those directly involved in the raising and killing of animals, such as farmers and slaughtering operations, those involved indirectly in the food business, such as food retailers, those involved in the dairy industry, those involved in various industries such as fast-food restaurants,

the pet food industry, the pharmaceutical industry, and the leather goods and wool industries, those involved in agricultural and veterinary research incidental to agriculture, those involved in publishing books about animal agriculture, and those involved in advertising the products of animal agriculture, and so forth. (Gaard, 2002, p. 6)

In *theory,* Earth jurisprudence would care little for the economic pitfalls of unraveling industrialized agriculture. In practice, however, it would be difficult to prove in a court of law, where all current precedent points to the necessary protection human rights to "liberty," that the deaths of tens of billions of cows per year would outweigh the economic pitfalls of *not* exploiting animals. Unless and until Earth jurisprudence admits that humanity, through its own invasiveness, ought to totally restructure its own self-image such that the loss of jobs, material comfort, and food sources is a potentially acceptable outcome of legislation and judicial decisions (unlikely given that legislators and judges are elected by complicit exploiters), then animals would not seem to secure any benefit from Earth jurisprudence's "holistic" utilitarianism. An inability to predict the future, to calculate the potential alternative farming operations that might result from a vegan lifestyle, from lab-based meat, from synthetic human flesh made for pharmaceutical testing, once again demonstrates how, in human-on-animal, and human-on-*domestic*-animal conflicts in particular, Earth jurisprudence cannot possibly live up to its own expectations.

Earth jurisprudence is a radical strand of environmental legal thought that, in its theory and praxis, suggests that kingdom *Animalia* ought to be granted legal rights and legal guardianship. In one sense, it fits easily into the canon of animal rights law through its extensive critique of legal anthropocentrism, of oppressive property law, and of "rights" as legal trump cards exclusive to the divinely blessed human species. At the same time, it offers an intriguing alternative to "prototypical" animal rights law that focuses exclusively on animal bodies, often at the expense of broader ecological issues, that excludes non-Western thought and human-oriented social justice issues, and that perceives rights as something to be extended to animals but not necessarily reconceptualized in favor of a relational, nonadversarial form of justice. This book therefore argues that environmental legal thought in the form of Earth jurisprudence is not only a type of animal right law but also a theoretically superior genre of it in many ways, given its staunch critique of prototypical liberal humanist ideologies.

Nonetheless, for all the benefits of integrating animal-exclusive legal theories and praxis with an ecological, holistic "Wild" orientation, legal theorists and practitioners must be mindful of the pitfalls of Earth jurisprudence. For those primarily interested in the rights of kingdom *Animalia,* and even for those more interested in ecological sustainability as a whole, Earth jurisprudence carries with it theoretical contradictions and moral ambivalences regarding individual versus community rights, the rhetorical construction of nature as pristine, and the mathematic/moral improbabilities of holistic utilitarianism. This book does not argue that environmentalist thought and animal rights praxis are incompatible. However, just as Wise's and Francione's conceptualizations of animal rights ultimately risk harming the beings they claim to want to protect, so too does Earth jurisprudence risk backfiring upon itself in efforts to promote animal personhood and rights. While Earth jurisprudence is perhaps the *closest* of this book's case studies to adhering to an ecofeminist legal theory, it ultimately misses the mark. The following chapter will aim to articulate how a critical vegan rhetoric, as both a theory and a praxis, offers a way to combine Wise, Francione, Earth jurisprudence, and other philosophies, strategies, and tactics of animal rights that, when filtered through an ecofeminist legal framework, offer a more fruitful path toward animal rights and, subsequently, total liberation.

Envisioning a Critical Vegan Rhetoric

Oppression is intersectional, but all oppressions are not identical in design or impact. . . . The goal of diversity in claimsmaking and institution-building is not to erase difference in a "melting pot," but rather to respectfully acknowledge differences in access, interests, and needs.

—Corey Wrenn, "Trump Veganism: A Political Survey of
American Vegans in the Era of Identity Politics"

This book summarized, analyzed, criticized, and reconceptualized prevailing rhetorics of U.S. American animal rights law. Specifically, it attempted to reframe "the law" from its legal positivist, liberal humanist, hyper-rationalist roots toward a critical, contextual, relational, empathetic, pragmatic, and ultimately *ecofeminist* understanding of legality, rights, and justice. It did so by critiquing the welfarist anticruelty paradigm, the classical rights paradigm, and the green ecological paradigms of animal rights through the theoretical lens of ecofeminist legal theory and a methodology of ideological rhetorical criticism.

An ideological rhetorical critique reveals how prototypical discourses of animal law too often rely upon highly patriarchal, logocentric, and ultimately colonial conceptualizations of what constitutes a "who" in a moral community, and subsequently which "who" ought to receive what rights in legal settings. While animal rights practitioners such as Steven Wise and Gary Francione rightly and vehemently argue against mere "welfarist" rhetorics of animal law and excoriate speciesist discourses of human exceptionalism, they are not immune from the far-reaching, longstanding dominant ideologies that have allowed for legal and extralegal domination of animals (and those humans deemed closer to animal) vis-à-vis Western colonial ontologies. And, while alternative discourses such as Earth jurisprudence may seemingly "decolonize" animal law by drawing upon Indigenous knowledges, moral contextualism, and ecocentric ideologies, this mode of radical environmentalism's de-emphasis of the "individual" in favor of the "system" actually reifies notions of a "pristine" wilderness that does little to account for a world of complex moral conundrums that lie in the realm of the liminal.

To summarize, all three of my case studies offered a unique stance on how to procure animal liberation in the form of legal rights for species other than the *Homo sapiens*. However, a rhetorical ideological criticism of Wise, Francione, and Earth jurisprudence's rhetorics demonstrates that without a solid grounding in the principles of ecofeminist legal theory, all three ultimately fall short in the pursuit of total liberation. It further reveals animal liberationists' need for a different orientation toward liberationist rhetoric to measure the strategic and tactical merits of their legal discourses.

Steven Wise and the Nonhuman Rights Project demonstrate one contemporary attempt to revolutionize the status of animals in the U.S. American legal system. Specifically, Wise and his organization litigate on behalf of more-than-human clients facing unjust imprisonment. Through writs of habeas corpus and other like statutes, the NhRP seeks to attain "legal personhood" for animals, one client at a time, to abolish the legal "thinghood" and thus the legal disenfranchisement maintained through the chattel status of animals. Through litigating highly mediated cases and appealing court decisions time and time again, Wise continually reminds the justice-minded of the distinct similarities that his clients have to *Homo sapiens* litigants, thus rhetorically breaking the pernicious human/animal binary for Tommy, Kiko, and other NhRP clients. However, Wise's particular rhetorics of personhood are not as critical as they need (and claim) to be. Rather, his and the NhRP's emphases on "practical autonomy" and cognitive prowess as the bases for a being's inclusion in a larger moral community ultimately invoke a troublesome principle of "sufficient similarity," wherein humanity actually *reclaims* its place atop the "Great Chain of Being" that Wise claims to fight against. While a legal victory for Tommy, Kiko, and the NhRP's other clients would be liberating for the particular individuals in court that day, I argue that Wise's rhetoric would likely set a legal precedent more *damaging* to animal liberation than not—a precedent wherein great apes, cetaceans, and elephants matter, but only via their relationship to a liberal humanist understanding of rationality. Thus, not only do Wise's tactics morph into anthropocentrism and risk leaving millions of "insufficiently similar" species unprotected, his legal strategy consistently veers between rhetorics of animal welfarism and animal rights.

Gary Francione's vegan abolitionist stance is more fruitful than Wise's orientation in that it simultaneously advocates for top-down judicial decisions to abolish animals' property status and bottom-up grassroots *praxis* in the form of outreach, education, and a vegan lifestyle. Furthermore, in contrast to Wise's hyper-humanist insistence that cognitive capabilities ought to be considered the most important asset for being granted personhood, and thus consideration in a larger moral and legal community, Francione roots his animal ethics in *sentience,* a broad mode of "being" that, if set into legal precedent, would encompass far more beings than would the NhRP. His is an ethic based firmly in the camp of animal rights as opposed to mere welfarism, as emphasized in Francione's disavowal of even the most infamous vegan theorists, such as Peter Singer, for not going "far enough" in pursuing larger structural changes. However, for all Francione's radicalness in comparison to men like Wise, he continually invokes pernicious nature/culture, human/animal binaries that simultaneously essentialize the category of "human" and disavow any and all liminal animal bodies existing in states of binary "in-betweenness" vis-à-vis the act of domestication. I therefore argue that for all the theoretical and practical benefits of a vegan abolitionist stance in comparison to "mere welfarism," Francione's purported radicalness merely reifies colonial, patriarchal, Whiteness-bound rhetorics at the nexus of speciesism, racism, and ableism. His rhetorical strategies and tactics align, but they are neither particularly radical nor in accordance with an ethic of total liberation.

Earth jurisprudence is a radical strand of environmental legal thought that, in its theory and praxis, suggests that kingdom *Animalia* ought to be granted legal rights and legal guardianship. In one sense, it fits easily into the canon of animal rights law through its extensive critique of legal anthropocentrism, of oppressive property law, and of "rights" as legal trump cards exclusive to some divinely blessed human species. At the same time, it offers an intriguing alternative to "prototypical" animal rights law that vexingly focuses exclusively on animal bodies, often at the expense of broader ecological issues, excludes non-Western thought and human-oriented social justice issues, and perceives rights as something to be extended to animals, but not necessarily reconceptualized in favor of a relational, nonadversarial form of justice. For all the benefits of integrating animal-exclusive legal theories and praxis with an ecological, holistic "Wild" orientation, legal theorists and practitioners must be mindful of the pitfalls of Earth jurisprudence. For those primarily interested in the rights of kingdom *Animalia,* and even for those more interested in ecological sustainability as a whole, Earth jurisprudence carries with it theoretical contradictions and moral ambivalences regarding individual versus community rights, the rhetorical construction of nature, and the mathematic and moral improbabilities of holistic utilitarianism. While its rhetorical strategies are perhaps the most "radical" out there, they contain pernicious incoherence regarding more "difficult" legal scenarios—those without a clear, mustache-twirling corporate villain. Additionally, tactical applications of Earth jurisprudence have little pragmatic basis in a U.S. American legal system.

So what can we ultimately conclude by setting these schools of animal rights law side by side? What, besides critiquing the imperfections of the NhRP, vegan abolitionism, and Earth jurisprudence, is the benefit of a rhetorical ideological critique of these legal doctrines? I argue that deconstructing the rhetorics of these legal movements through the lens of ecofeminist legal theory not only provides insight into the danger of adopting one of these doctrines unquestioningly but also demonstrates the good that might come from obligating these disparate schools of environmental, moral, and legal thought to work together to form new ideas and praxes. In many ways, the rhetorical "solution" I will now articulate is not so much a set of ultimatums, but rather a series of working hypotheses open to revision by multiple actors in different social spheres. It is ultimately an example of ideological rhetorical criticism's exhortation to prescriptively meld theory and praxis.

In line with ecofeminism's disdain for moral universalisms, I do not articulate the "ultimate Truth" or "purest Morality," but rather what I see as the "purest impurity" or "most perfect imperfection" in a messy world composed of infinitely diverse, disparate bodies hindered by material inequalities. Having dissected these case studies of animal rights law, I propose an alternative line of thinking and doing that attempts to dialectically connect theories of human and animal justice, environmentalism and animal rights, individualism and communitarianism, and humanism and posthumanism. An impossible task? Perhaps. Nonetheless, I argue

that these case studies have exemplified the issues that come with strict adherence
to unflinching moral cliquishness, to strict agendas set forth by rhetors, to derision
of self-reflexivity and intermovement critique, thus necessitating a considerably
"messier" dialectic approach to more-than-human (and at the same time, human)
rights. The application of ecofeminist legal theory and of ideological rhetorical
criticism ultimately leads me to a rhetorical approach to animal rights law called
critical vegan rhetoric.

Critical Vegan Rhetoric: Engaging Diverse Legal Subjectivities

To reiterate, my ecofeminist legal framework draws from a series of diverse disciplines, including feminist legal studies, ecofeminism, critical animal studies,
and rhetorical criticism. However, its application in the "real world" requires
engaging diverse voices inside *and* outside of the academy, necessitating a shift
from an animal *Whites* movement (Wise, 2005)—that is to say, a liberal humanist,
essentialist, individualistic, consumerist, postracial, patriarchal, heteronormative,
ableist, class-exclusive, and ultimately *species-essentialist* orientation to rights—
toward a decolonial and intersectional animal rights ethic. Engaging with diverse
subjectivities is not merely a matter of "expanding" animal rights demographics
or recruiting "token" minority spokespersons. Rather, it is a matter of articulating
animal rights and vegan ethics in a way that rhetorically decenters hegemonic
ideologies and allows for a more complex view of how "humans" and "animals"
(and yes, even "natural objects") interact and "intra-act" (Barad, 2010) through
complex systems of power. Eliminating those "monocultures of the mind" (Shiva,
1993) that normalize liberal humanist rights orientations as the "one way" to
properly "do" animal ethics is essential to creating an environment suited to total
liberation—noting, of course, that such liberation requires the simultaneous
pursuit of human and more-than-human rights, even when such pursuits are not
apparently in relation to one another.

In much the same way that "Whitestream feminism" (Grande, 2003) has been
critiqued and feminist thought rehabilitated by decolonial and women-of-color
feminisms, animal liberation must shed its colonial presumptions and instead argue
in favor of critical and definitively *radical* orientations to the pursuit of justice. This
does not mean that notions of the "individual," of "freedom," or of "rights" have no
place in this rhetorical framework. Decolonizing animal rights rhetorics necessitates

a *complication* of those terms, defamilarizing and subsequently resituating such ideographs within broader historical systems of power relations stemming from the rise of the West as dominant force and Westerners as embodiments of the premier mode of being in the world. Animal rights cannot be rhetorically articulated as an "animals first!" movement if it is to be successful. Neither can human-oriented social justice pursuits achieve ethical coherence without a critical engagement with "animality-as-injuring" (Belcourt, 2014). Total liberation requires a multi-pronged approach to justice and rights that notes how features such as "animality," "Blackness," or "femininity" have been not only historical markers of "inferiority" but also intertwined to such an important extent that even social justice issues seemingly unrelated to, or at times at odds with, one another are all part of the same longstanding colonial ontology that must be dissolved to make room for intersectional, genuine justice.

This rhetorical revolution means that seemingly human-bound movements must fight for animals and that animal rights practitioners must advocate on behalf of humans. Feminists must fight animal experimentation with the same vigor that they campaign for abortion rights—after all, both are based on the control of an oppressed subject on behalf of a dominant body (Adams, 1990). At the same time, animal rights practitioners must insist that "Black Lives Matter!" with the same vigor with which they proclaim animal equality, for police brutality against and the mass incarceration of Black American subjects is based in the same colonial derision of difference that casts certain bodies as no better than amoral brutes and chattel (Ko & Ko, 2017). To some extent, one could argue that this approach is even more of an all-or-nothing methodology than that of abolitionists like Francione or the holistic deep ecologists in Earth jurisprudence. If we concede, however, that contemporary manifestations of systemic oppression are based in the same ontological roots, the same existential struggle (Sanbonmatsu, 2011), then social justice truly is a zero-sum game. To legitimate one mode of oppression, even for the purpose of ending a different oppression, merely reifies the same ideologies that "got us here" in the first place. To invoke a dialogical metaphor, while something like this book might cast its *spotlight* on speciesism, it does not articulate animal rights as a social justice *monologue,* but rather an antispeciesist, intersectional, and decolonial *dialogue.*

Furthermore, utilizing this critical rhetorical approach opens scholars and activists to differential manifestations of "the law" and "justice" in U.S. American contexts, particularly where those manifestations might engage with Indigenous voices. Tribal jurisprudence and restorative justice, while not the focus of this book, are nonetheless boons to understanding potential directions for multidirectional animal rights legal rhetoric and praxis engaged with decoloniality. However, to do so requires a disengagement with the notion of the "ecologically noble Indian" (Nadasdy, 2005)—an essentialist construction of the indigenous subject that assumes an inherent, mystical expertise regarding environmental sustainability and animal welfare. Yet, at the same time, engaging with tribal jurisprudence and restorative justice necessitates looking beyond hyper-rational, instrumentalist constructions of animal ethics during times of interspecies conflict as well as veering away from perceptions of prototypical, courtroom-based legal formations as the only ways to envision the law.

Veering away from legal positivist approaches to jurisprudence allows animal liberationists to explore the possibilities of tribal jurisprudence and how indigenous orientations toward interspecies relationships might function under a framework of total liberation. There are, of course, multiple tribes with different histories and thus multiple manifestations of what is called "tribal jurisprudence," so to invoke this concept as a unified field would be intellectually shallow. Nonetheless, vegan indigenous activists worldwide remain adamant that their particular cultural contexts have much to offer vegan thought and praxis, if only the mainstream animal rights movement would listen. For example, vegan scholar/activist Margaret Robinson has used her upbringing in the Mi'kmaw tribe along Canada's eastern coast to explain her decolonial animal liberation orientation: "Being vegan has become a way I practice the values of my ancestors, such as respect for the personhood of other animals, albeit differently from how my ancestors practiced them" (Robinson, 2017, p. 73). Among these traditions is, according to Robinson (2014), the Mi'kmaw orientation toward animal personhood due to interspecies cosmologies based in reciprocity and mutual respect. As this book has aimed to demonstrate, such a conceptualization of personhood is a necessity for the achievement of animal liberation. A nuanced understanding of particular indigenous cosmologies, tribal laws, and native treaty rights is therefore essential in navigating cross-cultural (and most particularly Indigenous versus settler) controversies regarding "best practices" in animal liberation. To quote Christine Black:

> To come into the Indigenous world and its fluxing *physis,* the outsider must first enter the cosmology of the particular group with which they wish to engage, otherwise the knowing of the people is only superficial. This is because a people's

cosmological Creation story and events define their principles, ideals, values and philosophies, which, in turn, inform the legal regime. (Black, 2011, p. 15)

Engaging with critical vegan rhetoric allows total liberationists to better fight against the strategic rhetorical construction of "Indigenous peoples" as a coherent whole with unified interests, zero intertribal conflicts, and no moral debates regarding matters of treaty rights and restorative justice. This move not only fights against strawman antivegan arguments that regard animal liberation as antinative but also notes how Eurocentric rhetorics can interfere with processes of total liberation in cross-cultural conflicts. As Greta Gaard articulated in her analysis of the 1990s Makah whale hunt, wherein media discourses portrayed a conflict between "animal rights activists" against whale hunting and "Indigenous peoples" against settler interventions opposing their enactment of treaty rights, every marginalized group has its own domineering voices, and the disenfranchised have differential opinions over what restorative justice ought to entail. In the case of the Makah whale hunt, for instance, many Indigenous voices opposed the return of the Makah whale hunt on the grounds not only that the pursuit of restorative justice need not involve the return of traditions that exploit animal Others but also that the debate's silencing of Indigenous women's voices did not represent a process of decolonization but rather manifested a "new tribal identity that is both masculinist and elite" (Gaard, 2001, p. 16). In other words, while the context of the Makah whale hunt represented a noble attempt at decolonization via the reassertion of cultural identity, the content was not at all an agreed-upon practice, but rather one that engaged solely with traditions hitherto associated with male tribal elites: "In the case of the Makah, the whale hunting practices of a certain elite group of men have been conflated with the practices and substituted for the identity of an entire culture" (p. 17). This aspect of the content was conveniently ignored by both "animal rights activists" and "Indigenous peoples and allies" in mainstream media narratives, necessitating a shift in perspective that notes how restorative justice cannot be interpreted as a simple matter of "one" right versus "one" wrong. Rather,

in situations involving matters of cross-cultural justice, we should seek out, build relationships with, and support cultural border crossers whose values and goals coincide with the values of feminism and ecofeminism. With the leadership and collaboration of such border-crossers and cultural insiders, feminists and ecofeminists can contribute to envisioning and creating social and economic practices free from oppression of any kind—gender, race, class, sexuality, or species. (Gaard, 2001, p. 22)

This rhetorical approach decenters discourses of animal ethics steeped in normative Whiteness in that it "means that participants from the dominant culture must be willing to listen to and take on the perspectives of the non-dominant Other, and requires a genuine commitment to building cross-cultural solidarity" (p. 19), even if this means that, in certain moral controversies, it is not the place of a dominant culture to impose its values on one seeking to empower itself. And, at the same time, "culture" must not be understood as a coherent, unified, static, timeless whole with nonporous borders and an inability to adapt to changing contexts (Chang, 1999).

While this book does not purport to have the singular legal solution to animal rights controversies as they intersect with disputes over native treaty rights and/ or customary laws, it does note how engaging with critical vegan rhetoric can, by virtue of a decolonial orientation open to Indigenous perspectives, help explain why and how normalized judicial practices and discourses regarding liberal democratic notions of sovereignty and citizenship may in fact be insufficient for total liberation. As Belcourt (2014) asserted, decolonizing projects are inherently intertwined with antispeciesist projects insofar as settler colonial ontologies include a "falsely naturalized relationship between the animal body and colonized spaces" that must "become a point of decolonial intervention" because "settler colonialism itself operates through a militant and racist politics of territoriality whereby Indigenous lands are physically and symbolically evacuated to be re-made into settler spaces" (p. 5). The complexity of cross-cultural conflict and the multilayered phenomenon of "culture" in and of itself must therefore be central to a critical rhetorical approach to animal law and liberation. The contrasts between the situated contexts of colonialism versus the contents of decolonization tactics must be used to combat "those spaces for animal activism that center Whiteness [and] thus further impossibilize decolonization and leave intact *the* power relation that makes speciesism possible" (p. 5). Robinson is therefore correct to claim that engaging with indigeneity must involve a reflection upon the "way indigenous peoples are treated as if we are more like other animals than Settlers [non-Indigenous peoples] are and therefore ill-equipped to make good decisions about our territories, our bodies, or our lives" (qtd. in Brueck, 2017, p. 10).

Even if animal liberationists interested in animal rights law have little expertise in tribal law, indigenous jurisprudence, or native treaty rights, these complex cultural controversies must be considered essential to composing "alternative ways of knowing" (Cochran et al., 2008) the law and its relationship to constructing culture, humanity, and animality. An emphasis upon in-group voices as opposed to out-group orders affords power to "cosmologies," which Black (2011) defined as "safe places: they are the circle that encompasses all one perceives to be reality. It is from these safe places that people get a sense of who they are and how they fit into the grand plan (p. 27). In the case of Indigenous jurisprudence, for instance, law is not always a series of codified precedents emerging from a formal court proceeding, but rather "tribal cultural practices and customs as unwritten *laws*" that, when understood as a form of ritualized justice-seeking, can offer "a series of steps that can be considered in responding to the sometimes strained relationship between people and animals in tribal communities [and beyond] that also acknowledges the harm that has been done to the animal-human relationship in general" (Deer & Murphy, 2017, p. 705). To use or do critical vegan rhetoric effectively, one must take seriously the idea that decolonial processes require rhetorical strategies of coalition-building across cultural boundaries, necessitating a decentering of domineering voices steeped in Eurocentric norms and instead embracing multiple ways of "knowing" and subsequently "doing" animal liberation and veganism. Among these multiplicities is an engagement with the contemporary sociopolitical issues of the modern settler state—engagement not through mere tokenism, but through a serious partnership with and commitment to marginalized peoples still reeling from past and present colonial projects.

For some readers, I anticipate that this approach to animal rights may seem radical, even incoherent. However, such surprise only affirms the dominance of "White veganism" (Harper, 2012) and liberal humanist rights rhetoric in mainstream animal rights discourse. For others, this approach might be quite familiar, for as I articulated in the introduction, I am far from the first writer to note the need for the decolonization of animal rights ontologies and the diversification of voices "allowed" to participate in discussions of total liberation in animal-oriented circles. As I articulate the rhetorical strategies and tactics guiding my critical rhetorical methodology, I continue to draw from the work of such academic animal intersectionalists. As I place the rhetorics of Francione, Wise, and Earth jurisprudence in direct conversation with (rather than in total opposition to) these "nontraditional" (by which I mean systemically silenced) voices in animal rights, and as I filter these conversations through the theoretical lens of ecofeminist legal theory, the rhetorical strategies and tactics required by my critical vegan rhetoric begin to take shape.

Critical Vegan Rhetoric: Prophetic Legal Strategies

Strategically, I conceive of a critical vegan rhetoric as a rhetorical approach to "ethical" living that acknowledges the impossibility of total truth, justice, and moral purity today, if *ever*, while not giving up on a considerably better tomorrow. It is an approach that looks to the past to find where social, political, and legal notions of rights come from, identifying which can be kept as is, which are flawed but can be redeemed, and which may need to be done away with altogether in order to pursue an equitable future world. The "veganism" inherent in my approach is at once a set of principles, a pattern of consumption, a refusal to ignore the role of "animality" in justifying oppression, and a commitment to creating a future composed of minimal harm, unabashed honesty, and explicit empathy. It is not a present-oriented approach that hopes for a better future, but rather a future-oriented approach that advocates for present-day tactics consistent with that future—a future that, while admittedly idealistic and perhaps even unrealistic, embodies an ethic of total liberation that is not species essentialist, is not anthropocentric, is not animals-first, and embodies a vision of ideological decolonization to undermine those mechanistic, humanistic processes by which speciesism, racism, sexism, and other such isms have been allowed to flourish.

As I demonstrated in my previous chapters, moving toward a critical vegan rhetoric therefore requires breaking away from (although not necessarily killing off) traditional, mechanistic, hyper-rational understandings of the law, of rights, and of justice as seen in the works of Francione and Wise. At the same time, it requires a principled existence that emphasizes individual agency and personal transformation, as explained in vegan abolitionism—but not in a manner that ignores the very real inequalities among *Homo sapiens* that make behavioral changes much easier, even much more preferable, for certain groups. It requires a rhetorical deconstruction of legal positivism that takes seriously Wise's claim that the "thinghood" of certain beings is not a designated reality but an outdated social construction of Western philosophy, but it must go further than suggesting that justice might be achieved through granting "sufficiently similar" animals legal personhood. Be it a dog or a river, one must not neglect species outside of kingdom *Animalia,* even for rhetorically strategic purposes, for the survival of the Earth community in its entirety requires individual and societal changes that extend beyond bodies with beating hearts—but an environmentalist orientation must not turn into anthropocentrism *disguised* as environmentalism, wherein humans decide who should live or how they should die in accordance with a vague utilitarian "environmental" ethic of the "greater good."

In short, embracing a critical vegan rhetoric embodies a commitment on the part of individuals, groupings, and broader institutions to stem the flow of cruelty as much as is reasonably possible today—cruelty to animals, cruelty to ecosystems, and cruelty to other humans; cruelty in its epistemic, economic, and physical forms; and cruelty enacted by one or many parties upon one or many others in such a way that the latter's flourishment is no longer possible.

Rhetorical strategies must be ecofeminist and decolonial. First and foremost, they must embrace principles of intersectionality, acknowledging that abuses in the human and more-than-human world are, more often than not, justified on the part of the abuser by conceiving of the abused as less-than-human, and thus more-animal. At the same time, it does not pretend that a purely consumeristic veganism is the inevitable panacea to all social ills, for taking a discursively species-essentialist approach to society writ large would likely have the same downfalls as the willful ignorance put forth in postracial approaches to relationships, law, and politics. In this way, a legal orientation that embraces a critical vegan rhetoric *must be consistent* with the mode of intersectional veganism espoused by women-of-color feminists and so often overlooked or ignored by the animal rights "mainstream"—or, more specifically, an intersectional orientation toward animal rights that forces Whiteness-bound arenas such as the law to confront the consequences of defining Man and Not-Man within a White supremacist racial caste system (Broad, 2013; Brueck, 2017; Deckha, 2012; Harper, 2009; Ko & Ko, 2017; Twine, 2010; Wrenn, 2017). It must simultaneously embrace a "vegan ecofeminism" (Adams, 1991; Curtin, 1991; Gaard, 2001, 2002, 2011) that decenters capitalistic consumer culture as the premier site of human and more-than-human justice (while still acknowledging purchasing power's strategic force in a devastatingly violent world) and instead centers ethics of care and flourishing, emotions of empathy and compassion, and vegan living that is at once secure in its politics and morally contextual (Curtin, 1991).

This critical rhetorical approach to animal rights law is cross-cultural and contextual, acknowledging that everyone has different restrictions and different needs. A First Nations girl in rural Canada would not be held to the same set of consumption practices as a wealthy hedge fund manager on Wall Street. Merely their *ethic,* their *vision for a just and sustainable future* and that vision's *necessary influence on animal rights praxis,* would remain the same. In tune with ecofeminist discourse, cold rationality ought to be superseded by love and empathy. Utilizing critical vegan rhetoric does not neglect Francione's and Wise's emphasis on agency, choice, and the sentient subject, remembering the value of the *individual* in composing a compassionate ideology. An owl ought to be protected on the basis that it is an owl, a being with an innate interest in staying alive and a right to legal personhood, and each individual person should be brutally honest with themselves about what they can reasonably do to enrich the lives of themselves, the owl, and other beings. At the same time, in the spirit of Earth jurisprudence, it does not place the individual in aggressive confrontation with others, but sees the individual as an agent in a complex web of relationships that, when given an appropriate emotional toolkit, can expand its "compassion footprint" (Bekoff, 2013). True, the protected owl will not reciprocate the compassion shown to it by human beings by swearing off mice and other rodents. Nor will the coyote thank compassionate humans by boycotting loose cats and dogs. All individuals are individuals in relation, products of networked subjectivities that change across time, space, and place. Far from envisioning a word where all species live in perfect reciprocal harmony, legal and extralegal approaches to animal protection, then, are not solely meant to protect innocent beings from evildoers, but to dissuade the reproduction of destructive colonial ontologies that have long pitted humanity against an abstractly defined "nature."

However, there is always a difference between idealism (what we would do in a perfect set of circumstances) and pragmatism (what we have to do in an imperfect world). In a world full of moral quandaries and ethical entanglements, it is important to, where necessary, engage in strategic essentialisms in the short-term when those essentialisms might open doors to long-term change. The ends do not always justify the means, but means are always constrained by the options available to the protestor at a particular moment in time (Alinsky, 1972). For instance, working "within the law" to procure intersectional justice may, at first glance, appear to be a hypocritical stance. If the U.S. American justice system was formulated through liberal humanist conceptualizations of justice that did and does systemically exclude bodies from moral consideration, if law schools continue to train lawyers from a legal positivist paradigm that values reason and universality over empathy and contingency, and if legal practitioners are necessarily implicated in broader functions of capitalist state violence, then what is the point of using the dirty arm of the law to achieve equality?

The "impure politics" (Pezzullo, 2011) of animal rights law is a matter of pragmatism, of using the limited options available to fight for a common goal when an alternative system is not yet readily available for mainstream use. However, such impure politics ought to be *prophetically* pragmatic (Hamington, 2009; West 1989): "Pragmatism at its best because it promotes a critical temper and democratic faith without making criticism a fetish or democracy an idol" (West, 1989, p. 186). Prophetic in this sense does not require the invocation of some biblical prophecy, but rather an engaged effort to "foresee a new being . . . foresee a society"—not in terms of "the removal of social constructs and the restoration of the way things were always meant to be," but rather as the "production of a better set of social constructs than the ones presently available and thus as the creation of a new and better sort of human being" (Rorty, 1990, p. 35). As Sanbonmatsu (2011) explained, "human existence is a work in progress, a becoming, we are never fully 'what we are,' since we are always leapfrogging our identity in time. Consequently, I am always free to adopt different attitudes toward my transcendent nature" (p. 32). In other words, animal rights praxis, legally and extralegally, bottom-up and top-down, individual and collective, must work within existing systems in those moments wherein other systems are not readily apparent. But the means within which one utilizes those systems must be consistent with an agenda that *denies* the supremacy of those systems as such and opens doors to their reform or dissolution as time goes on. This battle is not to be confused with the fight between radicalism or welfarism, but rather the fight between doing something imperfect for now versus doing nothing until perfection presents itself.

To reiterate, an *ideal* does not equate to the *universal,* not when there are infinite mechanisms in place to prevent the adoption of a critical vegan rhetoric, such as cheap meat through factory farming, food deserts, an extensive history (and thus naturalization of) animal testing, of zoo marketing campaigns that defend captivity as a twisted "love" for animals, and of a seeming collective unwillingness to conceive of real alternatives for those individuals who, for whatever medical reason, cannot sustain themselves on current vegan food products' overreliance on soy and other common allergens. Positive animal rights legislation, favorable court decisions, and beneficial moral reconsiderations of human exceptionalism will not happen overnight—however, just because an ideal cannot be achieved immediately, or even easily, does not mean the ideal ought to be abandoned. Instead, one rhetorically sets concrete goals for the future while acknowledging the imperfections and inequalities of the present. Critical vegan rhetoric demands only that "everyone who can do *something* must do what they *can* do *right now*" (Bekoff, 2017, para. 16, emphasis mine), but that those "doings" be done in the spirit of and with discourses representative of a future compatible with total liberation.

Critical Vegan Rhetoric: Multidirectional Legal Tactics

But what encompasses a critical vegan rhetoric outside of the realm of the abstract? Tactically, the list of possible practices is too large to list, particularly on the individual level, for "what to do" is largely contingent upon one's own brutal honesty and self-reflexivity regarding what, in this moment, can be done and what, if circumstances change, should be done next. What is most important to remember, however, is that animal rights law must function via top-down *and* a bottom-up approaches, within *and* outside of established legal institutions, through experts *and* laypersons, against *and* in pursuit of human empowerment. In other words, although this book has emphasized ecofeminist legal theory as the necessary basis for fruitful animal rights law, the law cannot possibly adjust its deep-seated ideological frameworks without substantial extralegal assistance. Animal rights law's success is therefore contingent upon a critical vegan rhetoric's application both on the expert level (for instance, lawyers setting socially responsible legal precedents) and on the everyday level (antispeciesist actions pursued by individuals or small groups that appear at first glance to be personal, not political).

Not only is the personal political, but the political is also personal. Tactically, then, does the pursuit of animal justice (and by extension human justice) in the United States require human residents to embrace a vegan lifestyle? Someone embracing a critical vegan rhetoric would say "yes"—*but,* with the understanding that "vegan" must be understood to mean a nonspeciesist ethic that attempts to cause the least possible harm to others while at once allowing oneself to flourish. Someone with the means to be a vegan abolitionist ought to do so but at the same time must commit in theory and in discourse to ethics of antiracism, antisexism, etc.–even when these stances might be at odds with the "big speakers" in the animal rights community or might involve "vegan products" like dark chocolate harvested through child slavery ("About F.E.P.," n.d.). As the saying goes, "there is no ethical consumption under capitalism." A total liberationist agrees, with an important caveat: while there may be no ethical consumption under capitalism, there is a distinctively *more* ethical consumption. Until such time as a "revolution" comes, an ecofeminist, decolonial critical vegan rhetoric seeks to find this elusive "more" and move it slowly to its historically situated "most."

An ideal example of such a bottom-up approach to a critical vegan rhetoric is the California-based Food Empowerment Project. The FEP, founded in 2005 by Lauren Ornelas, is an animal rights, food justice, and racial equality organization that, per its mission statement, "seeks to create a more just and sustainable world by recognizing the power of one's food choices" ("About F.E.P.," n.d., para. 1). The organization advocates heavily for a vegan diet and ethic but does so through the lens of intersectional violence against vulnerable interspecies communities. Founded and run by women of color, the organization encourages "healthy food choices that reflect a more compassionate society by spotlighting the abuse of animals on farms, the depletion of natural resources, unfair working conditions for produce workers, and the unavailability of healthy foods in low-income areas" (para. 1). An interesting rhetorical trope of the FEP is its dismissal of the phrase "lactose intolerance" by noting that most people, particularly people of color, cannot actually digest dairy products comfortably. To work outside of normative Whiteness, the organization argues, being lactose intolerant is better dubbed being "lactose *normal*"—dairy is unethical, unnecessary, and for most persons' digestive systems, quite undesirable. Such a move embodies a necessary commitment to the rhetorical reversal of established concepts in arenas such as health and medicine that allow for the continuation of oppressive speciesist, racist, sizeist, etc. ideologies.

The FEP does not have an active litigation arm, although it does have social justice attorneys on its advisory board. The organization's grassroots efforts and legal advisors prefer to take on powerful, well-funded institutions from the bottom up in an effort to spur social and, ideally, legal change. For instance, FEP consistently runs a "Shame on Safeway!" campaign to highlight unethical business practices that create food deserts in vulnerable communities, such as the Safeway supermarket chain's tendency to use arcane legal clauses to prevent new grocery stores from opening on old Safeway grounds. It responds to concerns about horrific treatment of workers not only in slaughterhouses (as many animal rights organizations do), but also on produce farms, by calling for people to grow their own or to buy organic produce when possible, or at least to actively seek out ethical farms in the absence of mainstream labeling practices. Noting, however, that while individual purchasing power is a helpful way to put pressure on more farms to adopt change in worker conditions, "Comprehensive federal reform is still desperately needed to protect all field workers from known safety hazards and to promote equality in the workplace" ("Produce Workers," n.d., para. 25). Further, the FEP emphasizes the use of legalized slavery in other countries that, through conscripted labor, bring purportedly "vegan" products like dark chocolate and coffee beans to the United States, and ultimately provides lists of legitimately "cruelty-free" versions of these foods to not only promote animal-free products to conscious consumers, but slavery-free ones as well. While U.S. Americans cannot change the laws of overseas governments, they can at least protest the "importation of slavery" (symbolically accepting slave labor by importing slave-produced products) allowed by the U.S. government through complicity and complacency. With enough education into these practices and enough outrage, boycotts, and buycotts, perhaps stricter trade laws might emerge in the future.

Ultimately, the FEP embodies a bottom-up approach to a critical vegan rhetoric for three reasons: First, it proposes a vegan diet, lifestyle, and ethic as the ideal, but, because it is conscious of material inequalities based in longstanding ideologies of racism, classism, etc., it acknowledges that, while ideally, veganism would be a "moral baseline," for the already marginalized to adopt a further marginalized lifestyle is exceptionally more difficult than for privileged bodies. Thus, while consuming/using animal byproducts (in a U.S. American context) is not under this ethic "acceptable," it can in certain cases be "understandable" unless and until the world and its systems catch up to larger projects of total liberation. Second, it directly connects issues of animal oppression to issues of human oppression vis-à-vis larger narratives of food justice. And third, it envisions a future of total liberation that, while seemingly improbable now, might be achieved through bottom-up actions, such as careful consumer decisions and attention to/visible protest against corporate greed, and top-down approaches, such as worker protection legislation and the complete abolition of factory farms and, ideally, speciesism.

This book has attempted to describe animal-oriented ethics in the "expert," "top-down" legal sphere. Thus, it would be remiss not to steer the conversation toward an application of critical vegan rhetoric in top-down, prototypically *legal* arenas. Given the dearth of animal rights lawyers in general—of whom ecofeminists constitute an even smaller proportion—it is difficult to come up with a "picture perfect" example of this critical rhetorical approach in "legalese." There is, however, a burgeoning call within wildlife management discourses—not in formal legal studies, but rather in cognitive ethology—that attempts in no small way to embrace and apply something resembling a critical vegan rhetoric to federal, state, and local conservation discourses and practices.

This theory is called compassionate conservation (Bekoff, 2013, 2014, 2015; 2017; Bekoff & Pierce, 2009, 2017). It is a strand of thought that works across social and institutional spheres, encompassing the personal, the political, the scientific, and the legal. It is primarily attributed to the works of cognitive ethologist Marc Bekoff and bioethicist Jessica Pierce, whose primary argument is that the cold, calculated

violence of human-on-human, human-on-animal, and human-on-nature relationships has violently overshadowed the innate, shared capacity among sentient
species for empathic, compassionate relationships, thus naturalizing destructive
behaviors among humanity that risk ending the world as we know it.

A compassionate conservation approach to human-animal relationships
necessitates a substantial paradigm shift—a shift that is in many ways synonymous
to the shifts demanded by Francione, Wise, and Earth jurisprudence. The three
principles at its core are as follows: First, do not harm; second, all individuals matter;
and third, the ultimate goal of environmental politics and policy should be the
peaceful coexistence among Earth's residents. A paradigmatic shift of this nature
requires that humans decenter themselves from the moral universe, refuse cold and
calculated approaches to animal "management," and reimagine themselves as part
of an Earth community whose members share, among other things, the potential
for love and compassion for one another (Bekoff & Pierce, 2009). And, even while
recognizing the capacity of the more-than-human world to engage in ethical
behaviors previously attributed only to Man, the "moral animal," compassionate
conservation demands that we respect the innate and beautiful difference between
species as well, a process of biophilic curiosity that should ideally awaken our
"innate drive to connect with (M)other nature" (Bekoff, 2017, para. 6). Bekoff and
Pierce referred to this process as a "rewilding" of the human heart, a process based
on the "12 P's" of "being proactive, positive, persistent, patient, peaceful, practical,
powerful, passionate, playful, present, principled, and proud" (para. 14). While it is
primarily drawn from contemporary scientific discoveries regarding the moral lives
of animals, this approach calls for *practical solutions* over procrastinating with *more
research,* as "we don't need 'more science' to know we must change our ways, and
we already have enough information to mandate making positive changes" (para. 8).

Compassionate conservation, from a strictly legal perspective, has not been
explored fully by Bekoff, Pierce, or their adherents. Nonetheless, its tenets give
a solid indication of where lawmakers, lawyers, judges, and other likeminded
individuals might take it. Legally, a compassionate conservation approach would not
permit the wanton destruction of one species in the name of another: cormorants
would not be killed to "save" salmon, barred owls slaughtered to "save" spotted owls,
or coyotes exterminated to "save" livestock or domestic pets, as killing is no way
to "manage" species in an ethical, or even scientifically accurate way. Legislative
foci would switch from the existence of "problem" animals to that of "problem
locations" that, in their specific contexts, lead to unwanted human-on-animal

conflict. Instead of extermination or translocation, local ordinances might be passed to control domestic dog populations, appropriately dispose of kitchen and medical waste, and provide considerably better amenities to people—particularly tribal and socioeconomically disadvantaged people—in the form of lighting, housing, and sanitation. In other words, laws and procedures regarding human-on-animal conflict need not be reactive and violent, but preemptive and based on an ethic of compassion and coexistence, allowing humans and more-than-humans to share, not compete for, the landscape (Bekoff, 2015).

Compassionate conservation meets the qualifications of a critical vegan rhetoric for three reasons: First, it negates the patriarchal narrative of conservationism wherein humans have the right and duty to exterminate animals "for the greater good." It further embraces ecofeminist narratives of empathy and emotionality over cold rationality as the basis for ethical environmental thought. And finally, it integrates problems of privilege and disadvantage when articulating human and more-than-human conflict, providing possible solutions that would benefit both parties immensely.

Again, given the current state of animal law and legal narratives as a whole, there are very few "lawyers proper" that have the necessary support to initiate a clear, concise legal strategy consistent with a critical rhetorical approach to animal rights law. However, it would be remiss not to mention the work of Mariann Sullivan. Sullivan, a lawyer, acts as cohost and executive director of the animal rights podcast *Our Hen House* and the host of the podcast *Animal Law*. She has taught law at both Columbia Law School and Lewis & Clark College and serves as a board member of Animal Welfare Trust and Animal Welfare Advocacy. For Sullivan:

> To be vegan is not simply to adopt a more compassionate way of eating—it is to embrace the future by moving to the next chapter in humanity's story, and to attempt to write that story in the only way that can save our incredibly fragile, beautiful world and the extraordinary web of conscious perception of which we are a part. ("Why?," n.d., para. 2)

Her podcast thus invites intersectional activists and scholars such as Carol Adams, Aph Ko, and Hana Low to talk about the interconnections between, for instance, speciesism, sexism, antiblackness, and prison abolition, while simultaneously discussing current issues in animal law. The organization's social media pages highlight activists of color, not merely as tokens to show how "x and y groups can be vegans too!," but as active participants in a movement that must connect racism and speciesism. Sullivan's work further meets the requirements for a critical vegan rhetoric in that, though she identifies as a lawyer and expert, she articulates the need for top-down and bottom-up approaches to instigate lasting social change: "Change making requires a multiplicity of methods to reach the hearts and minds of a multiplicity of people, we need activists of all stripes—artists, academics, lawyers, students, business moguls, media darlings, everyone" ("100 Ways to Change the World for Animals," n.d., para. 1). To exemplify this mode of change-making, in 2016, her organization hosted, in tandem with the law student division of the Animal Legal Defense Fund, an event at the University of Texas at Austin School of Law entitled "Advocacy for Animals: Beyond the Law."

Engaging with critical vegan rhetoric thus invites a variety of rhetorical tactics from the top down and the bottom up. What is most important to note is the type of rhetoric employed by those tactics, specifically discursive emphasis on the need for intersectional and decolonial invocations of animal rights that not only point out the interconnections between speciesism and other isms but also invite possible solutions (by both legal experts and laypersons) that account for material differences in life circumstances and situated knowledges. Total liberation thus requires as vegan lifestyle-as-ideal, but one in which veganism-as-ethic is not as simple as avoiding animal products. Veganism must be understood and rhetorically constructed as an animal rights project that, both legally and extralegally, necessitates the abolition of human suffering without anthropocentrism and the abolition of more-than-human suffering without species essentialism. While "the law" proper has a lot of work to do to catch up to such intersectional projects, change is in the works.

Critical Vegan Rhetoric as Rhetorical Analytic: Directions for Future Communication Scholarship

I further hope that the critical rhetorical approach articulated in this chapter might serve as an analytic paradigm for future academic work on the subject of animal rights rhetoric in both its formal and informal legal forms. For example, critiquing failed legal campaigns by animal rights organizations from such a perspective might shed light as to what "went well," what "went wrong," and what must be done in future campaigns in order to attain a more desirable result both in terms of court hearings and in terms of setting a legal precedent in line with the goals of total liberation.

One could, for instance, analyze the failed PETA lawsuit against SeaWorld in 2011. This suit, which made national headlines from 2011 to 2012, involved PETA, three marine-mammal experts, and two former orca trainers asking a federal court to declare five of SeaWorld's wild-caught orcas as "slaves," and thus held unconstitutionally in violation of the United States Constitution's Thirteenth Amendment. According to PETA's counsel, the plain text of the Thirteenth Amendment prohibited the condition of slavery without reference to personhood or even any particular class of victim: "Slavery is slavery, and it does not depend on the species of the slave any more than it depends on gender, race, or religion" (PETA, 2011, para. 2). According to PETA president Ingrid Newkirk:

> All five of these orcas were violently seized from the ocean and taken from their families as babies. They are denied freedom and everything else that is natural and important to them while kept in small concrete tanks and reduced to performing stupid tricks. . . . The 13th Amendment prohibits slavery, and these orcas are, by definition, slaves. (PETA, 2011, para. 4)

The filing was particularly notable in three respects: First, it was the first ever seeking to apply this Constitutional amendment to the more-than-human world. Second, it (like the Nonhuman Rights Project) specifically named the five orcas as plaintiffs in the case, demanding their release either to the ocean or to seaside sanctuaries. Third, among the plaintiffs was the orca Tilikum, who would become famous two years later as one of the main subjects of the infamous anti-SeaWorld documentary *Blackfish*.

Perhaps unsurprisingly, a federal judge dismissed the case in February 2012. U.S. District Court Judge Jeffrey Miller ruled that "the only reasonable interpretation of the Thirteenth Amendment's plain language is that it applies to persons, and not to non-persons such as orcas" (qtd. in Zelman, 2012, para. 3). Although he did praise PETA's desire to protect complex creatures such as orcas, he found that the Thirteenth Amendment "affords no relief" (qtd. in para. 7). SeaWorld celebrated the decision, writing in a statement to the *Huffington Post*:

> The speed in which the Court issued its opinion provides reassurance of the sanctity of the 13th Amendment and the absurdity of PETA's baseless lawsuit. . . .

SeaWorld remains the standard for zoological stewardship of marine animals and
we reject any challenge to the conditions and quality of care for these remarkable
animals. (qtd. in para. 5)

Of course, neither PETA nor SeaWorld could predict the viral success of the
documentary *Blackfish* two years later, which would not only relaunch plaintiff
Tilikum to national fame as a sympathetic victim but also would also do enough
public damage to SeaWorld that it would lose profits, endure mass protests, and
eventually promise to cease its captive breeding program. Would the results of
PETA's lawsuit have changed were it filed today? That is impossible to say. However,
an application of critical vegan rhetoric as analytic sheds light onto the strengths
and weaknesses of the suit and the necessary strategic/tactical shifts that, were a
suit of this nature refiled, would need to occur in order to maximize the possibility
of success and set a precedent for total liberation.

Steven Wise, Gary Francione, and the affiliates of Earth jurisprudence would
likely identify the first major rhetorical sticking point of PETA's flawed suit: namely,
that PETA's counsel presumed that personhood status should be irrelevant to orca
liberation. Slaves are slaves, claimed PETA, regardless of legal personhood. As this
book has hopefully demonstrated, a premier strength among all of my featured
animal rights lawyers is their understanding of property status as necessarily
detrimental to the pursuit of any type of legalized liberation. Any talk of inherent
rights or value is rendered irrelevant under the law without personhood designation, for in circumstances of person vs. chattel, person will always be victorious
by virtue of the former's conceived value to a larger moral community and the
latter's legal irrelevance apart from instrumental value. Thus, PETA's legal strategy
and rhetorical tactics were totally incoherent. To attempt to grant "slave" status to
subjects not legally considered "persons" is next to impossible when, within and
outside of the law, animals are still considered chattel first—a point articulated
in the presiding judge's rejection of the case. In order for orcas to be liberated
from captivity, it is not enough to discursively designate them as slaves, and thus
in violation of the Thirteenth Amendment. They must be simultaneously named
as *persons* under the law not only to be legitimate plaintiffs for a presiding judge
but also to qualify for the status of subject to be freed as opposed to object to be
used by a subject.

By engaging with critical vegan rhetoric, a critic would take into account this
personhood argument and extend it by placing it beside the struggle for legalized

and extralegalized personhood among different humans in U.S. American contexts. Firstly, it would recognize that legal decisions are not ahistorical, objective decisions based in some higher rule of law; they are contingent upon changing times, places, spaces, and prevailing cultural norms. To argue that Black slaves were freed as a result of objective decision-making on the part of lawmakers would be a massive historical anachronism. Rather, the Thirteenth Amendment emerged as a result of decades of protest—written, spoken, and embodied—and even a colossal war between peoples unwilling to let go of prevailing ideologies that limit full human status to Whiteness. Even after the abolition of de jure slavery, de facto slavery persisted, exemplified via race-based segregation and discrimination even after legal decisions such as *Brown v. Board of Education* in 1954. Academic fields like critical race theory, postcolonial studies, and carceral studies exist and persist because, though many engaged with normative Whiteness and postracial rhetorics like to argue otherwise, the movement of Black Americans from de jure chattel to de facto personhood status is still incomplete.

PETA must therefore grapple with two important rhetorical decisions moving forward. First, has enough of a cultural antagonism opened in the United States for lawyers, judges, legislators, etc. to even begin to accept that animals-as-chattel equates to animals as immorally detained? Post-*Blackfish,* perhaps yes. SeaWorld has encountered massive pushback against its captive breeding programs and, as articulated in my chapter on Earth jurisprudence, countries like India are taking the lead on cetacean personhood. Meanwhile, divorcing parties fight for custody of canines as though they were human children; vegan diets in the United States have increased by 600 percent in the last three years; and the Whanganui *River—a "natural object"*—in New Zealand is legally a person. Perhaps the binaries of nature/culture, of human/animal, and even of subject/object are beginning to deteriorate. Perhaps the time is right for PETA to try again—in the same vein as the Nonhuman Rights Project—to sue for orca liberation. However, there is still a long way to go for a majority population to perceive even the most "cognitively advanced" animals as persons, and to argue in court for orca liberation requires setting a responsible precedent not based in highly exclusive personality characteristics that center human exceptionalism. Gary Francione would suggest, and PETA would likely agree, that a top-down courtroom approach to freeing orcas from SeaWorld will necessarily fail without sufficient prior, simultaneous, and ongoing grassroots activism (like advocating for a vegan lifestyle) to delegitimize de jure and de facto speciesism.

And, perhaps most importantly, were this case to reemerge, PETA would also need to grapple with its own normative Whiteness in its advocacy tactics. As rhetoricians like Wendy Atkins-Sayre have indicated, PETA thrives on shock-based, affective advocacy tactics to garner external attention through the public screen. These campaigns are often visual, such as nude protest, but are also legal, such as a case where PETA counsel sued a photographer for copyright infringement by profiting off of a "selfie" photo taken by a primate. Likely, PETA did not intend to win that case, but rather sought to secure public attention to issues of animal exploitation. Perhaps the 2011 SeaWorld case is representative of another shock value case, although the counsel's rhetoric does not imply a lack of seriousness on PETA's end. These legal and extralegal performances have not gone unnoticed, and the organization thrives on its infamy. According to the organization's website:

> We will do extraordinary things to get the word out about animal cruelty because we have learned from experience that the media, sadly, do not consider the terrible facts about animal suffering alone interesting enough to cover. It is sometimes necessary to shake people up in order to initiate discussion, debate, questioning of the status quo, and, of course, action. (PETA, n.d., para 1)

As a result, its shock campaigns and mass mediated "image events" (Delicath & DeLuca, 2003) often rely upon analogies that compare historically momentous moments of human suffering to animal suffering such as the transatlantic slave trade. These campaigns have not been received positively among people of color and their allies. Among the group's most infamous analogical displays was the 2005 exhibition "Animal Liberation," which used sensational visual panels to directly compare the historical treatment of Black African slaves to the contemporary treatment of animals in agriculture, research, and entertainment. One panel juxtaposed pictures of Black persons in chains with those of shackled elephants. Another showed a civil rights protestor being beaten alongside a seal being bludgeoned to death. Yet another panel, entitled "Hanging," showed a graphic, explicit photo of lynched Black bodies surrounded by a White mob in conjunction with a cow's carcass hanging in a slaughterhouse (AP, 2005). Some groups, particularly antiracist organizations, excoriated PETA for its misanthropy, insensitivity, and ignorance. The Connecticut chapter of the NAACP condemned "Animal Liberation" on the grounds that "black people are being pimped" (qtd. in Bailey, 2007, p. 41). A spokesman for the group incredulously asked, "They're comparing chickens to black people?" (AP,

2005, para. 19). Racial justice activist and essayist Tim Wise angrily upbraided PETA's efforts not only for insulting Black people but also for undermining its own cause:

> The very legitimate goal of stopping the immense horror of factory farming . . . gets conflated with the extermination of millions of people . . . thereby ensuring that damn near everyone who hears the analogy will conclude that PETA is either completely insensitive, at best, or bull-goose-loony. (qtd. in Associated Press, 2005, para. 10)

The 2005 "Animal Liberation" vignettes and the 2011 SeaWorld lawsuit are far from the only PETA campaigns—or even animal rights campaigns—to invoke the transatlantic slave trade as a moral analogy for animal liberation. And, to a large extent, the analogy is a good one. Both parties were considered chattel; both were used for unpaid labor; both endured suffering en masse on the ground that the affected parties were not fully "human." And, if racism is necessarily entwined in the concept of humanness, and if humanness a construction based in colonial conceptions of species, then the slave/animal trade analogy holds even more analytic value. As Seshadri (2012) explained, "We can discover the origins of the practice of racial dehumanization in our long history of managing the nonhuman animal world" via "a strict colonialist homology or similarity between our exploitation of nature and animals and of 'inferior peoples'" (p. 7). Indeed, to be offended by the comparison of Black American slaves to animals might merely lend credence to author Marjorie Spiegel's unwavering stance that "those who are offended by a comparison to fellow sufferers have fallen for propaganda spewed forth by the oppressors" (Spiegel, 1988, p. 25).

And yet, as the old adage goes, "You have to *give* respect to *get* it." In terms of engaging with humans outside of an essentialist conceptualization of the *Homo sapiens,* PETA has been perhaps even more unsuccessful than vegan abolitionism in acknowledging how colonial ideologies both reproduce and reinforce human inequality. Indeed, it is perhaps the premier organization representative of Harper's claim that mainstream representations of veganism are "far from race neutral" (Harper, 2012, p. 155). Animal rights discourses of race neutrality most typically invoke *postracial* rhetoric, touched upon in chapter 3 as a style of postracial discourse in which rhetors argue that racism no longer exists and skin color no longer has social significance—or, perhaps, that racism definitively exists, but that a vegan lifestyle will *necessarily* lead to the eradication of racist systems

(Harper, 2011). Acknowledging PETA's (and prototypical liberal humanist animal rights groups') tendencies toward postracial tactics requires a broader revision of animal rights strategies in both top-down and bottom-up legal spheres that deal with rhetorics of chattel.

Slavery analogies, when used postracially, inevitably orient slavery as *backward* in time. After the passing of the Thirteenth Amendment, the slavery-era stopped and the era of racial restitution slowly but surely began. However, this orientation is shallow at best. Outrage to slavery invocations by many people of color and social justice allies thus cannot be reduced to speciesists rejecting being called out on their speciesism. Perhaps (in fact, almost certainly) there is an element of latent speciesism in critiques of campaigns that invoke human histories to promote animal liberation. However, mixed in it is the long-espoused and long-ignored proclamation of purportedly "freed" individuals that their struggles are not over, but in fact go on. The term "racism," after all, "is synonymous with the practice of dehumanization, whereby the victim is disqualified from being a full member of the elite company of human beings" (Seshadri, 2012, p. ix). And, despite the omnipresent "triumphalist narratives" of White heroism and Black survival, "blacks continue to fight for full membership in humankind" (Kim, 2001, p. 326).

In other words, should the 2011 PETA suit emerge again, then the organization must reflect and respond *honestly* to its reputation of exploitation of "Othered" human subjects in the pursuit of animal liberation. Invocations of Blackness, femininity, and other typically oppressed human "differences" cannot be done as mere tokenism or for pure "shock value." Intersectionality and decoloniality do not emerge purely by invoking analogies of sufficient similarity. In fact, as my critique of Wise and the Nonhuman Rights Project has shown, principles of sufficient similarity must be closely interrogated for what ideologies those similarities deemed most valuable enforce. For PETA to invoke the Thirteenth Amendment, then, is a risky endeavor not only because orcas are not persons under the law but also because the organization itself has a messy reputation regarding putting marginalized groups' contemporary experiences of inhumanity on display, seemingly without concern for intergroup reciprocity. Unidirectional activism is incompatible with such analogical argumentation, for, as Seshadri (2012) eloquently observed, PETA and other likeminded individuals and groups "cannot do anything at all about the appalling ways human beings treat other human beings or animals without rethinking and renewing our norms, presuppositions, platitudes, and morals with regard to life and what is living." (Seshadri, 2012, p. 11)

I do not go so far as to suggest that animals ought not to be protected under the Thirteenth Amendment—such a top-down legal victory would be monumental for animal rights. I neither suggest that using the term "slaves" to describe, say, circus elephants or dairy cows is a misnomer—they are chattel subjects under oppressive regimes of bio- and necropolitical control, with tens of billions executed each year in the name of capitalist profit and individual consumption. However, animal rights cannot function unidirectionally; intersectionality and decoloniality do not result by insisting that "species" is as important as "race" or "gender" and calling it a day. Coalition-building is not a matter of "recruiting more x people" to visually show diversity.

Of course, one could easily argue that human-oriented social justice groups rarely make the more-than-human world a priority—thus, the animal rights movement owes little to groups that would "take offense" to being asked to confront their speciesism like animal groups are demanded to confront their racism and other isms. I postulate, however, that animal rights must consistently take a "higher ground" and fight for *total* liberation, necessitating modes of legal and extralegal activism that not only *analogize* the historical exploitation of humans to the contemporary exploitation of animals but also consistently *fight against* the present manifestations of those oppressions deemed to be "in the past," those discriminations that have moved from de jure to de facto.

A critical vegan rhetoric thus functions simultaneously as a rhetoric, an ethic, and an analytic, allowing scholars to investigate animal rights rhetorics—legal or extralegal, top-down or bottom-up, individual or group-led—from a paradigm that deviates from liberal humanist essentialisms and universalisms. It is, in a sense, a way of making analytics messier, of producing more questions than answers, of insisting upon the *complication* of strategic thought as opposed to the production of coherent answers. It is not so much a way of proving that "x group is right" or "y group was wrong," but rather a dialectic style of both/and thinking that prefers to make impure politics slightly purer without presupposing that, at the present moment, an "ultimate purity" exists. Ultimately, this analytical approach necessitates the identification and critique of strategic, tactical, and overarching ethical incoherence in the naming of making better, not tearing down; of opening dialogues, not perpetuating the same old monologues; and, ultimately, of rejecting speciesism and species essentialism simultaneously.

In a world of increasing environmental degradation and interspecies exploitation, I anticipate that this project will contribute to the ever-growing call for academic scholarship that offers prescriptive advice as opposed to description alone. In my case, I integrated the theoretical fields of ecofeminism, feminist legal studies, critical animal studies with ideological rhetorical methodologies to understand the complex and interrelated ideologies guiding legalized human and more-than-human oppressions and to offer suggestions for future legal (and necessarily interconnected extralegal) praxis. This book serves as an interdisciplinary prototype for animal-interested rhetorical scholarship. It further offers a new theoretical paradigm with which to view animal legal rhetorics in ecofeminist legal theory. And finally, it calls for a critical vegan rhetoric as a guiding rhetorical framework for animal rights theorizations and applications. Central to this project was the decentering of "prototypical" (read: liberal humanist) animal rights legal rhetoric in order to point to its roots in complex systems of exploitation—not necessarily to *eradicate,* but rather to *complicate* the use of rights rhetoric in various animal liberationists' rhetorical strategies and tactics.

To conclude, animal rights law is not even close to an ideological monolith. It carries with it a set of competing ontologies that are often morally ambivalent and contradictory to each other. The three dominant paradigms that I have identified—Francione's vegan abolitionism, Wise's NhRP, and Earth jurisprudence—are, by themselves, too internally incoherent to amount to "animal rights" in any legitimate sense. However, by adopting a both/and approach and reconciling what *appear* to be conflicting ideologies—for instance, individualistic vegan abolitionism with bio-egalitarian green ecology—some of this incoherence actually *lessens.* And finally, by insisting that such theoretical combinations stay true to the intersectional values of ecofeminist, decolonial ideologies, (ir)rational legal positivism might be replaced with a critical, more-than-humanist legal framework that fights for justice via broad ontological shifts in conceptions of humanity, animality, nature, culture, domesticity, and rights. There is a long road ahead for animal rights law, but perhaps the right combination of ideologies, strategies, and tactics might get us there a little bit faster. We must remember, however, that "there" must be envisioned as a land of *total* liberation.

References

Abram, D. (2012). *The spell of the sensuous: Perception and language in a more-than human world.* New York: Vintage.

Adams, C. J. (1990). *The sexual politics of meat: A feminist-vegetarian critical theory.* New York: Bloomsbury.

———. (1991). Ecofeminism and the eating of animals. *Hypatia, 6*(1), 125–145.

The Advocacy for Veganism Society. (n.d.). Mission. http://www.abolitionistvegansociety.org/about/mission/#.Wq6lC5ch02w

Albright, K. M. (2002). The extension of legal rights to animals under a caring ethic: An ecofeminist exploration of Steven Wise's "Rattling the Cage." *Natural Resources Journal, 42*(4), 915–937.

Alexander, S. (2010). Earth jurisprudence and the ecological case for degrowth. *Journal Jurisprudence, 6,* 131–148.

Alinsky, S. D. (1972). *Rules for radicals: A pragmatic primer for realistic radicals.* New York: Vintage.

Alley-Young, G. (2008). Articulating identity: Refining postcolonial and whiteness perspectives on race within communication studies. *Review of Communication, 8*(3), 307–321.

American Bar Association. (2017). ABA national lawyer population summary. https://www.americanbar.org/resources_for_lawyers/profession_statistics.html

American Pet Products Association. (2017). Pet industry market size and ownership statistics. http://www.americanpetproducts.org/press_industrytrends.asp

Animal Charity Evaluator. (2017). The Nonhuman Rights Project: NHRP. https://animalcharityevaluators.org/charity-review/the-nonhuman-rights-project/.

Armstrong, P. (2002). The postcolonial animal. *Society and Animals, 10*(4), 413–420.

Artz, L., Macek, S., & Cloud, D. L. (Eds.). (2006). *Marxism and communication studies: The point is to change it.* New York: Peter Lang.

Associated Press. (2005, August 14). PETA rethinks slavery analogy *Los Angeles Times.* http://articles.latimes.com/

Atkins-Sayre, W. (2010). Articulating identity: People for the Ethical Treatment of Animals and the animal/human divide. *Western Journal of Communication, 74*(3), 309–328.

Backus, M. (2013, November 13). Fur flies in West Hollywood showdown over city ban. Animal Legal Defense Fund. http://aldf.org/

Bailey, C. (2007). We are what we eat: Feminist vegetarianism and the reproduction of racial identity. *Hypatia, 22*(2), 39–59.

Barad, K. (2010). Quantum entanglements and hauntological relations of inheritance: Dis/continuities, spacetime enfoldings, and justice-to-come. *Derrida Today, 3*(2), 240–268.

Bartlett, K. T. (1990). Feminist legal methods. *Harvard Law Review, 103*(4), 829–888.

Bekoff, M. (Ed.). (2013). *Ignoring nature no more: The case for compassionate conservation.* University of Chicago Press.

———. (2014). *Rewilding our hearts: Building pathways of compassion and coexistence.* Novato, CA: New World.

———. (2015, February 9). Compassionate conservation: More than "welfarism gone wild." *Huffington Post.* https://www.huffingtonpost.com/marc-bekoff/compassionate-conservatio_1_b_6639964.html

———. (2017, September 11). A journey to ecocentrism: Earth jurisprudence and rewilding. *Psychology Today.* https://www.psychologytoday.com/blog/animal-emotions/201709/journey-ecocentrism-earth-jurisprudence-and-rewilding

Bekoff, M., & Pierce, J. (2009). *Wild justice: The moral lives of animals.* University of Chicago Press.

———. (2017). *The animals' agenda: Freedom, compassion, and coexistence in the human age.* Boston: Beacon.

Belcourt, B. R. (2014). Animal bodies, colonial subjects: (Re)Locating animality in decolonial thought. *Societies, 5*(1), 1–11.

Bell, M. (2003). Thomas Berry and an Earth jurisprudence. *Trumpeter, 19*(1), 69–96.

Bentham, J. (1789/1970). *An introduction to the principles of morals and legislation.* London, UK: Athlone.

Berdik, C. (2013, July 14). The "animal personhood" movement believes dolphins, great apes, and elephants deserve to be able to sue—and now it has a plaintiff. *Boston Globe.* https://www.bostonglobe.com/ideas/2013/07/13/should-chimpanzees-have- legal-rights/ Mv8iDDGYUFGNmWNLOWPRFM/story.html

Berman, R. (2018, March 2). Why philosophers say chimps have to be considered persons. *Big Think.* http://bigthink.com/robby-berman/why- philosophers-say-chimps-have-to-be-considered-persons

Berry, T. (1988). *The dream of the earth.* San Francisco: Sierra Club Books.

———. (1999). *The great work: Our way into the future.* New York: Broadway.

———. (2001, April 21–24). *The origin, differentiation and role of rights.* Paper presented at the Earth Jurisprudence Conference at the Airlie Centre, Warrenton, Virginia.

———. (2006). *Evening thoughts: Reflections on the Earth as sacred community.* San Francisco: Sierra Club Books.

Best, S. (2007). The killing fields of South Africa: Eco-wars, species apartheid, and total liberation. *Fast Capitalism, 2*(2). https://www.uta.edu/huma/agger/fastcapitalism/2_2/ best.html

———. (2009). The rise of critical animal studies: Putting theory into action and animal liberation into higher education. *Journal for Critical Animal Studies, 7*(1), 9–52.

Bhabha, H. K. (2006). Third space. *Multitudes, 26*(3), 95–107.

Birkeland, J. (1993). Ecofeminism: Linking theory and practice. In G. Gaard, (Ed.), *Ecofeminism: Women, animals, nature* (pp. 13–59). Philadelphia: Temple University Press.

Black, C. F. (2011). *The land is the source of the law: A dialogic encounter with indigenous jurisprudence.* New York: Routledge.

Black, J. E. (2003). Extending the rights of personhood, voice, and life to sensate others: A homology of right to life and animal rights rhetoric. *Communication Quarterly, 51*(3), 312–331.

———. (2009). Native resistance rhetoric and the decolonization of American Indian removal discourse. *Quarterly Journal of Speech, 95*(1), 66–88.

———. (2012). Native authenticity, rhetorical circulation, and neocolonial decay: The case of Chief Seattle's controversial speech. *Rhetoric & Public Affairs, 15*(4), 635–646.

Blosh, M. (2012). *The history of animal welfare and the future of animal rights* (Master's thesis). Electronic Thesis and Book Repository. (803)

Bradford, W. (1856). *History of Plymouth plantation.* Published for the Massachusetts Historical Society.

Broad, G. M. (2013). Vegans for Vick: Dogfighting, intersectional politics, and the limits of mainstream discourse. *International Journal of Communication, 7*, 780–800.

————. (2016). Animal production, ag-gag laws, and the social production of ignorance: Exploring the role of storytelling. *Environmental Communication, 10*(1), 43–61.

Brown, S. R. (2017, June 8). Captive chimps Tommy and Kiko are not entitled to human rights, judges rule. *New York Daily News.* http://www.nydailynews.com/

Brueck, J. F. (2017). *Veganism in an oppressive world.* Sanctuary Publishers.

Brulliard, K. (2016, May 24). This man is trying to help chimps—and soon, elephants sue their owners. *Washington Post.* https://www.washingtonpost.com/news/

Buck v. Bell, 274 U.S. 200. (1927).

Buescher, D. T., & Ono, K. A. (1996). Civilized colonialism: *Pocahontas* as neocolonial rhetoric. *Women's Studies in Communication, 19*(2), 127–153.

Buff, E. (2014, December 29). The ten biggest animal rights and welfare victories of 2014. *One Green Planet.* http://www.onegreenplanet.org/animalsandnature/biggest-animal-rights-and-welfare-wins/

Burdon, P. (2010a). Wild law: The philosophy of earth jurisprudence. *Alternative Law Journal, 35*(2), 62–65.

————. (2010b). The rights of nature reconsidered. *Australian Humanities Review, 49,* 69–90.

————. (2011). Earth rights: The theory [E-journal issue]. *ICUN Academy of Environmental Law, 2011*(1), 1–12.

California Academy of Sciences. (2011, August 24). How many species on earth? https://www.calacademy.org/explore-science/how-many-species-on-earth

Cao, D. (2014). Crimes against animality: animal cruelty and criminal justice in a globalized world. In B. Arrigot and H.Y. Bosat (Eds.), *Routledge handbook of international crime and justice studies* (pp. 169–190). New York: Routledge.

Cassidy, A., & Mills, B. (2012). "Fox tots attack shock": Urban foxes, mass media and boundary-breaching. *Environmental Communication, 6*(4), 494–511.

Center for Earth Jurisprudence. (n.d.). Our History. http://www.earthjurist.org/our-history.

Cerulli, T. (2014, March 14). A caretaker and a killer: How hunters can save the wilderness. *Atlantic.* https://www.theatlantic.com/

Chang, H. (1999). Re-examining the rhetoric of the cultural border. *Electronic Magazine of Multicultural Education, 1*(1), 1–7.

Choplin, L. (2017, March 23). Why rights? Tommy and Kiko appellate hearing. Nonhuman Rights Project [Blog post]. https://www.nonhumanrights.org/blog/chimpanzee-rights-appellate-court/

————. (2018, February 26). Philosophers offer support on chimpanzee rights cases. Nonhuman Rights Project [Blog post]. https://www.nonhumanrights.org/blog/update-motion-philosophers-brief/

Client: Kiko. (n.d.). Nonhuman Rights Project. https://www.nonhumanrights.org/client-kiko/

Client: Tommy. (n.d.). Nonhuman Rights Project. https://www.nonhumanrights.org/client-tommy/

Cloud, D. L. (1999). The null persona: Race and the rhetoric of silence in the uprising of '34. *Rhetoric & Public Affairs, 2*(2), 177–209.

Cochran, P. A., Marshall, C. A., Garcia-Downing, C., Kendall, E., Cook, D., McCubbin, L., & Gover, R. M. S. (2008). Indigenous ways of knowing: Implications for participatory research and community. *American Journal of Public Health, 98*(1), 22–27.

Coelho, S. (2013, May 24). Dolphins gain unprecedented protection in India. *Deutsche Welle.* http://www.dw.com/en/

Conaghan, J. (2009). Intersectionality and the feminist project in law. In E. Grabham, D. Cooper, J. Krishnadas, & D. Herman (Eds.), *Intersectionality and beyond: Law, power and the politics of location* (pp. 21–48). London: Routledge

Cordeiro-Rodrigues, L. (2017). Animal abolitionism and "racism without racists." *Journal of Agricultural and Environmental Ethics, 30,* 745–764.

Cotroneo, C. (2016, March 24). Jane Goodall pleads for the release of two very special chimps. *The Dodo.* https://www.thedodo.com/hercules-leo-chimps-goodall-1684907023.html

Cowles, I. (2011, May 31). Real environmentalists eat meat. *Huffington Post.* https://www.huffingtonpost.com/isabel-cowles/real-environmentalistseab521084.html

Cox, R. (2007). Nature's "crisis disciplines": Does environmental communication have an ethical duty?. *Environmental Communication, 1*(1), 5–20.

Crenshaw, K. (1991). Mapping the margins: Intersectionality, identity politics, and violence against women of color. *Stanford Law Review, 43,* 1241–1299.

Cronon, W. (1996). The trouble with wilderness: Or, getting back to the wrong nature. *Environmental History, 1*(1), 7–28.

Cullinan, C. (2008). Do humans have standing to deny trees rights?. *Barry Law Review, 11,* 11–22.

Cupp, R. L. (2016, June 3). Gorilla's death calls for human responsibility, not animal personhood. *The Conversation.* https://theconversation.com/gorillas-death-calls-for-human-responsibility-not-animal-personhood-60360.

Curtin, D. (1991). Toward an ecological ethic of care. *Hypatia, 6*(1), 60–74.

Daly, N. (2017, February 6). U.S. animal abuse records deleted—what we stand to lose. *National Geographic.* https://news.nationalgeographic.com/2017/02/wildlife-watch-usda-animal-welfare-trump-records/

Deckha, M. (2007). Animal justice, cultural justice: A posthumanist response to cultural rights in animals. *Journal of Animal Law & Ethics, 2,* 189–229.

————. (2008). Intersectionality and posthumanist visions of equality. *Wisconsin Journal of Law, Gender & Society, 23,* 249–266.

————. (2010). The subhuman as a cultural agent of violence. *Journal for Critical Animal Studies, 8*(3), 28–51.

————. (2011). Critical animal studies and animal law. *Animal Law, 18,* 207–236.

————. (2012). Toward a postcolonial, posthumanist feminist theory: Centralizing race and culture in feminist work on nonhuman animals. *Hypatia, 27*(3), 527–545.

Deer, S., & Murphy, L. (2017). Animals may take pity on us: Using traditional tribal beliefs to address animal abuse and family violence within tribal nations. *Mitchell Hamline Law Review, 43,* 703–742.

Definition of veganism (n.d.). The Vegan Society. https://www.vegansociety.com/go-vegan/definition-veganism

DeGrazia, D. (1996). *Taking animals seriously: Mental life and moral status.* New York: Cambridge University Press.

Delicath, J. W., & Deluca, K. M. (2003). Image events, the public sphere, and argumentative practice: The case of radical environmental groups. *Argumentation, 17*(3), 315–333.

DeLuca, K. M. (1999). Articulation theory: A discursive grounding for rhetorical practice. *Philosophy & Rhetoric, 32*(4), 334–348.

DeLuca, K. M., & Demo, A. T. (2000). Imaging nature: Watkins, Yosemite, and the birth of environmentalism. *Critical Studies in Media Communication, 17*(3), 241–260.

DeLuca, K. M., & Peeples, J. (2002). From public sphere to public screen: Democracy, activism, and the "violence" of Seattle. *Critical studies in media communication, 19*(2), 125–151.

DeLuca, K. M., & Slawter-Volkening, L. (2009). Memories of the tropics in industrial jungles: Constructing nature, contesting nature. *Environmental Communication, 3*(1), 1–24.

De Lucia, V. (2013). Towards an ecological philosophy of law: A comparative discussion. *Journal of Human Rights and the Environment, 4*(2), 167–190. doi: 10.4337/jhre.2013.02.03

Dell'Amore, C. (2013, December 16). 20,000 species are near extinction: Is it time to rethink how we decide which to save? *National Geographic.* https://news.nationalgeographic.com/news/2013/12/131216-conservation-environment-animals-science-endangered-species/

Department of the Interior. (2017, September 7). New 5-year report shows 101.6 million Americans participated in hunting, fishing & wildlife activities [Press release]. https://www.doi.gov/pressreleases/new-5-year-report-shows-1016-million-americans-participated-hunting-fishing-wildlife

Dhamoon, R. K. (2011). Considerations on mainstreaming intersectionality. *Political Research Quarterly, 64*(1), 230–243.

————. (2015). A feminist approach to decolonizing anti-racism: Rethinking transnationalism, intersectionality, and settler colonialism. *Feral Feminisms, 4,* 20–37.

Derrida, J. (1992). "Eating well" or "the calculation of the subject." In E. Cadava, P. Connor, & J. Nancy (Eds.), *Who comes after the subject?* (pp. 96–119). New York: Routledge.

———. (2002). The animal that therefore I am (more to follow). *Critical Inquiry, 28*(2), 369–418.

Donaldson, S., & Kymlicka, W. (2011). *Zoopolis: A political theory of animal rights.* New York: Oxford University Press.

———. (2011). *Zoopolis: A political theory of animal rights.* 1st ed. Oxford, UK: Oxford University Press.

Donovan, J. (1990). Animal rights and feminist theory. *Signs: Journal of Women in Culture and Society, 15*(2), 350–375.

Donovan, J., & Adams, C. J. (Eds.). (2007). *The feminist care tradition in animal ethics: A reader.* New York: Columbia University Press.

Doyle, J. (2016). Celebrity vegans and the lifestyling of ethical consumption. *Environmental Communication, 10*(6), 777–790.

Dvorsky, G. (2013, August 15). No, India did not just grant dolphins the status of humans. *Gizmodo.* http://io9.gizmodo.com/

———. (2014, December 4). Why an appeals court was wrong to say this chimp isn't a person. *Gizmodo.* http://io9.gizmodo.com/

———. (2017a, June 9). Appeals court says chimps are not legal persons—here's why they're wrong. *Gizmodo.* http://gizmodo.com/

———. (2017b, November 14). Connecticut lawsuit is the first to claim elephants as legal persons. *Gizmodo.* https://gizmodo.com/

Dwyer, C. (2018, March 8). Trump administration quietly decides—again—to allow elephant trophy imports. *NPR.* https://www.npr.org/

Edmonds, D., & Warburton, N. (Producers). (2012, October 13). Gary Francione on animal liberation. *Philosophy Bites* [Audio podcast]. http://philosophybites.com/2012/10/gary-l-francione-on-animal-abolitionism.html/

Eisler, R. (1987). *The chalice and the blade.* San Francisco: Harper Collins.

Elder, C. (2015, September 30). Whitesplaining: What it is and why it matters. *The Conversation.* https://theconversation.com/whitesplaining-what-it-is-and-how-it-works-48175.

Enck-Wanzer, D. (2012). Decolonizing imaginaries: Rethinking "the people" in the Young Lords' church offensive. *Quarterly Journal of Speech, 98*(1), 1–23.

Endres, D. (2009a). The rhetoric of nuclear colonialism: Rhetorical exclusion of American Indian arguments in the Yucca Mountain nuclear waste siting decision. *Communication and Critical/Cultural Studies, 6*(1), 39–60.

————. (2009b). From wasteland to waste site: The role of discourse in nuclear power's environmental injustices. *Local Environment, 14*(10), 917–937.

————. (2009c). Expanding notions of scientific argument: Understanding and communicating science. In L. Kahor & P. Stout (Eds.), *Understanding and communicating science: New agendas in communication* (pp. 187–208). New York: Routledge.

————. (2013). Animist intersubjectivity as argumentation: Western Shoshone and Southern Paiute arguments against a nuclear waste site at Yucca Mountain. *Argumentation, 27*(2), 183–200.

Ereshefsky, M. (1998). Species pluralism and anti-realism. *Philosophy of Science, 65*(1), 103-120.

Fanon, F. (1967). *Black skin, white masks* (C. L. Markmann, Trans.). New York: Grove.

Fermino, J. Nonhuman rights project argues for chimpanzees' rights, release to sanctuary in New York appellate court. Nonhuman Rights Project. https://www.nonhumanrights.org/media-center/03–16–17-nonhuman-rights-project -argues-for-chimpanzees-rights/

Ferre, F. (1994). Personalistic organicism: Paradox or paradigm? *Royal Institute of Philosophy Supplements, 36*, 59–73. doi: 10.1017/s1358246100006457

Ferrell, J. (1997). Against the law: Anarchist criminology. In D. Milanovec (Ed.), *Thinking critically about crime* (pp. 146–154). Piscataway, NJ: Transaction.

Fischer, B. (2018). Is abolitionism guilty of racism? A reply to Cordeiro-Rodrigues. *Journal of Agricultural and Environmental Ethics, 31*(3), 295–306.

Food Empowerment Project. (n.d.). About F.E.P. http://www.foodispower.org/about-f-e-p/

————. (n.d.). Produce workers. http://www.foodispower.org/produce-workers/

Fox, N., & Ward, K. (2008). Health, ethics and environment: A qualitative study of vegetarian motivations. *Appetite, 50*(2–3), 422–429.

Francione, G. L. (1993). Personhood, property, and legal competence. In P. Cavalieri & P. Singer (Eds.), *The great ape project: Equality beyond the law.* New York: St. Martin's Griffin.

————. (1995). *Animals, property, and the law.* Philadelphia: Temple University Press.

————. (1996). *Rain without thunder: The ideology of the animal rights movement.* Philadelphia: Temple University Press.

————. (1997). Animal rights theory and utilitarianism: Relative normative guidance. *Animal Law, 3*, 75–101. https://law.lclark.edu/law_reviews/animal_law_review

————. (2006a, December 20.). The Great Ape Project: Not so great [Blog post]. http://www.abolitionistapproach.com/the-great-ape-project-not-so-great/

————. (2006b, December 26). Animals as property and the rape analogy: A postscript [Blog post]. http://www.abolitionistapproach.com/animals-as-property-and-the-rape-analogy-apostscript/#.Vk-WhLs45o

————. (2006c). Taking sentence seriously. *Journal of Animal Law & Ethics, 1*, 1–18.

————. (2007a). The use of nonhuman animals in biomedical research: Necessity and justification. *Journal of Law, Medicine & Ethics, 35*(2), 241–248.

————. (2007b, January 10). Animal rights and domesticated nonhumans [Blog post]. http://www.abolitionistapproach.com/animal-rights-and-domesticated-non-humans/

————. (2008). *Animals as persons: Essays on the abolition of animal exploitation.* New York: Columbia University Press.

————. (2009, March 16). Peter Singer and the welfarist position on the value of nonhuman life [Blog post]. http://www.abolitionistapproach.com/peter-singer-and-the-welfarist-position-on- the-lesser-value-of-nonhuman-life

————. (2010a). Animal welfare and the moral value of nonhuman animals. *Law, Culture, and the Humanities, 6*(1), 24–36.

————. (2010b). *Introduction to animal rights: Your child or the dog?.* Philadelphia: Temple University Press.

————. (2012a, January 4). Animal rights, animal welfare, and the slavery analogy [Blog post]. http://www.abolitionistapproach.com/animal-rights-animal-welfare-and-the-slaveryanalogy/#.VkW4rs45o

————. (2012b, July 31). Pets: The inherent problem with domestication [Blog post]. http://www.abolitionistapproach.com/pets-the-inherent-problems-of-domestication/#.VkS-L-s45p

————. (2012c, August 12). Only sentience matters [Blog post]. http://www.abolitionistapproach.com/only-sentience-matters/

————. (2013, November 23). Abolitionist animal rights/abolitionist veganism: In a nutshell [Blog post]. http://www.abolitionistapproach.com/abolitionist-animal-rights-abolitionist-veganism-ina-nutshell/#.VhqiNCus7rQ

————. (2015, December 10). Sexism and racism in the "animal movement": A reply to Ruby Hamad [Blog post]. http://www.abolitionistapproach.com/sexism- and-racism-in-the-animal-movement-areply-to-ruby-hamad

————. (2016, January 10). Essentialism, intersectionality, and veganism as a moral baseline: Black Vegans Rock and the Humane Society of the United States [Blog post]. http://www.abolitionistapproach.com/essentialism- intersectionality-and-veganism-as-a-moral-baseline-black-vegans-rock-and-the humane-society-of-the-united-states/

————. (n.d.). Quotes by Gary L. Francione. *The Abolitionist Approach.* http://www.abolitionistapproach.com/quotes/

Francione, G. L., & Charlton, A. (2010). Abolitionist approach to animal rights. In M. Bekoff (Ed.), *Encyclopedia of animal rights and welfare* (pp. 1–5). Santa Barbara, CA: ABC-CLIO.

————. (2015). *Eat like you care: An examination of the morality of eating animals.* Logan, UT: Exempla.

————. (2016, September 8). The case against pets. https://aeon.co/essays/why-keeping-a-pet-is-fundamentally-unethical

Francione, G. L., & Garner, R. (2010). *The animal rights debate: Abolition or regulation?* New York: Columbia University Press.

Freeman, C. P. (2009). This little piggy went to press: The American news media's construction of animals in agriculture. *Communication Review, 12*(1), 78–103.

————. (2010a). Embracing humanimality: Deconstructing the human/animal dichotomy. In G. Goodale & J. E. Black (Eds.), *Arguments about animal ethics* (pp. 11–30). Lexington, MA: Lexington Books.

————. (2010b). Meat's place on the campaign menu: How US environmental discourse negotiates vegetarianism. *Environmental Communication, 4*(3), 255–276.

Freeman, C. P., Bekoff, M., & Bexell, S. M. (2011). Giving voice to the "voiceless": Incorporating nonhuman animal perspectives as journalistic sources. *Journalism Studies, 12*(5), 590–607.

Gaard, G. (Ed.). (1993). *Ecofeminism: Women, animals, nature.* Philadelphia: Temple University Press.

————. (1997). Toward a queer ecofeminism. *Hypatia, 12*(1), 114–137.

————. (2001). Tools for a cross-cultural feminist ethics: Exploring ethical contexts and contents in the Makah whale hunt. *Hypatia, 16*(1), 1–26.

————. (2002). Vegetarian ecofeminism: A review essay. *Frontiers: A Journal of Women Studies, 23*(3), 117–146.

————. (2011). Ecofeminism revisited: Rejecting essentialism and re-placing species in a material feminist environmentalism. *Feminist Formations, 23*(2), 26–53.

Garner, R. (2006). Animal welfare: A political defense. *Journal of Animal Law & Ethics, 1,* 161–221.

Giroux, H. (1997). Rewriting the discourse of racial identity: Towards a pedagogy and politics of whiteness. *Harvard Educational Review, 67*(2), 285–321.

Goodale, G. (2015). *The rhetorical invention of man: A history of distinguishing humans from other animals.* Lexington, MA: Lexington Books.

Goodale, G., & Black, J. E. (Eds.). (2010). *Arguments about animal ethics.* Lexington, MA: Lexington Books.

Gordon, J. G., Lind, K. D., & Kutnicki, S. (2017). A rhetorical bestiary. *Rhetorical Society Quarterly 47*(3), 222–228.

Grande, S. (2003). Whitestream feminism and the colonialist project: A review of contemporary feminist pedagogy and praxis. *Educational Theory, 53*(3), 329–346.

Green, A. (2016, June 16). Pets not "mere" property: Oregon Supreme Court upholds dog starvation conviction. *OregonLive: The Oregonian.* http://www.oregonlive.com/portland/index.ssf/2016/06/pets_arent_just_property_ orego.html/

Greenpeace. (n.d.). "Eating less meat, more plants helps the environment." https://www.greenpeace.org/usa/sustainable-agriculture/eco-farming/eat-more-plants/.

Griffin, L. M. (1952). The rhetoric of historical movements. *Quarterly Journal of Speech, 38*(2), 184–188.

Grillo, T. (1995). Anti-essentialism and intersectionality: Tools to dismantle the master's house. *Berkeley Women's Law Journal, 10*(1), 16–30.

Grimm, D. (2014). *Citizen canine.* New York: Public Affairs.

———. (2015, July 30). Judge rules research chimps are not "legal persons." *Science.* http://www.sciencemag.org/news/2015/07/judge-rules-research-chimps-are-not-legal-persons

———. (2016, May 23). When animals were put on trial [Blog post]. http://davidhgrimm.com/2016/05/23/when-animals-were-put-on-trial/

Habermas, J., Lennox, S., & Lennox, F. (1974). The public sphere: An encyclopedia article. *New German Critique,* (3), 49–55.

Hamblin, M. (2011). Wild law and domesticated animals: A wild law approach to the regulation of farming industries in Australia. Presentation at the 3rd annual Wild Law Conference at Griffith University, 16–18 September.

Hamington, M. (2009). Feminist prophetic pragmatism. *Journal of Speculative Philosophy, 23*(2), 83–91.

Haraway, D. J. (2003). *The companion species manifesto: Dogs, people, and significant otherness.* Chicago: Prickly Paradigm.

Harper, A. B. (2009). *Sistah vegan: Black female vegans speak on food, identity, health, and society.* Brooklyn, NY: Lantern.

———. (2011). Vegans of color, racialized embodiment, and problematics of the "exotic." In A. H. Alkon & J. Agyeman (Eds.), *Cultivating food justice: Race, class, and sustainability* (pp. 221–238). Boston: MIT Press.

———. (2012). Going beyond the normative white "post-racial" vegan epistemology. In P. Williams-Forson & C. Counihan (Eds.), *Taking food public: Redefining foodways in a changing world* (pp. 155–170). New York: Routledge.

———. (2013, June 5). On Trayvon Martin, PETA, and being a black critical race researcher in white spaces [Video file]. https://www.youtube.com/

———. (2014, October 9). Of [post]race consciousness, food justice, and hip-hop vegan ethics [Blog post]. http://sistahvegan.com/2014/10/09/on-ferguson-thug-kitchen-and-trayvon-martin-intersections-of-postrace-consciousness-food-justice-and-hip-hop-vegan-ethics/

———. (2015a, December 20). [Facebook update]. http://www.sistahvegan.com/2015/12/21/this-is-the-impact-gary-francione-and-ruby hamads-moment-in-time-had-on-my-engaged-buddhist-practice/

———. (2015b, December 21). This is the impact Gary Francione and Ruby Hamad's "moment in time" had on my engaged Buddhist practice [Blog post]. http://www. sistahvegan.com/2015/12/21/this-is-the-impact garyfrancione-and-ruby-hamads-moment-in-time-had-on-my-engaged-buddhist-practice/

———. (2016a, January 20). Ruminating on perpetually being labeled a "white hating racist" and other thoughts [Blog post]. http://www.sistahvegan.com/2016/01/20/ruminating-on-perpetually-being- labeled-as-a-white-hating-racist-and-other-thoughts/

———. (2016b, February 9). [Vegan special edition]: A possessive investment in whiteness ("non-racist" "cruelty-free" donor power) [Blog post]. http://sistahvegan.com/2016/02/09/vegan-special-edition-a-progressive-investment-in-whiteness

———. (2017, November 26). Return of the n*gger breakers: The [white racist] vegan playbook [Blog post]. http://www.sistahvegan.com/2017/11/26/the-return-of-the-ngger-breakers-the-white-racist-vegan-playbook/

Harvey, F. (2016, March 21). Eat less meat to avoid dangerous global warming, scientists say. *Guardian.* https://www.theguardian.com/

Hasian, M. A. (1996). *The rhetoric of eugenics in Anglo-American thought.* Athens, GA: University of Georgia Press.

———. (1993). Myth and ideology in legal discourse: Moving from critical legal studies toward rhetorical consciousness. *Legal Studies Forum, 17,* 347–365.

———. (2001). Rhetorical studies and the future of postcolonial theories and practices. *Rhetoric Review, 20*(1/2), 22–28.

Hasian, M., Condit, C. M., & Lucaites, J. L. (1996). The rhetorical boundaries of "the law": A consideration of the rhetorical culture of legal practice and the case of the "separate but equal" doctrine. *Quarterly Journal of Speech, 82*(4), 323–342.

Hawhee, D. (2011). Toward a bestial rhetoric. *Philosophy and Rhetoric, 44*(1), 81–87.

Helsinki Group. (2010, May 22). Declaration for the rights of cetaceans: Dolphins and whales. https://www.cetaceanrights.org/

Hogan, B. (2015, December 31). India declares dolphins "non-human persons." *EcoRazzi.* http://www.ecorazzi.com/2015/12/31/india-declares-dolphins-non-human-persons/

Holt-Gimenez, Eric, & Harper, A. B. (2016). Food-systems-racism: From mistreatment to transformation. Institute for Food & Developmental Policy. https://foodfirst.org/wp-content/uploads/2016/03/DR1Final.pdf

hooks, b. (1984). *Feminist theory: From margin to center.* London: Pluto.

Humane Society of the United States. (2015, June 30). Complaints filed with FDA and FTC over Costco egg supplier's chicken cages. http://www.humanesociety.org/news/ news_briefs/2015/06/ftc-fda-costco- complaint-063015.html?credit=web_id89991628

Jackson, C. (1993). Women/nature or gender/history? A critique of ecofeminist "development." *Journal of Peasant Studies, 20*(3), 389–418.

Kahumbu, P., & Halliday, A. (2016, April 23). Why it makes sense to burn ivory stock piles. *Guardian.* https://www.theguardian.com/

Kaufman, A. (2016, June 24). The lawyer fighting for animal rights in "Unlocking the Cage" asks: What kind of being are you? *Los Angeles Times.* http://www.latimes.com/

Keim, B. (2012, July 19). New science emboldens long shot bid for dolphin, whale rights. *Wired.* https://www.wired.com/

———. (2013, December 6). A chimp's day in court: Inside the historic demand for nonhuman rights. *Wired.* https://www.wired.com/

———. (2014, December 4). Case for chimpanzee rights rejected by appeals court. *Wired.* https://www.wired.com/

Kelly, C. (2012). Neocolonialism and the global prison in National Geographic's locked up abroad. *Critical Studies in Media Communication, 29*(4), 331–347.

Kelman, M. G. (1984). Trashing. *Stanford Law Review, 36*(1/2), 293–348.

Kennedy, G. A. (1992). A hoot in the dark: The evolution of general rhetoric. *Philosophy & Rhetoric, 25*(1), 1–21.

Kim, C. J. (2011). Moral extensionism or racist exploitation? The use of holocaust and slavery analogies in the animal liberation movement. *New Political Science, 33*(3), 311–333.

Kleiner, B. (2002, September 5). "Drawing the Line" by Steven Wise. *Salon.* https://www.salon.com/

King, B. (2014, October 27). Humans, chimps, and why we need personhood for all. *TIME.* http://time.com/

Ko, A. (2015, September 18). 3 reasons black folks don't join the animal rights movement—and why we should. https://everydayfeminism.com/2015/09/black-folks-animal-rights-mvmt/

Ko, A., & Ko, S. (2017). *Aphro-ism: Essays on pop culture, feminism, and black veganism from two sisters.* New York: Lantern.

Koons, J. E. (2008). Earth jurisprudence: The moral value of nature. *Pace Environmental Law Review, 25,* 263–340.

———. (2011). Earth jurisprudence and the story of oil: Intergenerational justice for the post-petroleum period. *University of South Florida Law Review, 46,* 93–138.

Koopman, S. (2008). Imperialism within: Can the master's tools bring down empire?. *ACME: An International Journal for Critical Geographies, 7*(2), 283–307.

Laclau, E., & Mouffe, C. (2001). *Hegemony and socialist strategy: Towards a radical democratic politics.* New York: Verso.

Leahy, M. P. (1991). *Against liberation: Putting animals in perspective.* New York: Routledge.

Leenaert, T. (2015, March 4). I used to be a Francione fan (on Gary Francione and "abolitionists," part 2) [Blog post]. http://veganstrategist.org/2015/03/04/i-used-to-be-a-francione-fan-on-gary-francione-and-abolitionists-part-2/

———. (2015, March 6). Why I'm openly criticizing Francione (final post) [Blog post]. http://veganstrategist.org/2015/03/06/final-part-onfrancione/

Leopold, A. (1949). *A sand county almanac: With other essays on conservation from Round River.* Oxford, UK: Oxford University Press.

Lingis, A. (2003). Animal body, inhuman face. In C. Wolfe (Ed.), *Zoontologies: The question of the animal* (pp. 165–182). New York: Routledge.

Lockwood, R. (2010). Cruelty to animals: Prosecuting anti-cruelty laws. In M. Bekoff (Ed.), *Encyclopedia of animal rights and welfare* (pp. 158–160). Santa Barbara, CA: ABC-CLIO.

Lorde, A. (2003). The master's tools will never destroy the master's house. In R. Lewis & S. Mills (Eds.), *Feminist postcolonial theory: A reader* (pp. 25–28). New York: Routledge.

Loria, J. (2017, April 20). You can't eat meat and be an environmentalist. Period. http://www.mercyforanimals.org/you- cant-eat-meat-and-be-an-environmentalist

Lovelace, R. (2017, March 13). New York court to consider whether a chimpanzee is a "person." *Washington Examiner.* http://www.washingtonexaminer.com/

Lucaites, J. L. (1990). Between rhetoric and "the law": Power, legitimacy, and social change. *Quarterly Journal of Speech, 76*(4), 435–449.

Lugones, M. (2007). Heterosexualism and the colonial/modern gender system. *Hypatia, 22*(1), 186–219.

Lunceford, B. (2010). PETA and the rhetoric of nude protest. In G. Goodale & J. E. Black (Eds.), *Arguments about animal ethics* (pp. 97–112). Lexington, MA: Lexington Books.

MacKenzie, D. (1976). Eugenics in Britain. *Social Studies of Science, 6*(3/4), 499–532.

Maldonado-Torres, N. (2008). *Against war: Views from the underside of modernity.* Durham, NC: Duke University Press.

Maltby, G., & Mountford, R. (2012). The animal rights "bible." *Resurgence & Ecologist.* http://www.resurgence.org/magazine/article3614-the-animalrights-bible.html

Martendill, C.M. (2015, June 7). Of breeders, MOOs, and overpopulation: Eugenics in the animal rights movement [Blog post]. http://www.veganfeministnetwork.com/of-breeders

Matambanadzo, S. M. (2012). Embodying vulnerability: A feminist theory of the person. *Duke Journal of Gender Law & Policy, 20*(1), 45–83.

McCarthy, K. (2017, October 17). California becomes first state to require pet stores to sell rescue animals. *ABC News*. http://abcnews.go.com/

McClintock, A. (1992). The angel of progress: Pitfalls of the term "post-colonialism." *Social Text, 31/32*, 84–98.

McGee, M. C. (1975). In search of "the people": A rhetorical alternative. *Quarterly Journal of Speech, 61*(3), 235–249.

———. (1980). The "ideograph": A link between rhetoric and ideology. *Quarterly Journal of Speech, 66*(1), 1–16.

———. (1990). Text, context, and the fragmentation of contemporary culture. *Western Journal of Communication, 54*(3), 274–289.

McJetters, C. S. (2015, January 27). Is veganism a moral baseline? Bigotry wrapped in "new welfarist" accusations [Blog post]. https://strivingwithsystems.com/tag/intersectionality/

McKerrow, R. E. (1989). Critical rhetoric: Theory and praxis. *Communications Monographs, 56*(2), 91–111.

McKittrick, K. (2006). *Demonic grounds: Black women and the cartographies of struggle*. St. Paul: University of Minnesota Press.

Menon, N. (2004). *Recovering subversion: Feminist politics beyond the law*. Champaign: University of Illinois Press.

Merchant, C. (1980). *The death of nature: Women, ecology, and the scientific revolution*. New York: Harper Collins.

Merry, S. E., Levitt, P., Rosen, M. Ş., & Yoon, D. H. (2010). Law from below: Women's human rights and social movements in New York City. *Law & Society Review, 44*(1), 101–128.

Mignolo, W. D. (2011). Epistemic disobedience and the decolonial option: A manifesto. *Transmodernity, 1*(2), 44–46.

Mika, M. (2006). Framing the issue: Religion, secular ethics and the case of animal rights mobilization. *Social Forces, 85*(2), 915–941.

Milstein, T. (2008). When whales "speak for themselves": Communication as a mediating force in wildlife tourism. *Environmental Communication, 2*(2), 173–192.

Milstein, T., & Dickinson, E. (2012). Gynocentric greenwashing: The discursive gendering of nature. *Communication, Culture & Critique, 5*(4), 510–532.

Monyak, S. (2018, February 2). When the law recognizes animals as people. *New Republic*. https://newrepublic.com/

Moore, H. (2014, June 16). "Environmentalists" called out in Cowspiracy [Blog post]. https://www.peta.org/blog/environmentalists-caught-in-cowspiracy/

Muller, S. M. (2017). Elephant tracings: A critical animal/postcolonial genealogy of the Royal Museum for Central Africa. *Journal for Critical Animal Studies, 14*(2), 5- 41.

Munro, L. (2004). Animals, "nature," and human interests. In R. White (Ed.), *Controversies in environmental sociology* (pp. 61–76). Cambridge, UK: Cambridge University Press.

Mussawir, E., & Otomo, Y. (2013). Law and the question of the animal. In Y. Otomo, & E. Mussawir (Eds.), *Law and the question of the animal: A critical jurisprudence* (pp. 1–9). New York: Routledge.

Nadasdy, P. (2005). Transcending the debate over the ecologically noble Indian: Indigenous peoples and environmentalism. *Ethnohistory, 52*(2), 291–331.

Naess, A. (1973). The shallow and the deep, long range ecology movement: A summary. *Inquiry, 16,* 95–100.

Nakayama, T. K., & Krizek, R. L. (1995). Whiteness: A strategic rhetoric. *Quarterly Journal of Speech, 81*(3), 291–309.

Nedelsky, J. (1993). Reconceiving rights as relationship. *Review of Constitutional Studies, 1*(16), 1–16.

Newman, S. (2005). Anarchism and the politics of ressentiment. In J. Moore & S. Sunshine (Eds.), *I am not a man, I am dynamite!: Nietzsche and the anarchist tradition* (pp. 107–126). New York: Autonomedia.

Nonhuman Rights Project. (n.d.). "Who we are." https://www.nonhumanrights.org/who-we-are/

Norton, B. G. (1984). Environmental ethics and weak anthropocentrism. *Environmental Ethics, 6*(2), 131–148.

O'Brien, G. V. (2013). *Framing the moron: The social construction of feeble-mindedness in the American eugenic era.* Manchester, UK: Manchester University Press.

Olson, K. M., & Goodnight, G. T. (1994). Entanglements of consumption, cruelty, privacy, and fashion: The social controversy over fur. *Quarterly Journal of Speech, 80*(3), 249–276.

Ono, K. A. (2009). *Contemporary media culture and the remnants of a colonial past.* New York: Peter Lang.

Ono, K. A., & Sloop, J. M. (1999). Critical rhetorics of controversy. *Western Journal of Communication, 63*(4), 526–538.

Oravec, C. (1981). John Muir, Yosemite, and the sublime response: A study in the rhetoric of preservationism. *Quarterly Journal of Speech, 67*(3), 245–258.

Osterfeld, D. (1989). Anarchism and the public goods issue: Law, courts and the police. *The Journal of Libertarian Studies, 9*(1), 47–68.

Our Hen House. (n.d.). Why? http://www.ourhenhouse.org/why-2/

People for the Ethical Treatment of Animals. (2011, October 25). PETA sues SeaWorld for violating orcas' rights [Blog post]. https://www.peta.org/blog/peta-sues-seaworld-violating-orcas-constitutional-rights/

———. (2017, September 18). Updated: In a win for animals, federal judge declares Utah's 'ag-gag' law unconstitutional [Blog post]. https://www.peta.org/blog/victory-peta-aldf-challenge-utahs-ag-gag-law/

———. (n.d.). Uncompromising stands on animal rights. https://www.peta.org/about-peta/why-peta/

Pepinsky, H. E. (1978). Communist anarchism as an alternative to the rule of criminal law. *Contemporary Crises, 2,* 315–334.

Petrinovich, L. F. (1999). *Darwinian dominion: Animal welfare and human interests.* Cambridge, MA: MIT Press.

Pezzullo, P. C. (2003a). Touring "Cancer Alley," Louisiana: Performances of community and memory for environmental justice. *Text and Performance Quarterly, 23*(3), 226–252.

———. (2003b). Resisting "National Breast Cancer Awareness Month": The rhetoric of counterpublics and their cultural performances. *Quarterly Journal of Speech, 89*(4), 345–365.

———. (2009a). *Toxic tourism: Rhetorics of pollution, travel, and environmental justice.* Tuscaloosa: University of Alabama Press.

———. (2009b). "This is the only tour that sells": Tourism, disaster, and national identity in New Orleans. *Journal of tourism and cultural change, 7*(2), 99–114.

———. (2011). Contextualizing boycotts and buycotts: The impure politics of consumer based advocacy in an age of global ecological crises. *Communication and Critical/Cultural Studies, 8*(2), 124–145.

Pezzullo, P. C., & de Onís, C. M. (2018). Rethinking rhetorical field methods on a precarious planet. *Communication Monographs, 85*(1), 103–122.

Plec, E. (2007). Crisis, coherence, and the promise of critical rhetoric. *Environmental Communication, 1*(1), 49–57.

———. (Ed.). (2013). *Perspectives on human-animal communication: Internatural communication.* New York: Routledge.

Plumwood, V. (2002). *Feminism and the mastery of nature.* New York: Routledge.

Pollan, M. (2002, November 10). An animal's place. *New York Times Magazine.* http://michaelpollan.com/articles-archive/an-animals-place/

Puckett, T. (2017) Earth day 2017: How eating less meat helps the environment [Blog post]. *Reducetarian.* https://reducetarian.org/blog/2017/4/13/earth-day- 2017-how-eating-less-meat-helps-the-environment

Quijano, A. (2000). Coloniality of power and Eurocentrism in Latin America. *International Sociology, 15*(2), 215–232.

Rauber, P. (2018, March 21). Heartbreaking final moments of the last male northern white rhino. *Sierra.* https://www.sierraclub.org/sierra/

heartbreaking-final-moments-last-male-northern-white-rhino

Reading, R. P., & Miller, B. J. (2010). Captive-breeding ethics. In M. Bekoff (Ed.), *Encyclopedia of animal rights and welfare* (pp. 101–105). Santa Barbara, CA: ABC-CLIO.

Regan, T. (1985). The case for animal rights. In P. Singer (Ed.), *In defense of animals* (pp. 13–26). New York: Basil Blackwell http://www.animal-rights library.com/texts-m/regan03.htm

Rhodes, A. B. (2013). Saving apes with the laws of men: Great ape protection in a property based animal law system. *Animal Law, 20*(1), 191–228.

Robinson, M. (2014). Animal personhood in Mi'kmaq perspective. *Societies, 4*(4), 672–688.

———. (2017). Intersectionality in Mi'kmaw and settler vegan values. In J. F. Brueck (Ed.), *Veganism in an oppressive world* (pp. 71–88). Sanctuary Publishers.

Rogers, R. A. (1998). Overcoming the objectification of nature in constitutive theories: Toward a transhuman, materialist theory of communication. *Western Journal of Communication, 62*(3), 244–272.

———. (2008). Beasts, burgers, and Hummers: Meat and the crisis of masculinity in contemporary television advertisements. *Environmental Communication, 2*(3), 281–301.

Rorty, R. (1990, December 7). Feminism and pragmatism. Lecture given as part of the Tanner Lectures on Human Values at the University of Michigan, Ann Arbor. https://tannerlectures.utah.edu/_documents/a-to-z/r/rorty92.pdf

Rosenberg, M. (2014, May 13). Environmentalists sue to list bumble bee as an endangered species. *Scientific American.* https://www.scientificamerican.com/

Rosenblatt, K. (2017, March 14). Do apes deserve "personhood" rights? Lawyer heads to N.Y. Supreme Court to make case. *Wired.* https://www.nbcnews.com/news/

Rutberg, A. T. (2010). Wildlife contraception. In M. Bekoff (Ed.), *Encyclopedia of animal rights and welfare* (pp. 610–615). Santa Barbara, CA: ABC-CLIO.

Sanbonmatsu, J. (2011). The animal of bad faith: Speciesism as an existential project. In J. Sanbonmatsu (Ed.), *Critical theory and animal liberation* (pp. 29–45). Plymouth, UK: Rowan & Littlefield.

Scales, A. (1989). Militarism, male dominance and law: Feminist jurisprudence as oxymoron. *Harvard Women's Law Journal, 12,* 25–73.

Scheer, R., & Ross, D. (2011, December 28). How does meat in the diet take an environmental toll? *Scientific American.* https://www.scientificamerican.com/

Schillmoller, A., & Pelizzon, A. (2013). Mapping the terrain of earth jurisprudence: Landscape, thresholds and horizons. *Environmental & Earth Law Journal, 3,* 1–32.

Schipani, S. (2018, March 10). At rattlesnake roundups, cruelty draws crowds. *Sierra.* https://www.sierraclub.org/sierra/rattlesnake-roundups-sweetwater-texas-cruelty

Schutten, J. K. (2008). Chewing on the *Grizzly Man:* Getting to the meat of the matter.

Environmental Communication, 2(2), 193–211.

Seegert, N. (2014). Play of sniffication: Coyotes sing in the margins. *Philosophy & Rhetoric, 47*(2), 158–178.

———. (2016). Rewilding rhetoric with animate others. *Review of Communication, 16*(1), 77–79.

Seshadri, K. (2012). *HumAnimal: Race, law, language.* Minneapolis: University of Minnesota Press.

Shiva, V. (1988). *Staying alive: Women, ecology and development.* Chicago: Zed Books.

———. (1993). Monocultures of the mind. *Trumpeter: A Journal of Ecosophy, 10*(4). http://trumpeter.athabascau.ca/index.php/trumpet/article/view/358/562

Shome, R. (1996). Postcolonial interventions in the rhetorical canon: An "other" view. *Communication Theory, 6*(1), 40–59.

Shome, R., & Hegde, R. S. (2002). Postcolonial approaches to communication: Charting the terrain, engaging the intersections. *Communication Theory, 12*(3), 249–270.

Silby, S. (1997). "Let them eat cake": Globalization, postmodern colonialism, and the possibilities of justice [1996 presidential address]. *Law & Society Review, 31*(2), 207–236.

Simons, H. W. (1970). Requirements, problems, and strategies: A theory of persuasion for social movements. *Quarterly Journal of Speech, 56*(1), 1–11.

Singer, P. (1975). *Animal liberation.* New York: Random House.

Singer, R. (2016). Neoliberal backgrounding, the meatless Monday campaign, and the rhetorical intersections of food, nature, and cultural identity. *Communication, Culture & Critique, 10*(2), 344–364.

Smith, N. D. (1983). Plato and Aristotle on the nature of women. *Journal of the History of Philosophy, 21*(4), 467–478.

"Sistah Vegan Anthology" (2012). The sistah vegan project: A critical race feminist's journey through the "post-racial" ethical foodscape . . . and beyond. http://sistahvegan.com/sistah-vegan-anthology/

Solnit, R. (2014). *Men explain things to me.* Chicago: Haymarket.

Spade, D. (2015). *Normal life: Administrative violence, critical trans politics, and the limits of law.* Durham, NC: Duke University Press.

Spiegel, M. (1988). *The dreaded comparison: Human and animal slavery.* London, UK: Mirror Books.

Spivak, G. C. (1990). *The post-colonial critic: Interviews, strategies, dialogues.* Sussex, UK: Psychology Press.

———. (2003). Can the subaltern speak?. *Die Philosophin, 14*(27), 42–58.

Stewart, C. J. (1980). A functional approach to the rhetoric of social movements.

Communication Studies, 31(4), 298–305.

———. (1999). Championing the rights of others and challenging evil: The ego function in the rhetoric of other-directed social movements. *Southern Journal of Communication, 64*(2), 91–105.

Stewart, C. J., Smith, C. A., & Denton, R. E., Jr. (1984). *Persuasion and social movements.* Prospect Heights, IL: Waveland Press.

Stringham, E. P. (2011). *Anarchy and the law: The political economy of choice.* Piscataway, NJ: Transaction Publishers.

Stone, C. (1972). *Should trees have standing? Law, morality, and the environment.* Oxford, UK: Oxford University Press.

Stuckey, M. (2012). On rhetorical circulation. *Rhetoric & Public Affairs, 15*(4), 609–612.

Sztybel, D. (2007). Animal rights law: Fundamentalism versus pragmatism. *Journal for Critical Animal Studies, 5*(1), 1–35. http://journalforcriticalanimalstudies.org

Taylor, C. (2002). Modern social imaginaries. *Public Culture, 14*(1), 91–124.

Taylor, S. (2017). *Beasts of burden: Animal and disability liberation.* New York: New Press.

Thompson, C. (2006). Back to nature? Resurrecting ecofeminism after post-structuralist and third wave feminisms. *Isis, 97*(3), 505–512.

Torres, B. (2007). *Making a killing: The political economy of animal rights.* Oakland, CA: AK Press.

Torrez, M. (2013). Combatting reproductive oppression: Why reproductive justice cannot stop at the species border. *Cardozo Journal of Law & Gender, 20,* 265–306.

Twine, R. (2010). *Animals as biotechnology: Ethics, sustainability and critical animal studies.* New York: Routledge.

———. (2010). Intersectional disgust? Animals and (eco) feminism. *Feminism & Psychology, 20*(3), 397–406.

Unferth, D. O. (2011). Go vegan or go home. *UTNE.* https://www.utne.com/politics/gary-francione-animal-activist-rights-exploitation

Varner, G. E. (2002). *In nature's interests?: Interests, animal rights, and environmental ethics.* Oxford, UK: Oxford University Press.

Verchick, R. (2001). A new species of rights. *California Law Review, 89*(1), 207–229.

von Essen, E., & Allen, M. P. (2017). Solidarity between human and non-human animals: Representing animal voices in policy deliberations. *Environmental Communication,* 1–13.

Wadiwel, D. (2015). *The war against animals.* Leiden, Netherlands: Brill.

Wander, P. (1983). The ideological turn in modern criticism. *Communication Studies, 34*(1), 1–18.

———. (1984). The third persona: An ideological turn in rhetorical theory. *Communication*

Studies, 35(4), 197–216.

Wanzer, D. A. (2012). Delinking rhetoric, or revisiting McGee's fragmentation thesis through decoloniality. *Rhetoric & Public Affairs, 15*(4), 647–657.

West, C. (1989). *The American evasion of philosophy: A genealogy of pragmatism.* New York: Springer.

White, S. (2011, September 17). Wild law and animal law: Commonalities and differences. Presentation given at the 3rd Wild Law Conference at Griffith University, Queensland, Australia.

White, T. I. (2013). Humans and dolphins: An exploration of anthropocentrism in applied environmental ethics. *Journal of Animal Ethics, 3*(1), 85–99.

Wise, S. M. (1996). Legal rights for nonhuman animals: The case for chimpanzees and bonobos. *Animal Law, 2,* 179–186.

———. (1999). Animal thing to animal person: Thoughts on time, place, and theories. *Animal Law, 5*(1), 61–68.

———. (2000). *Rattling the cage: Toward legal rights for animals.* Cambridge, MA: Perseus.

———. (2002). *Drawing the line: Science and the case for animal rights.* Cambridge, MA: Perseus.

———. (2003). The evolution of animal law since 1950. In D. J. Salem & A. N. Rowan (Eds.), *The state of the animals II* (pp. 99–105). Washington, DC: Humane Society Press. from http://animalstudiesrepository.org/sota_2003/1/

———. (2010). Legal personhood and the Nonhuman Rights Project. *Animal Law, 17*(1), 1–10.

———. (2011, November 10). PETA's slavery lawsuit: A setback for animal rights. *Nonhuman Rights Project* [Blog post]. https://www.nonhumanrights.org/blog/petas-slavery-lawsuit-a-setback-for-animal-rights/

———. (2017, March 16). What chimpanzees deserve: Attorney who represents Tommy and Kiko makes the case for their legal personhood. *New York Daily News.* http://www.nydailynews.com/

Wise, T. (2005, August 13). Animal whites: PETA and the politics of putting things in perspective. *Counterpunch.* http://www.timwise.org/2005/08/animal-whites-peta-and-the-politics-of-putting-things-in-perspective/

Wolfe, C. (2003). *Animal rites: American culture, the discourse of species, and posthumanist theory.* Chicago: University of Chicago Press.

Wrenn, C. L. (2011). Resisting the globalization of speciesism: Vegan abolitionism as a site for consumer-based social change. *Journal for Critical Animal Studies, 9*(3), 9–27.

———. (2015). *A rational approach to animal rights: Extensions in abolitionist theory.* New York: Springer.

————. (2016). An analysis of diversity in nonhuman animal rights media. *Journal of Agricultural and Environmental Ethics, 29*(2), 143–165.

————. (2017). Trump veganism: A political survey of American vegans in the era of identity politics. *Societies, 7*(4), 32.

Wright, G. (2013). Animal law and earth jurisprudence: A comparative analysis of the status of animals in two emerging critical legal theories. *Australian Animal Protection Law Journal, 9.* https://www.animallaw.info/sites/default/files/australia_journal_vol9.pdf

WWF [World Wildlife Fund]. (2016). "WWF position on ivory trade." https://d2ouvy59p0dg6k.cloudfront.net/downloads/wwf_and_elephant_ivory_trade.pdf

Wynter, S. (2003). Unsettling the coloniality of being/power/truth/freedom: Towards the human, after man, its overrepresentation—An argument. *CR: The New Centennial Review, 3*(3), 257–337.

Zelman, J. (2012, February 8). PETA's SeaWorld slavery case dismissed by judge. *Huffington Post.* https://www.huffingtonpost.com/2012/02/09/peta-seaworld-slavery_n_1265014.html

Index

136; law regulates, 11; power and, 137; solidarity across, 137. *See also* Indigenous cultures

Cupp, Richard L., 46–47

Curtin, Deane, 9

D

Darwin, Charles, 83

Davis, Michelle, 78

Dawkins, Richard, 59

Deckha, Maneesha, 2

Declaration of Human Rights (UN), 119

"Declaration on Great Apes," 59–61

decoloniality, 11, 12; animal liberation and, 135; animal rights law and, 17, 30, 135; Belcourt and, 16–17, 124, 137; essence of, 14, 15; and intersectionality, 14–17, 21, 154, 155; metaphor of, 16; social justice and, 26; speciesism and, 113, 137; theories of, 26

decolonization, 15; of artifacts, 29; Indigenous, 135–36; process of, 136, 137

deconstruction, 12, 28; by Derrida, 53; feminist, 8; of Francione, 62; rhetorical, 24, 26, 139

deer, 84, 103, 104

DeGrazia, D., 85

dehumanization, 10, 153, 154

De Lucia, V., 114, 118

democratization, 12, 24

Derrida, Jacques, 53, 62

Descartes, Rene, 37, 54, 98; dualism and, 6, 26, 55; objectivism of, 4

Dhamoon, Rita, 14

Diamond, Jared, 59

difference, 3, 5, 75; as wrongness, 16

discourse: animal law and, 4; in animal liberation, 30, 52, 72, 76; Wise as subject of, 43, 52–57

dogs, 55, 83; as food, 65; personhood for, 38, 51, 85, 93; as pets, 85, 87, 147; rights of, 36, 86, 90; sterilization of, 84, 88–89; value of, 86, 88, 90, 92, 122

dolphins, 36, 39, 53; "advanced" rights of, 50

domestication, 42, 117, 122–23; Francione on, 67, 85–88, 90–91, 131

domination: of humans, 6; intersectional and, 12–13; logics of, 7, 10; of Not-Man, 10; violence and, 16

Donaldson, Sue, 85, 87

Donovan, Josephine, 4

Drawing the Line (Wise), 39, 46, 52, 53

Dream of the Earth, The (Berry), 107

dualism, 6–7, 25

Dvorsky, George, 45, 46

E

Earth jurisprudence, 99; Alexander and, 114; animal rights thinking in, 111–12; *Animalia* and, 117; benefits of, 111, 114; "deep ecology of law" and, 110, 111, 112, 120, 124; ecocentric communitarianism and, 117–18; ecofeminist legal theory and, 127; environmental legal thought as, 126; goal of, 110, 118, 124; holistic, 126; Indigenous perspectives in, 124; liberation and, 117, 130; moral authority and, 123; nature and, 118–19, 120, 121; as radical, 106, 126, 131; "recognition route" in, 118; relational view of rights in, 115, 116, 117–18, 124–27; rhetorical pivots of, 121, 132; risk of, 124; science and,

vehement, 62, 70, 75–77, 81, 82, 92; Indigenous jurisprudence and, 135; liberal humanist, 155; rejection of, 8, 14; rhetoric of, 13, 67, 81, 82, 140, 141; speaker defines, 75; "species," 62, 70, 79, 80, 81, 133, 148, 155; strategic, 51, 54, 75, 141. *See also* species essentialism

"Essentialism, Intersectionality, and Veganism as a Moral Baseline" (Francione, blog), 75

essentialist *species* category, 77, 79

essentialist veganism, 71, 75–77, 79, 82, 92

"ethic of care" ideal, 9, 10

ethical veganism, 20, 21

ethics, 4; American legal system and, 11; animal, 17, 137, 145; New Welfarism as, 63–64, 67, 75, 93; total liberation, 71; Whiteness and, 137

eugenics: ableism and, 82; companion animal, 84, 91; essentialist, 82; extinction and, 82; Hasian on, 2, 3, 24, 30, 82–83; human, 84; rhetoric of, 67, 82, 84; rights control and, 90; roots of, 83; sterilization and, 83, 89; technologies for, 7

euthanasia, 38, 87, 89

existentialism, 89, 134, 142

experimentation, animals used for, 9, 10, 66, 134

extinction, 47, 57, 70, 91, 93, 100; environmentalism and, 101, 102, 113; rates of, 109; rhetoric of, 82; *Sierra* on, 101

extinctionism, 82, 87, 93

F

fashion, animals used for, 10, 64

Favre, David, 47

FDA (Food and Drug Administration), 100

"feeble-minded," 85, 86, 90

Feldman, Steve, 47

feminism, 6, 8; "ethic of care" ideal of, 9; legal studies and, 5, 17, 30; in legal theory, 11, 12; veganism and, 73

feminist theories: women-of-color, 12, 71, 76, 133, 140; "whitewashing" and, 14

Fenton, Andrew, 44

FEP (Food Empowerment Project), 143, 144–45

Ferre, Frederick, 96

Florida, 96; chimpanzees in, 33, 34

Florida Springs and Aquifer Protection Act, 96

Food and Drug Administration, 100

Food Empowerment Project, 143, 144–45

food industry: activists and, 38, 71; animals in, 9, 10, 19–20, 46, 64–65, 104, 125–26, 142; capitalist, 79; carbon emissions and, 100–101; justice in, 145; meat in, 104–5, 142; plant-based, 6, 74, 79, 142–44; power in food choices and, 144; safety in, 7, 100, 144; Safeway supermarket practices in, 144; slavery and, 145, 155; sustainable, local, 104–5

Forks over Knives (documentary), 100–101

fragmentation theories, 28

Franciobots, 68, 69, 80, 82

Francione, Gary L.: ableist rhetoric of, 89, 90, 91; abolitionism and, 63–65, 69, 70, 73–81, 85, 91–92, 131, 134; academia activity of, 68; activist discourse of, 62, 66, 69; against "humane treatment," 63; animal groups and, 77; on animal rights, 66–68, 73, 120, 127; on animals as chattel, 63, 67;

on animals-as-property, 113, 117; binary
natures and, 62, 70, 82, 122, 131; critics
of, 68–70, 72–77; critiqued deer hunters,
103; "Declaration on Great Apes" signer,
59–61; deconstruction of, 62; disparaged
Wise, 52; domestication critiqued by, 67,
85–88, 90–91, 131; ecofeminist theory
and, 130, 138; essentialist veganism and,
71, 75–77, 79, 82; eugenics and, 89, 90,
91; on euthanasia, 87, 89, 91; extremism
of, 85; on feminism, 73; Fracnciobots
and, 68, 69, 80, 82; grassroots and, 71; on
Harper's veganism, 74; on human legal
advantage, 124; as liberal humanist, 82,
90; liminal views of, 121; moral baseline
and, 64, 69, 74, 75, 79, 92, 145; moral
values and, 66, 71, 75, 76, 77, 79, 82; on
New Welfarists, 93; paternalism of, 90;
on personhood, 60, 92, 93, 111, 150; PETA
and, 65–66, 150; postracial legal theory
of, 71; radical rhetoric of, 67–69, 71–72,
80, 82, 86, 91, 131; on SeaWorld orca
freedom, 151; on sentience and animal
rights, 50, 63, 65, 131; on "similar minds
approach," 52; social media and, 63,
68; "species blindness" of, 70; species
essentialism and, 79, 82, 89, 92; on
sterilization, 88, 89; utilitarianism and,
125; as vegan abolitionist, 62–65, 68,
70–71, 75, 80–81, 91–92, 119, 131, 156; on
vegan Whiteness, 71, 75; violence rejected
by, 65, 66; website of, 63; welfare rhetoric
and, 65, 66, 67, 130–31; whiteness
framework of, 71, 75, 131. Works: *Animals,
Property, and the Law*, 63; *Animals as
Persons*, 63; *Introduction to Animal
Rights*, 63; "Personhood, Property, and
Legal Competence," 60; *Rain without
Thunder*, 63; "The Great Ape Project,"
60–61. Coauthored works: *The Animal
Rights Debate*, 63; *Eat Like You Care*, 63
Freeman, Carrie Packwood, 25, 37, 54, 56, 104
Frey, Raymond, 125

G

Gaard, Greta, 7, 125, 136
Gaia Foundation, 96, 106
Galton, Francis, 83, 89
Garner, R., 68
gender: as "category," 16; colonial history and,
27; critical animal studies ad, 21; justice,
7; legal rhetorics and, 12; Man/Not-Man
binary and, 8, 9; neoliberalism, 15
Gizmodo (website), 35, 45
Global Climate Change Movement, 96
Goodale, Greg, 24, 25, 37
Goodall, Jane, 39, 44, 48, 59
gorillas, 50, 59, 60
Grande, Sandy, 14
Great Ape Project, The (Cavalier & Singer),
59–60, 61
"Great Ape Project" (Francione), 60–61
great apes: chimpanzees as, 59, 60;
"Declaration on Great Apes," 59–61;
gorillas as, 50, 59, 60; human beings as,
60; legal status of, 39, 56, 131; orangutans
as, 59, 60; personhood and, 59–61;
as primates, 53, 60, 61, 152. *See also*
chimpanzees: bonobos
Great Chain of Being, 42, 49, 51, 131
Great Legal Wall, 40, 42, 43
Great Work, The (Berry), 107

11; legal rights in, 40–41, 118; legitimacy
of, 13; liberal conception of, 2; as *logos*,
11; *nomos* created by, 11; NRDC as, 101;
political change and, 3; queer, 11; rhetoric
and, 5, 11, 12, 13; as rhetorical culture, 24;
rule of, 11, 24; as science, 11; social change
and, 5; *telos* of, 14; theory of, 3, 5, 6, 11, 12,
41; tribal, 137; U.S. American courts and,
44; U.S. Constitution and, 35, 149; welfare
statues in, 41; "Wild," 97–98, 108, 117, 121,
127, 132; wisdom of, 11

lawsuits, 22; climate change, 96; by NhRP
for elephants, 51; nonpersons and, 40;
by PETA against SeaWorld, 149–50, 153;
police brutality, 21

Leadership Council of Women Religious, 96

Leahy, M. P., 85

Leenaert, Tobias, 69

legal personhood, 3, 118, 139; for artificial
humans and robots, 42, 45, 46, 47; for
cetaceans, 36, 39, 44, 50, 53, 56, 131,
136, 149–51, 154; for chimpanzees, 45;
for corporations, 42; courts and, 120,
130; Cupp on, 46; for dogs, 38, 51, 85,
93; domestication and, 88, 93; for great
apes, 60–61; indigenous practice and,
135; levels of, 40–41; as misguided, 37,
47–48, 55; in New York state, 33–36,
46; for New Zealand Whanganui River,
151; nonhuman, 44, 45, 47; in PETA's
SeaWorld lawsuit, 149–53; rationality
test and, 56; rights linked to, 42, 60, 63,
69; value of individual and, 141; veganists
and, 135. *See also* NhRP

legal positivism, 1, 11, 71, 139, 156

legal protection, 41

legal rights: definition of, 118; of natural
objects, 106–7; of trees, 55, 106, 108, 109,
116

legal scholarship, 24

legal theory: American colonial roots of, 41;
ecofeminism and, 5–6, 11; feminist, 3,
5–6, 11, 12, 41

Leo. *See* chimpanzees

Leopold, Aldo, 110

liberal humanist, 1; ideals, 2

liberalism, 2–3; animal rights and, 4; pitfalls
of, 10

liberation: animal, 15, 18–19; personhood
and, 135; pet keeping and total, 85, 90, 91;
total, 36, 41, 71, 135, 143, 145, 155

linguistics, 30, 50, 54

litigation: animal rights, 1, 4, 6; animal
welfare, 1

logic, anthropocentric, 17

Lorde, Audre, 31

Los Angeles Times (newspaper), 38, 51

Low, Hana, 147

Lucaites, John, 2, 4, 24

M

Makah whale hunt, 136

man over nature, 4, 9

Man/Not-Man binary, 8, 9, 10, 15

"mansplaining," 80

Marxism, 23, 74

Matambanadzo, Saru, 33, 37

Matsuzawa, Tetsuro, 44

Maynell, Letitia, 44

McClintock, A., 17

McGee, Michael Calvin, 23, 28

McKittrick, Katherine, 124